WITHDRAWN

SAIL

FAR AWAY

Robert S. Carter

SAIL
FAR AWAY

W · W · NORTON & COMPANY · INC ·
NEW YORK

Copyright © 1978 by Robert S. Carter
Published simultaneously in Canada by George J. McLeod Limited,
Toronto. Printed in the United States of America.
ALL RIGHTS RESERVED
FIRST EDITION
Library of Congress Cataloging in Publication Data
Carter, Robert S.
Sail far away.
1. Cynthia R (Yacht) 2. Carter, Robert S.
3. Voyages and travels—1951–   I. Title.
G530.C98C37   1978   910'.41'0924   [B]   78–3859
ISBN 0–393–03214–0

1 2 3 4 5 6 7 8 9 0

To Cynthia

Who has gracefully tolerated both
my sailing and my writing these many years.

Contents

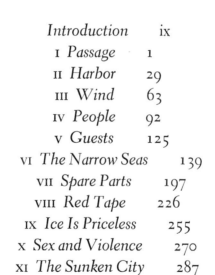

Introduction

This is not a How To Do It book. A great number of them have been written, some of which are even quite useful. This is meant to pick up where they leave off. In short, it is meant to show you what's likely to happen after you have read those books and bought your boat and sailed off over the edge of your known world, when familiar shores have dropped out of sight astern and you must pit your own wits against whatever lies beyond the next horizon. It is not written for the lone circumnavigator or the Cape Horner, but for us run-of-the-mill sailors who have pried ourselves away from home and office enough to taste the spray of unfamiliar waters.

It presumes that you already have some fundamental knowledge of sailing and seamanship, of piloting, and perhaps even of navigation. If you know the fundamentals of mechanics and electronics as well, you are already one up on the author. The question we address is not learning to sail, but what the hell you do next.

There is the old story of the fishing smack, drifting in the fog off the Massachusetts coast when, in the eerie light of dawn, a majestic clipper ship loomed out of the mist.

"Ahoy," hailed the smack, "What ship is that?"

"Ahoy," came the reply. "This is the *Shooting Star*, eighty-six days out of Canton. What ship is that?"

"This is the *Lizzie and Maggie* of Gloucester, out *all* night."

We may dream of being on the *Shooting Star*, but most of us wind up on the *Lizzie and Maggie,* and it is from this point of view we write.

In the years before launching the *Cynthia R* we had cruised the East Coast between Halifax and Miami, the West Coast between Vancouver Island and San Diego, the Great Lakes between New York and Chicago, and the West Indies for a month. Since then, in the ten years between launching the *Cynthia R* and the chronicling of these reflections on the sea, we have lived half our lives on board her. We have sailed to twenty-three countries on four continents, have logged over 38,000 miles, have passed through 540 locks, have made up bunks for perhaps two hundred arriving guests, and have repaired pumps about the same number of times.

I am sure the reader will appreciate not having to accompany us on a day-by-day account of each mile sailed, each harbor visited over these years. My wife, Cynthia, less fortunate than the reader, perhaps, has been dragged along on those miles, to all those harbors, escaping only the longer ocean passages. Both of us were older when we commenced this present venture than Columbus was when he finished his fourth and final voyage, but I don't dare tell her so, because she might think it time to stop. She has been a wise counsel on plans, a cautionary voice on challenging the fates, a calm and steady hand on the helm when the going was rough.

Instead of following our every day, let us try to capture some moods of the sea, some experiences afloat, some of those moments which tempt one, as Mephistopheles tempted Faust, to say, "Just linger on! Thou art so beautiful!" and others which seem to be our punishment for saying this, moments or hours best forgotten. For together they are typical of what one will encounter on the water, and together they make up the great experience of cruising.

One evening when the *Cynthia R* was lying at anchor below a club in George Town in the Exumas, one of the group we had joined at the outdoor bar, who had just flown down in his private aircraft, looked down at our boat and said, "Now *that's* the way to travel. You just put up the sails and go!"

It isn't always like that. Things don't always run smoothly afloat, but perhaps the biggest contribution I can offer in these pages is the knowledge that when they are not running smoothly for you, you are not alone. I would like to think that a lifetime of mistakes, if properly documented, would serve to prevent their repetition by our readers, but then I think of our old friend, Bert Sinnett, of Bailey Island, Maine, where I first ventured onto the water. Bert was called up as a witness at the county seat, and after he had been sworn in and identified himself as Bert Sinnett, the attorney asked him, "Where do you live?"

"Down to Baileys Island," Bert answered thoughtfully.

"Lived there all your life?" came next.

Bert reflected a moment and then said, "Not yit."

So no doubt I don't have my full quota of mistakes behind me yet, and you and I can continue making them and feeling stupid about them as long as we continue to venture. But still, if in the course of describing what it is like to be out there over the horizon, some educational hints creep in, accept them. After all, you paid for them when you bought the book. If you don't waste time making the same mistakes over again, you will have that much more time free to make your very own.

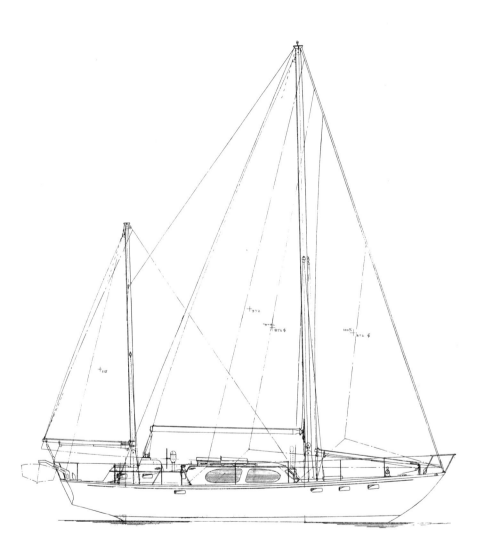

SAIL
FAR AWAY

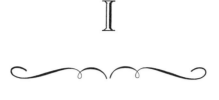

Passage

Roll on, thou deep and dark blue ocean, roll.
Byron, "The Ocean"

A rectangle of sunlight travels back and forth across the chart table to starboard in the space below the bridge deck, illuminating in turn a page of H. O. 214, a plotting sheet on which several pencil lines parallel each other or converge and cross; and a sheet of notebook paper, half covered with all those little figures associated with a morning sun sight and a meridian altitude at noon. There is a swivel chair at this chart table, facing outboard, and looking up from working our noon position I see, for the most part, a pale blue sky and fair weather clouds, as we are broad reaching on the starboard tack. As we roll off each wave in turn the nearest breaking crest of the endless procession that has been overtaking us for days and will continue to do so for days to come flashes above the porthole, or maybe smothers it for a moment in backlit suds. And as we roll to port the patch of sunlight travels across the cabin to hover over a plastic wash basin filled with rising bread dough, resting in the sail bin to port. The sail bin is a good place to let dough rise, because you can nest the bowl into the sail bags at an angle which compensates for the average heel.

When a crest passes under our stern I can judge the alertness of the helmsman, for if he lets the boat be thrown too much the patch of sunlight will travel across the aft bulkhead of the navigating cabin across the recording fathometer (of no use at sea, as it reaches only to 40 fathoms) and the transistor transfer switch, which permits us to shift the pulse to a flashing repeater visible from the helm, and to the radio-telephone panel, also a seldom-used instrument on our boat. If the helmsman has anticipated too much or overcompensated, it will circle back across the forward bulkhead, illuminating the shelf of navigating books and instruction manuals or, if we are pitching upwards, the typewriter, portable-radio direction finder, and hand-bearing compass, which, by good fortune, exactly fit into the space below the bookshelf. Or it may lift on a deep roll to blind my eyes just as I am picking little numbers out of little columns.

The boat is full of sound, although mostly muted: all the rushing noises of the water passing the hull, a sizzling of bubbles, the slap and thud of waves at the bow, the soft, foamy sound of a crest alongside; it all sounds as if we are traveling even faster than we are. From aloft comes the crack of the topping lift against the main; there is a chinking of dishes in the dish rack, the tick of the chain drive of the pedestal steerer over my head. Only the rising dough is silent. A boat at sea, even were we becalmed, is never silent.

When one is facing athwartships and leaning into the back of the swivel chair, the physical sensation is rather like sitting in a rocking chair on whose rockers a willful child is tramping with erratic rhythm. A rhythm there is, but with no regularity in the applied force, and I am at times rocked deeply back and grab the papers on the chart table to keep them from sliding into my lap, and again I am lulled by a pleasant period of even rolling, only to be jerked out of this relaxing condition by some rogue sea. Then one can feel the acceleration, the swooping drive forward, as our stern lifts and the whole boat is swept ahead with the rushing wave crest. Over the long run the sensory input from all these sources develops an endlessly repeated but endlessly varied pattern, a theme with variations of sound and light and motion. After some days of this I believe the sailor could tell from any one of these senses what the other senses would be simultaneously recording. It is a different world from a quiet room on land.

I can remember when my wife, Cynthia, who has sailed every trip with me except this Atlantic crossing, used to be unable to sleep on a boat even at night at anchor in a protected harbor in fair weather. I would wake to find her surreptitiously reading under the covers by the light of a flashlight. Then we went on a long cruise, not a passage, but harbor hopping in the Northwest Indian country as we circumnavigated Vancouver Island. It was a trip filled with the usual combination of new adventure, placid anchorages, and wild hours when the wind was up, and we slept like babies. And finally we were home again, in our own wide bed in a motionless room on a silent night. Cynthia tossed and turned, and at 2 A.M. she announced, "I can't sleep a wink." And turned on the light to read.

And so it is at sea. At first nerves and novelty stimulate one to wakefulness, but in due course one succumbs to the rhythm of the sea, to the rhythm of life at sea, and except for those rare wild nights, sleep comes as if one had returned to the womb. Even during harbor hopping, if we have experienced a sequence of windy nights, of groaning anchor lines and moaning rigging, of wavelets slapping the bow and the lurch and stagger as the boat is buffeted and sails around her anchor, we will find that the dead stillness of a calm night in an isolated harbor produces restlessness, not relaxation.

Sitting here at the chart table, despite the noise and the flicker of sunlight and the perpetual change of balance, one is relaxed. All these sensory stimuli become a part of normal life, and as long as no dramatic change in sound or motion or light occurs, one senses that all is normal. There on the overhead above the porthole a never-ending succession of light and shadow travels from aft forward, our own illuminated news display that the foam outside is traveling from forward aft, a reassuring thing to know.

Although full of sound and motion, the ship is almost odorless under these pleasant conditions today. The companionway is wide open at the risk of a few drops of salt water below, hatches or portholes are cracked open in every cabin, ventilators are trimmed to exhaust air from the head and forepeak and bilge, nothing is cooking on the stove, and the fruit and vegetables that had gone bad in the oilskin locker are overboard, the remainder under the dinghy in ventilated stowage, where they should have been from the start. (And we have not yet discovered that carton of margarine which has melted into the foam liner of the laundry locker.) Later I will light the oven, accompanied by the smell of alcohol and to be followed by the smell of freshly baking bread, but right now if I were to smell diesel oil or alcohol, it would be because in the back of my mind a voice had said, "Something's wrong; what can it be?"

This is the essence of a passage as opposed to just sailing, to the daytime trip and harbor hopping. The ship's work goes on, from the hourly recording to the patent log reading and course made good, to the daily working of sights, their comparison with dead-reckoning results, and the final satisfying circled dot on the plotting sheet which says, "This is where we were at Local Apparent Noon." And a cautionary voice in the back of the mind replies, "At least you hope you were there." It goes on from the thrice-daily preparation of a meal before waking the next watch to the occasional triumph of freshly baked bread in a rolling sea, from the routine scrutiny of lines and sails for chafe to the discouraging task of sewing up several feet of torn dacron. It is not only a sport, it is a life entire.

This navigating cabin is directly beneath the bridge deck which, in *Cynthia R*, substitutes for a cockpit. When I am sitting at the chart table, the steering cables from the pedestal steerer are a couple of feet over my head; standing up, one just clears them. By dropping the sole of this cabin almost into the shaft alley, the architect had achieved a full-headroom walk-through from the main cabin house amidships to the aft stateroom, an arrangement arrived at in many later boats by molding a broad cockpit coaming into the fiberglass deck structure, providing a passage with headroom beneath it as well as a good base for winches.

Forward of me and three steps up in the main cabin, Parker, one of the two men on watch, is doing up the lunch dishes in a bucket of seawater, while his watchmate, Skip, is at the helm.

Parker is not going to throw the top of Cynthia's favorite Dansk casserole overboard with the dirty dishwater today, because he did it yesterday.

Cynthia might have caught it, but Cynthia is not with me on this trip. As I said, she has sailed with me everywhere before, "everywhere" being up and down the East Coast and the Bahamas, throughout the Great Lakes, and for years of cruising in the northwest. She is to visit another twenty countries and make every coming passage in European waters with me, but she didn't really relish this trip across an ocean.

"I don't like open spaces," she says. "I suffer from agoraphobia, and the Mediterranean, which is only a few hundred miles across, is big enough for me."

"But if you're a hundred miles from land, what difference does it make if you're a thousand?" I ask, always practical.

"Nine hundred miles," she answers, topping me for practicality.

Hard to argue that one, isn't it?

Her rationale is that she can assist at the launching of a new grandchild at home, which is true, but what she doesn't know is that she is missing a smooth trip and that the few storms we will encounter in our cruising are all waiting until she is back on board.

Beyond my range of vision in the forward stateroom, one of the off watch, John, who shares that cabin with Skip, is getting his afternoon nap, while John's watchmate, Paul, who shares the aft stateroom with me, is in the sack there, two steps up from the navigating space. Parker sleeps in the wide lower berth to starboard in the main cabin. This means a bit of coming and going, but, you see, it means only one person at a time up forward, the most difficult cabin to ventilate at sea, and also means that, if necessary, the leeward bunk there is always available. In fact, our crew has found that by wedging up the mattress of the windward bunk with a spare sail, it has stayed perfectly comfortable. And all the other bunks have adequate dacron bunk boards to lie into under any conditions, although this has been a good-luck passage and conditions have never been severe.

If we are talking about a passage I ought to define my terms. The professional deep-sea sailor may think only of an ocean crossing as satisfying his concept of a passage, but for our purposes here I will call any run of about 100 miles or more a passage. It almost always requires a night at sea, you are generally out of sight of land, some routine of watch systems and duties are established, and usually you are moving, if not from country to country, at least into a changing environment. Your boat is generally alone at sea, and you have pitted it and yourselves against the vagaries of nature. And these, too, are a part of the essence of passage, the anticipation, the low-key excitement of finding something new and different, the reward for your endeavor. The excitement ceases to be low key if those vagaries of nature produce the unexpected; noise levels rise noticeably, abetted by considerable shouting on the part of the crew, while with ports and hatches closed the fresh sea air is replaced by the concentrated funk of food and bilge, of diesel and drain, of wet clothes and wet human bodies, of toothpaste and toilet. That too is a part of passage, but not a part we relish.

But now we are in the middle of a very planned and organized passage, an ocean crossing that is working out well. We are midway between Bermuda and the island of Fayal in the Azores, a run of 1,900 miles, and, as I said, it is a good-luck passage. The accepted route is to avoid the calms associated with the Mid-Atlantic High, which normally lies between these islands, by sailing north from Bermuda to the thirty-ninth parallel to pick up the prevailing westerlies of these higher latitudes. But on leaving Bermuda we had found light northwesterlies by day and calms by night and had cut corners on a northeasterly course. At 38 degrees north, four days out of Bermuda, we had come into a pleasant west wind, after a minor front had passed over, and we had put up the helm and borne off east before it for the Azores, sailing fast ever since. Our crew is well rested; we are even clean (not always the case at sea), because in the calms we could swim or bucket off on deck, and when the only rain came through it was so torrential and lasted so long that we all had soap and fresh-water showers under the runoff from the mainsail. They are settled into the watch system and happy with it.

There are various schools of thought on watch setting; some argue that routine is desirable and, in the long run, more restful, while others hold that an alternation of duties is more fair. Still others solve the problem by sailing single handed. I had opted for the middle course, adding the thought that variety is more restful than routine for the active mind, and my crew was made up of four bright college students, all enthusiastic sailors and all with at least some experience at being offshore, of night sailing, and of moderately heavy weather. So I had set up a variation of the so-called Swedish system, allowing for two six-hour watches by day, followed by three four-hour watches by night, when the hours seem longer. Succumbing to Daylight Saving psychology, I had shifted the whole cycle one hour back, and the daily routine was supposed to go rather like this: At 0600 the on watch would start preparing breakfast; at 0630 they would wake the off watch and feed them, so that at 0700, fed and happy, the new watch (let us call it the starboard watch) would take over. One of them would feed the offcoming port watch, who were then free to turn in, and the starboard watch would handle the cleanup. Generally the two men on watch were to relieve each other hourly at the helm, when the patent log was read and the mileage entered in the deck log, a steno notepad, together with average course made good. At noon, lunch would be started, and at 1230 the port watch called up, to eat and to relieve the starboard watch at 1300, when the reverse process of feeding the offcoming watch and cleaning up became their duty. My own lunch would be dictated by the time of Local Apparent Noon, when I had to be out on deck to take the meridian altitude. At 1800, 1830, and 1900 dinner was prepared and served and the watch changed again, and now we went onto the night schedule, changing watches at 2300 and 0300. No meals, and the watches would make themselves such snacks as growing boys at sea require to get through the night, aided by a thermos of hot water prepared with dinner. In this manner on succeeding days each watch would have alternately prepared two meals and cleaned up one and then prepared one and cleaned up two.

Fatigue being the great enemy in a passage, I had added one other quirk to the system, relieving one man every evening from 2100 to 2300, which meant that every fourth night each man could count on six successive hours in the sack. Since this was a fortunate trip, the man relieved was more than likely to stay on deck and enjoy the night sky with us throughout the watch.

Jupiter was in a fine position in the west for evening sights, and I generally worked out one of these, while Parker, who had just completed a navigation course, threw in a triangle of star sights and, when the moon was around, a moon sight or two, so that during these hours one of us was very often in the navigating cabin doing his computations. The light here doesn't bother the helmsman, as it is directly beneath the deck under him, and the off watch in the aft cabin can drop a curtain.

So evening would find someone quietly at work with the tables, someone else perhaps already snoring, and two or three in the cockpit. There would be talk in low voices, perhaps some music on the portable radio. At 2300 I would tumble into my own bunk, to wake up later, perhaps to the sound of the diesel being started, perhaps to the singing of wind in the rigging, a greater heel or swoop of the boat, and I would wonder if I should struggle up and look around. Then I would say to myself, "Hell, no, those guys know what they're doing." And I would cozy up to the side of the bunk (how snug and comfortable that trough between mattress and side can be when you are heeled over and driving hard), and in the morning one of the boys would report, "Say, skipper, it got a bit heavy in the night and we rolled in a reef at 0100." And I would think: "See, you knew you could rely on them." I hope I even said it.

In thinking about an ocean passage I had concluded that we should plan a minimum average day's run of 100 miles, the time-honored figure used by ocean cruisers. To do this we must avoid lying becalmed for days, consuming our 190 gallons of fresh water while we had 150 gallons of diesel fuel in our tanks, and I decided to use three knots as the minimum acceptable speed under sail. If the log reading at the end of any hour showed we had moved less than three miles through the water, the watch were to turn on the engine and run it at the advised minimum continuous rpm of 1200, which gave us nearly six knots. Once in a while I would get a half-apologetic report or confession at breakfast that it had been just too fine a night to spoil with the noise of an engine and that we had continued to ease along at two or one and a half knots. Beautiful! The crew was enjoying it, we were saving fuel, the currents were with us, and there was no fault to be found. But usually at under three knots the sails are slatting, gear is wearing out, nerves are raw, and it's time for power.

I gambled that this rule would allow us to average the desired 100-mile-per-day minimum without exhausting our fuel supply. As we had fuel for only 900 miles and a 1,900-mile run, I was obviously counting on some wind, and the same would be true on the 1,000-mile run from the Azores to Gibraltar. While we did in fact refuel at Bermuda and the Azores, it was hardly necessary. We would have had twenty-five gallons remaining of our original one hundred fifty when we got to Gibraltar, and we had averaged six knots for the entire distance, 144 miles per day. And since some of this had been sailed at 5, 4, and 3 knots, and since we motored at only 6 when under power, we clearly did a lot of sailing at 7 and 8 knots. As I said, it was a good-luck trip.

I don't know if a three-knot rule would stand up for all boats. Clearly it is based on an ample fuel supply, even if far from enough to motor all the way, and clearly that fuel must be burned with a bit of common sense in the effort to get one through to where the wind can be expected. Beyond that it is more a matter of comfort than of necessity, because, while one may be becalmed in the regions of prevailing winds for a day or two or three and can afford to sit it out, pretty well counting on the wind's return in due course, this is a very different prospect from lying becalmed in the horse latitudes where there is no assurance that the wind will soon be back.

Some cruising people will line their decks with drums or jerry cans of extra fuel, but there are disadvantages to this. The cluttered decks are more dangerous to get around on, drums have been known to break loose and inflict serious injury, fuel can leak and spill and be a slippery mess, there is even a fire hazard; but mostly it seems to me that the proper cruising boat should be designed with reasonably ample tank capacity and that the ocean voyager should then learn to live with what he has designed or bought, and not feel he must motor all the way. The purist will fault me for turning on power at less than 3 knots, and if I were going into areas where fuel supplies were unlikely to be found, I would be adopting some other rule. Or maybe I would be lining my decks with jerry cans.

The *Cynthia R* should theoretically average about six miles to the gallon, running at minimum rpm, but it appears that on this crossing we really made nine miles to the gallon. Since our sails were always up, they were adding a good boost to the engine, even in the light airs, and I suspect that while we never turned the engine on until our speed had dropped below three knots, there were often long periods when the progress under power dampened our perception of the wind, and we were still motorsailing, very economically, with the sails doing half the work. We would secure the engine to find we were doing four or five knots without it, a very easy situation to be lulled into, especially when the wind is aft. It is a safe rule that if you can smell your exhaust fumes with a following wind you ought to be sailing, not motoring.

This engine is a Perkins 6-354, rated at 95 horsepower, which is really too much for a boat this size, and I suspect we could attain our hull speed of 8 knots under power with the four-cylinder model, rated at sixty horsepower, and be more conservative with fuel. The only arguments I can make in favor of our choice is that a six is thought to be a smoother-running engine than a four, that I have never heard of anyone complaining about too much power, any more than complaining about his winches being too big, and that maybe when we were really punching into a high wind and head sea we would use some of that extra power. But just maybe.

The engine lives under the floor of the main cabin, and by sliding out of my swivel chair I can lift out the steps to that cabin and gaze fondly into the engine room, clean enough, but a mess of control cables, feed lines, tachometer cables, and wires of unknown purpose. (It would really be better if the sailor knew the purpose of each wire, and I was a bit distressed to find after ten years of use that we had one fine wire, covered with a lavender insulation, whose bare end proved it had broken adrift from something. The engine operates faultlessly and all the instruments read, and I still don't know where this wire goes after it disappears into a sheathing with many other vari-colored wires.) The engine room is heavily soundproofed with two inches of Ensolite under the floor, an impervious foam of non-interconnected cells, held in place with a sheathing of pegboard. The engine is mounted on fiber mounts, the hold-down bolts housed in fiber sheaths, to limit transmission of vibration, and under it is a lead-lined drip pan, to catch not only the drippings but the high-frequency sounds as well. The cabin floor is carpeted. All along the port side, lying against the fiberglass hull in neat rows, are tins of alcohol stove fuel. On the starboard side it looks messier, as laced around this space are the icebox drain hose; the bilge pump intake hose from the sump; the fuel lines and gross fuel filter; a coil of spare stainless-steel wire rope; plastic bottles of distilled water; and the clutch, throttle, shutoff, and tachometer cables.

I can check the oil and hydraulic fluid; change the oil filter; check the fuel filters, control fuel feed line, and return valves; and lock the shaft by just removing the steps. To check water or batteries, to add oil, or to make repairs, I must roll up the carpet and lift a large hatch over the entire starboard side of the engine. If we ever have to lift the engine, or remove the head or header tank, I will have to remove the galley and dinette joiner work over a similar hatch to port. The joiner work is designed for this, but I do not look forward to the day it must be done.

I would much prefer an engine room where one can sort of walk around the engine, or sit down beside it and hold its hand and take its temperature and pulse and give it a sponge bath, but on a 31-foot waterline you can't have everything.

But let us leave the Chamber of Horrors for now. I really get into it only seldom during a passage if I have cared for it properly in port, and this too is one of the relaxing qualities of the ocean voyage.

It was not always thus. Behind us lie not only the days from Bermuda, but the nearly 800-mile passage to Bermuda from Charleston, South Carolina, whence we had taken our departure, and those days in Charleston fitting out. Ah, those days in Charleston!

Those days in Charleston prior to sailing had been something else, referred to later by my crew as their days in purgatory. They were all strangers to each other, and Parker even a stranger to me, having been recruited from a Navy ROTC class at Harvard, so that someone could pinch hit in the navigation department. All of us had been offshore; none had crossed an ocean. None of us had used his navigation in earnest at sea.

Paul was not yet with us, as my daughter had signed on for the shakedown cruise to Bermuda, whence she would return, somewhat shaken down, to her home and husband. The daily temperature in Charleston was in the nineties and the humidity higher. Mosquitoes hummed about us in the evening. The boat, which had been a month in the yard at Charleston, showed some minor defects on our arrival; to wit, the engine had a breakdown and was unusable and the main boom had delaminated, so we could not use that sail. When these failures had been repaired and an overabundant supply of stores placed on board, and we had pulled out of the yard to the yacht basin, we found we couldn't use the stove. After a struggle to locate a replacement valve on a weekend and fit it, and being at last ready for sea, a hurricane was reported off Charleston. A hurricane there in June is almost unheard of. I can only say that it was to the credit of my crew that they did not desert when I decided not to sail until the hurricane was clear of the area, although I guess they agreed later when we learned that in 1968, for the first time in history, the start of the Bermuda Race had been postponed because of this very hurricane.

These doubts, these days of tension, the self-examination, asking oneself if everything has been done that should be done, the heat and the sweat and the mosquitoes are not conducive to sound sleep. Perhaps none of us felt as confident as he would have liked to feel. But by the twenty-third of June our work was finished. The 65-pound bower anchor, which comes over a roller chock fitted at the stemhead and houses there with its muddy flukes outboard, had been cleaned and sent below, where its weight would be amidships and below the waterline instead of out on the end of the overhang forward and six feet above the water. The 200 pounds of anchor chain had been drawn back through the pipe that drains the chain locker, so that it too now rested at the base of the mast step, below the waterline and amidships instead of resting just above the cutwater forward. The dinghy, for which there are davits aft, had been stowed bottom up on top of the house, bringing its 150 pounds amidships. I am as firm a believer in centering the weights for ocean passages, to prevent the pendulum motion which causes a boat to plunge and bury, as I am for doing the same in racing. A clutch of three-quarter-inch oak battens, eight feet long, had been stowed on the lazarette floor, in case we suffered a second delamination of the main boom at sea. (They have never been used.) The emergency tiller was on top of them and within reach of a panel in the aft stateroom which, when removed, reveals the rudder stock and the keyway and key for locking this tiller in place. The idea is that if the pedestal steerer should suffer a breakdown, we can steer from within the aft stateroom, placing a compass on the cabin sole. An old tire, carefully wrapped in plastic for cleanliness, was lashed to the lazarette hatch, to which a three-fathom chain and 200 feet of nylon anchor line could be shacked to serve as a drogue. Most modern boats are not docile lying to a sea anchor streamed from the bow and respond better to a drogue or warps astern, and I have no doubt *Cynthia R* would respond best this way. Her aft cabin and midships bridge deck leave less to be feared from a boarding sea aft than from another direction, and her very full forward sections and lack of forefoot under the water should serve to prevent burying the bow and pitchpoling or broaching when running off before a breaking sea. (But I hope I never have the opportunity of putting this to the ultimate test.) A six-man inflatable raft was lashed in its original envelope behind the bridge deck seat. The instructions say that if it is in the original factory packing it should not be inflated for testing, and I must say this leaves a certain doubt in one's mind. It is rather like testing your parachute to see if it will open. If it does, you have to repack it and start wondering again. Outboard of the lifeline was lashed a man-overboard kit, a dacron envelope, held shut by three bronze pins threaded through bronze rings on back and flap, containing the base of the pole with flag, connected by floating line to the strobe light and life vest. A firm pull on a lanyard within reach of the helmsman drops the lot into the sea where, if all is right, the flag waves and the light begins to flash. A carton of high-nutrient milkshakes had been placed in the deck box behind the helm, in case heavy weather prevented us from feeding the inner man. A plastic bag of thimbles, wire clamps, and 18-inch lengths of chain was in the bilge, in case a turnbuckle fitting let go. Safety harnesses had been tried on for size.

On the morning of June 23, then, it had been calm, hot, and muggy. A call to the weather bureau brought the news that Hurricane Brenda was now between Bermuda and Hatteras and moving away with accelerating velocity to the northeast. When I came back on board and announced that we would sail after breakfast, I wonder if my crew believed me. On the ebb tide we swept quickly down the river; Fort Sumter dropped astern; by the time docking lines and fenders were stowed and sails were raised we were already checking off the buoys of the entrance channel. As we rounded the outer sea buoy off the channel at 1130, a light southerly sprang up. The sails filled, the engine was secured, and now each of us, keeping his doubts and fears to himself, commended his future to his separate god or fortune, and looking no more behind us, but only straight ahead, we shaped a course for Bermuda, 800 miles to the east.

This, too, was a fortunate trip; had we but known, we could have nailed down the sheets outside the breakwaters and not touched them until Bermuda was in sight on the starboard bow. But of course we played them in and out, and we changed jibs, and we sailed out of our way to pick up a large drifting Japanese glass net float (the Japanese were fishing off Bermuda that year), but none of it was really necessary. We had covered those miles in six days with almost no use of the engine; we had shaped up to such problems as nature had tossed at us; Bermuda had been only a few miles from where it was supposed to be; nothing was amiss with boat or gear. At Bermuda my daughter's lovely face on the pillow across the cabin was replaced by Paul's. I missed her, although there is a feeling of relaxation with an all-male crew which is to some extent a compensation. Our self-confidence was restored, our tanks were refilled with water and the few gallons of fuel, the icebox was once again loaded with fresh food, and it was with a feeling of deep inward calm that we set out on the longer passage to Horta.

And now our noon position shows a run of 160 miles; Parker, who has long since finished the lunch dishes, has announced that we logged 7.2 miles in the past hour; he and Skip are on the bridge deck reading excerpts from Bill Snaith's *Across the Western Ocean* and chuckling over it; and the dough has risen and I must light the oven. We will have fresh bread at dinner, and a tinned stew, and after dinner the whole ship's company will sit on deck for a while and read from a paperback anthology of poetry and watch the sun go down and the waves turn from Gulf Stream blue capped with flashing white to a deep blue-black with creamy suds, until finally the sea is blacker than the black night sky and only the ghosts of breaking crests and the phosphorescence of our own wash reveal its surface.

Skip is a Jewish boy, the only son of one of Seattle's better-known sailors, and if we were to appoint a morale officer it would be Skip. The day I made up my mind I would like to have him on board we were racing off the west coast of Vancouver Island, crew for his father on their 73-foot yawl, and to give the other boats a chance he had chosen to tow a Boston Whaler. Well, it sometimes gets lumpy out there, the wind having a fetch all the way from Japan, and in due course we pulled the bow ring out of the Whaler and did a jibing maneuver to come back alongside, Skip preparing to board it. His father is the kind of person for whom we all jump when he says "Jump!", but this time, just as he said: "Don't jump till I tell you," Skip jumped with perfect timing. Anyone who jumps when Henry says "Don't jump," was the man for me, but I felt a particular responsibility for Skip. There is a strong family feeling for the only son, and his parents could hardly fail to have some misgivings about this venture, but they still encouraged him to come, and I really felt I ought to bring him back alive.

John, on the other hand, is one of six sons, and perhaps his parents would never notice if one was missing. All these men were eminently able to take care of themselves, of course, but John seemed always to be challenging fate, to be walking on the edge of the cliff. At the age of fifteen he and his father and I had been crew on a 48-foot ketch on a nonstop trip from Seattle to San Diego, and when the weather brought us to bare poles and we adults were maybe a little nervous, John brought out a 15-foot diameter nylon parachute to fly from the forestay.

Paul, who had sailed with John in the Northwest, was a good companion and foil. He seemed always amazed at finding himself sailing an ocean, at the life around us, at the busy navigators, at the landfalls.

Parker's sailing had been on the coast of Maine, a bond with me, as my early years of sailing were all there, and he had been off on the Monhegan races. Parker at times grew introspective, brooding over lost loves, I would surmise, and then Skip would cheer him up.

"So the answer is Chicken Chow Mein. What's the question?" Skip would say. And the question, of course, was: "Who is the world's greatest living *kamikaze* pilot?"

Innocent pleasures, tolerance, and consideration marked this group, and it was a great pleasure to be on the sidelines observing the coming generation on their own, much less discouraging than reading the press about them. Once, perhaps, I was concerned that their pleasures might become less innocent. Tied to the quay at Ponta Delgada a pimp was trying to pump up business for a local house. "All very nice girls, pretty girls, they very nice to you." The boys were interested, although maybe only in the pitch; working below, I could not be sure. "They cost you only five dollar." I could hear the boys saying, "Five dollars? That's really not so much. Where did you say this club is?" But I couldn't see their faces. Who was having whom on? And how, without being a prudish old fuddy, could I suggest that they avoid exposure when we had another 1,000 miles ahead of us?

The pimp came to my rescue: "Only five dollar," he repeated, "And the girls, they're all virgins."

"Grab it, fellows," I yelled from below. "Anytime you can get virgins at five dollars apiece you've got the best bargain of the year."

They broke up in the cockpit, the pimp retired with good grace, considering some of the comments on the virginity of his working girls. And somehow I felt the boys themselves were looking for some way out, too, without being prudish old fuddies.

It was John who had had to climb to the masthead in mid-ocean. Our jib halliard is loose ended, so that it can be tied off from the mast in harbor, and since the standing end when the jib is set is wire rope, the loose end must be passed through a hole in the cleat and a figure-eight knot tied in it to prevent it from climbing the mast. It was mercifully calm for the North Atlantic the day John forgot to do this, and in changing headsails he lost the halliard. While the crew cheered him on, he shinned barefoot up the mast to where the loose end had whipped itself around the masthead fitting, and slid down with the bitter end in his teeth. (No, the bitter end doesn't really taste bitter; it's just supposed to be secured to a bitt.)

Do we feel lonely? I think the answer is no. Alone, yes, but not really lonely. It's a hackneyed question and answer, which seems never to lose its fascination for the landsman and the dreamer. The truth may be that the types who wind up out there are not the types who feel its loneliness, while those who would feel it either have the good sense not to go or, having tried it, never return. And there must be some who feel loneliness is a small price to pay for the adventure.

Our ocean has been full of life, from the little plankton which wink and sparkle at you when you flush the toilet at night to the beautiful but silly tropic birds. Soon after the gulls forsook us these snow-white birds with the dramatically long swallowtails came, often singly, to hover around the sails and to get caught in the back eddies around the spinnaker. They seemed to have an affinity for this sail and would glide in from the side, invariably get caught in some unexpected air current, and fall clumsily into the bellying sail, to flap angrily away. Around the Azores we were to see shearwaters in numbers to darken the sky. Their aim was to settle on the log line, not sensing its rotation. Many a shearwater put on a comic show for us in this manner, his normal majestic grace affronted by his being dumped, chin first, into the sea. A few made a pass at eating the rotor, but it proved an elusive prey. One day a pod of whales emerged a mile to the north, blowing and rolling and lifting their great spade flukes high in the air, like scenes from prints of the old whaling ships, and John and Paul, who had been reading *Moby Dick,* were beside themselves. Whales are not at all uncommon. In channels of the Northwest we have been completely surrounded by killer whales, disporting themselves like porpoise; in the Gulf of Maine I have literally grabbed a boathook to push off from a 60-foot whale on collision course, who fortunately dropped under our keel and surfaced on the other side; in the Mediterranean we eased up to a sleeping whale so close that I felt tempted to slip into the water, swim over, and climb on board. Here in mid-Atlantic we have seen a few sea turtles, indeed we unintentionally hit one the other day, sending him swimming down and away at what in his mind was probably great haste, although it looked rather lazy to us. At night, streaks of phosphorescence in the water around us indicate the existence of the larger fish, dashing upon some less fortunate and smaller relative. Later, as we neared Cape St. Vincent on the coast of Portugal, we were to sail through several bands of luminous water in the dark night, hundreds of feet in width and seeming to stretch from horizon to horizon across our course, shoals of sardines by the millions, through which streaked the bigger fish feeding on this delicacy. Flying fish skitter away across the wavetops and many a one zoomed on board, usually at night, once or twice to land flopping on the cabin top. But none was big enough to bother cooking, and we were pulling desiccated miniatures out of hidden corners and ventilators for a year to come.

From time to time we have crossed a steamer lane and may see two or three ships at once, after days of empty horizon. We must seem to be in good shape, as none has altered course to look us over or to offer aid. Then Skip, our radio man, jumps to the radio telephone and on the ship-to-ship frequency tries to contact them. But it seems they are not standing radio watch, as we never get a reply. Or have we become a ghost ship, neither seen nor heard? We found out on arrival at Gibraltar why no ship had replied; we were not putting out. It was never quite clear to me whether the humidity had damped out our entire transmission or whether there was a fault in the ship-to-ship circuit (or whether the big ships were only guarding 2182), because by the time we were in Malta, where winter layup and servicing were scheduled, the radio was transmitting again. But since the Mediterranean ship-to-ship frequency is different from that installed, we were unable to prove much. As I mentioned in the Introduction, I am not an electronics man. But it had been a great comfort all the way across the Atlantic to know we had a radio telephone in case of need. Or at least it had been a comfort to wives and mothers at home. This radio-telephone was installed to avoid further argument with those who felt I was hazarding our lives in sailing without it, chiefly Cynthia.

"I think we ought to get a radio-telephone before we do any more cruising. Everybody has a radio-telephone these days," Cynthia would say.

"That's not true," I would reply, displaying my suave and soothing technique in discussion. "That sounds like our daughter in junior high days saying 'Everyone wears heels nows.' "

"But what are you going to do when you're in trouble?"

I know better than to say, "I never get into trouble." Cynthia has sailed with me too long to swallow that.

"What kind of trouble?" I ask.

"Any kind. Suppose you're aground or dismasted or on fire or caught in a storm?"

"Look," I'd say, "I can't think of any situation where I

shouldn't be doing something else. I ought to be pumping or
bailing or grabbing a fire extinguisher or rowing out an anchor
to kedge off or setting up a jury rig or launching a life raft or
something. Anything except yakking on the telephone while the
ship goes down under us."

"But you know the insurance rates are lower." She knows she
she has hit my sensitive spot when she talks about economies.

"I spent twenty years as a marine underwriter and I never saw
a claim which was in any way mitigated by the use of a radio-
telephone. All the use I know is by boats that manage to run
out of gas and call the Coast Guard to tow them home. Anyway, insurance credits were just a local gimmick to cut rates and
grab business. Utterly unjustified by statistics. In fact," I say,
waxing eloquent about a pet peeve of long ago, "I'll bet if the
facts were known more insurance claims are paid for damaged
radio-telephones than are saved by their use."

But I've run off the track with that argument. The insurance
companies' problems are not her problems. I would have to
have made up some story such as: "Cynthia, statistics prove
that radio-telephone aerials attract lightning," or "make the
boat topheavy," or "are a known source of the electrocution of
the crew." Precaution is her sensitive spot. None of these is true,
of course, but it might have carried the day, and if stated with sufficient conviction I don't think Cynthia would have challenged
me with a "Let's see you prove that hokum." So I had just continued to refuse to have one.

In Charleston I had one installed.

Since those days it hasn't done us much good, but then it
hasn't done us any harm, either, and it makes my navigating
cabin look very official. But, in all fairness, I have since run into
one case where lives were saved by the radio-telephone. Acquaintances of ours were sailed one night onto a remote coral
reef in the Bahamas by their hired crew, and before the boat
had quite broken up they got through on 2182 and were later
picked up from the desert island near this reef. And if I know of
one such case, there must be dozens. I do find, though, that the
majority of sailors who quietly come and go on long passages

(and the world is full of them) do so without benefit of a telephone.

Let's talk about sails instead. Sails will pull a boat faster than a radio.

Cynthia R is a ketch, although the ratio of mizzen to total sail area is not much greater than with some yawls. There is an argument that, with today's materials, the sloop is more suitable for cruising, but I don't subscribe to this view, and neither do the majority of cruisers we encounter in remote places, judging from the fact that most of them are in ketches. We are a conservative lot, aren't we? Or perhaps it is laziness, or old age. Anyway, I don't like to crawl forward and reef under those circumstances when reefing is indicated, and much prefer dropping a mizzen, which is no more trouble than trimming a sheet. Or, if there is a sudden squall, dropping the main. We must still reef at times, but I should guess it has cut the incidence of reefing to 25 percent of what it would be with a sloop rig.

The fore triangle is undivided, and here I have taken advantage of the strength of modern materials. My own experience with the divided fore triangle in the past was that hauling the jib around the staysail with every tack was a damn nuisance—I have admitted to laziness—and on *Cynthia R* we carry both a No. 2 genoa and a club jib. A club jib almost filling the fore triangle is as good a workhorse as a genoa once the wind is up to the middle of Force 4, and with more wind than that one benefits from its center of effort being farther forward than is true of an overlapping sail. When one is beating to windward, it is a joy to have no sheets to handle. When running off the wind it is a dog, the heavy club preventing the sail from lifting and filling, so that it slams back and forth on its track, crushing the stoppers and one's nerves. Best then to replace it with the genoa or, if it is a short leg downwind, to strap it in flat amidships. The genoa is the sail for reaching, as well as for windward work in light airs. We carry only the No. 2 because the No. 1 genoa is really a racing sail with a range of usefulness too limited to justify its stowage space on a small cruising boat. When the air is so light that a No. 2 won't keep us moving, the chances are that we will be on power anyway, or if off the wind, under spinnaker. And from our bridge-deck steering station, visibility is problem enough even with the No. 2 set on a short tack pennant. On a run the genoa and main can be set wing and wing, and with no sea it will hold itself full, but of course it is better to help it, either by poling it out, an excellent rig until you come to take it in shorthanded after the wind and sea have kicked up, or by leading the sheet through a snatch-block on the end of the mizzen boom.

A storm jib or spitfire is in its bag somewhere in the bottom of the sail bin. It has been used only once, and then because the outhaul fitting on the club pulled out, not because it was a storm. A storm trisail has also been sent up only once. A smaller mizzen, though, cut low and with a hollow roach and no battens, has been used for most of the Atlantic passage, as it gives us better balance on these reaching conditions.

The prize of this trip has been the spinnaker. We didn't get one with our original sails, partly because Cynthia is never happy when she hears the suggestion of "Let's pop the chute," and partly because I was already encountering cost overruns. (Don't we all?) But with four eager young men and an ocean it seemed essential to provide them with a spinnaker to play with, and I searched the used sail lists for one of approximately our size. They were being listed back then in 1968 at maybe $350 to $500 used. But look! Here is one of almost exactly our size, a Ratsey sail to boot, listed on a "make offer" basis. I picked up the phone, called the used-sail dealer, confirmed that it was still on his shelf, and then said, "If I send you a check for $75 today, will you ship the sail to Charleston on its receipt?" There was a moment's silence, then "Yes." So that's how we had gotten a masthead Ratsey spinnaker for a 44-footer for $75. I leave it to your imaginations to picture its age and condition, which rather resembled a star map of the heavens, entire constellations of patches, but in following winds of up to 10 knots it was a great sail. At 11 to 12 knots it would begin to come apart, the boys would drop it, and I would spend a few hours with ripstop, needle, and thread.

One gentle day of broad reaching across a barely rippled sea we had set it outside the jib, added the mizzen staysail, and still the crew called for more sail. The awning was rigged under the spinnaker pole as a square stunsail or water sail, and the main and mizzen sail covers run up and spread-eagled on the shrouds. Everything drew, and what had started out as a stunt became our sail plan for the entire day, a day which might have been spent grinding along under power without all this stuff up in the air.

The days come and go. The ripples are replaced by wavelets and the light stuff is sent below. The wavelets become rolling seas, and we are driving at nearly hull speed under jib and main, or jib and reefed main, and then that weather pattern passes, one day the reef is shaken out, the next day the mizzen

is added, and some evening at sunset we are becalmed again. Another chapter of an ocean passage.

The moon was approaching first quarter when we sailed from Bermuda. It had come to full and was waning as we approached the Azores. The Fourth of July had come while we still had fresh food and we had crossed the American flag and the CCA pennant over the fireplace. Skip had strung red, white, and blue streamers from overhead, and after bucket showers of salt water on the poop deck we had opened a bottle of Mouton Cadet and drunk a toast to freedom and then feasted on roast lamb rubbed with garlic, baked potatoes, spinach, and an orange layer cake, baked and frosted by Parker.

It was five days later that you first found us baking bread, and on that day we had crossed the halfway mark to the Azores and had celebrated both bread and progress with a pre-dinner drink for all hands, pouring suitable libations to Aeolus and to Poseidon, and carrying spinnaker and mizzen staysail all night under the full moon.

Another five days brought us to Bastille Day. We were now picking up the radio beacon on Flores, out of sight to the north, the ship's pool on sighting land was made up, and we marked the day with a bottle of Beaujolais with our dinner and liqueurs thereafter, a singing of *La Marseillaise*, which quickly degenerated into *Auprès de ma blonde*, and the off watch retired happily to restless sleep as the boat swung along through a night of rising wind and a lump of sea.

The final day was hazy and we were closing fast with our hoped-for landfall. The orders to the helm had not altered our compass course for 44 hours, as the slowly changing variation just balanced any change indicated by our sights or by the suspected set of the current. Shearwaters and petrels were thick around us. Suspense was high, and the crew reminded me again of Rule 17 of the Code of Oleron, coming down from Eleanor of Aquitaine of about A.D. 1150. "But when the ship arrives at the land where the wine grows the mariners ought to have drink and the master ought to find it." And there, at 1410, it was—Land, Ho! The sharp outline of a noble headland two miles distant on our port bow. And even as I regretted that it

was not dead ahead, there was another headland hardening out of the mist, the Castello Branco, our proper landfall, the forestay lining up on its seaward cliff.

Two hours later we were rounding the southeast corner of Fayal and making plans for a smart entry into the harbor of Horta. A pilot boat sheared alongside, and the pilot leaped on board, guiding us by hand signals. Rounding the end of the sea-wall, we came head to wind, and within sixty seconds and without a spoken word, the sails came down and were furled, the engine was on, the flag went up at the stern staff, fenders and docking lines appeared, and the crew stood by with lines and boathooks, as if we had done this daily. Good show! Good crew! I shall find them wine with their dinner tonight.

That was a long passage for us, but by world cruising standards it was only a run. Shorter passages fill our log books, but no two seem alike. Some are calm throughout; some start calm and end in a turmoil of wind and spray; others start with a plunging sea, with water breaking over the cabin top, and end in hours of motoring.

Perhaps the jolliest end of all was our approach to Gibraltar as we homed in from the Azores. Cape St. Vincent, our landfall, had not died away nobly in the sunset; it had been merely a winking light in the night, surrounded by shipping, and with morning we were again out of sight of land.

"Smallest continent I ever saw," Parker commented.

We drifted and swam in the Gulf of Cadiz; then, raising full sail and spinnaker, we eased past Trafalgar toward the Strait, preparing ship for the captain's dinner. Streamers and balloons decorated the cabin, place cards were set, a banner identifying the crew as Men of Infinite Resource and Sagacity was suspended over the table. A dinner of canned ham with canned asparagus hollandaise and rice, washed down with our last bottle of Pico Branco, was consumed, while the ship sailed majestically into the Strait of Gibraltar under spinnaker and on auto pilot, no soul visible at the wheel (but a sharp lookout through the forward windows of the cabin house). Toasts were drunk to the voyage, short speeches were made, and in the fading light after dinner the entire crew assembled in the cockpit for a final reading of Byron's "Ocean."

"Roll on, thou deep and dark blue ocean, roll. . . ." And in the morning we came to harbor in Gibraltar.

II

Harbor

To a stormy, tossing anchorage
Where yawls and ketches ride.
John Masefield,
"A Wanderer's Song"

Now I ask you! Who the hell wants that? What do you suppose Mrs. Masefield used to say after a rough day on the Channel when John asked: "Hey, Honeybun, which stormy, tossing anchorage would you like to try sleeping in tonight?" I know what Cynthia would say. She'd say, "You can get yourself another wife."

This doesn't mean that we don't wind up in them from time to time, but it is a mistake, psychologically, physically, and maritally.

There are all kinds of harbors, including Masefield's kind, but for the most part they fall into three groups in our minds: the artificial, the natural, and the open anchorage. At the end of a passage any one of them may look good. I don't know why we sailors, who so looked forward to breaking with the land and committing our fortunes to the open sea, should so anticipate coming to harbor at the end; perhaps the successful completion of another phase of the season's voyaging is reason enough, a relaxation, a novel change from the days at sea. Or more likely we are tired, cold, hungry, or maybe a little seasick, part of the price one pays for the thrill of a passage.

More often than not the harbor one reaches after the ocean passage is of the artificial type; it almost has to be a port of entry and a base for resupply, and this means a city, break-waters, pollution, traffic, and the other blessings of civilization. Throughout a large part of the world a seaport means just this; one's boat lies in oil-covered sewage, sloshed back and forth by whatever waves or wakes penetrate the opening to reflect from the vertical sides, illuminated by floodlights at night, and re-ceiving its daily coating of fallout.

Artificial harbors mean lying to a quay, and if the space is uncrowded you may lie broadside, in which case your decks and cockpit become a litter basket for the curious who stare at you as you go about your daily life, while dropping their gum wrappers and cigarette ashes and peanut shells upon you. Or you may moor bow or stern to the quay, as is the custom in the Mediterranean, where quayside space is always in short supply, in which case your anchor joins the knitting, as they say, of a dozen other anchors and chains across the bottom, to be lifted by the first big boat to move, while you struggle ashore over your gangplank, a cumbersome object to handle at best.

As we come into such a harbor we check its perimeter to learn where the yachts are lying, we estimate from observing the other boats what depth of water we can expect at the quay, we note how high the quay is above the water, where the floodlights and traffic may be the least objectionable, and where bollards or rings exist for mooring lines. With this we make our best deci-sion on coming in broadside or end on to the quay. If broadside, fenders are set out on one side and a bow and stern line made ready, led through a chock, and the coil laid handily on deck. All this time we may have been receiving peremptory whistles or hand signals from shore, if in the Mediterranean, and there is always a question of whether to heed them or not. Usually they are shoreside hangers-on, who have less idea than we as to a suitable place to lie, and who are just looking for a chance to catch our lines, for which they presumably expect a pack of cigarettes. If we are coming in alongside, it is particularly impor-

tant not to pass them one's lines. Give a man a line and he
pulls on it (it seems to be a reflex), just at that point when
steerageway is at a minimum, or he snubs it down as one tries
to glide forward for a perfect landing, skewing the boat obliquely
across the intended approach pattern. Of course, in ignoring the
importunities from the quayside one runs the risk that it may
be the harbor officials themselves (they don't wear uniforms
everywhere, you know).

But if the harbor is crowded, or a slop is rolling boats against
the quay, or the depth is not right, we will want to moor end
in. A sailboat maneuvers poorly in reverse, especially in a cross
wind. So all things being equal we will come bow in by preference. Fenders will be set out on both sides, two docking lines
made ready forward, and an anchor and anchor line prepared to
let go aft. When our bow is about 100 feet from the quay I
drop the anchor and scamper forward, calling over my shoulder,
"OK, come in slowly; hold her straight; keep steerageway." I
grab a bow line, ready to spring over the pulpit. "Fifty feet;
thirty feet; twenty feet; keep coming; KEEP COMING, DAMN
IT!"

"I can't; the anchor line's caught around a cleat."

That's why I prefer to come in alongside.

At times circumstances indicate back-in parking; perhaps the nature of the harbor requires chain, which is not transferable aft, instead of line; perhaps we know we will want to use our gangplank, not transferable forward, instead of climbing over the pulpit; perhaps the slap of wavelets under the stern will be an annoyance; perhaps we will sacrifice maneuverability on entering in order to gain it on getting clear. Now we must be ready to pay out chain forward, a job I assign to Cynthia, not because the chain is dirty to handle, but because the chances of botching the job of steering backwards are excellent and I find I would rather botch it myself. It usually requires repeated bursts of power ahead, with helm hard over, followed by backing down with helm reversed, in order to keep the boat backing into her slot, and at the right moment one must drop the controls and jump aft to a readied stern line. This time I am really grateful to anyone who catches it and gets a wrap on a bollard. By now uniformed men have joined the crowd on the quay, although we cannot yet sort out who is customs, quarantine, police, immigration, or harbor master, and while we are adjusting fenders to bear on the neighboring boats, setting up on docking lines and anchor chain, securing the engine, rigging the mizzen halliard as a topping lift for the gangplank, and getting it ashore, they are already firing questions: "Where you come from? How long you stay here? Where you go next? You got crew list?"

I am afraid we have run into many cruising people who have done the Med and who have probably seen little else than these artificial harbors, but at least they can say at home that, yes, they have sailed to Majorca and Monaco, to Capri and Corfu, to Piraeus and Rhodes, all the names that spell glamour and smell of sewage. To us they are necessary evils. One must enter and clear, get fuel and water and ice and stores, and one must pick up and discharge guests near airports, and one must see certain sights, but then let's be off to the natural harbor. That's what we came cruising for.

While some sailors are in the game for the ocean passages, some to satisfy their ego, most of us and nearly all our wives are

explorers at heart, harbor hopping in search of new discoveries. This harbor may be a very personal thing, the new acquaintance whose moods, whose reliability, must be tested, or an old friend welcoming us back to her embrace after a long absence. Perhaps it has no name and we must invent one for it. In due course we find we have joined that obnoxious class who feel that any later visitor to "our" harbor is an interloper with no right to intrude on our personal preserve where we have studied the winds and the holding ground and have become accustomed to sunbathing and skinny dipping in glorious solitude.

And to yet others a harbor means people, not tourists in the mass, but the small aggregation of inhabitants who can make of a visit a lifetime memory.

But there are different tastes in harbors, even amongst the explorers. One of our acquaintances is Eric Williams, author of that great story of escape *The Wooden Horse*, who now, with his wife, Sibyl, lives on the *Escaper*, a cutter of about our size. Conditioned by his lifetime association with escape, he seeks the open bay, preferably a windy one, although with an offshore wind, where he can lie in a smart breeze, cooling him in the heat of a Mediterranean summer and blowing the bugs away, but yet in calm water and with a clear, quick exit when he wants to get away.

We often find ourselves in a similar situation, although it is less from choice than from absence of choice. If I suggest such an open anchorage, Cynthia will say, "Suppose the wind shifts?" To which I may reply: "Look, the wind hasn't shifted here for two months." And of course that may turn out to be the very night the wind shifts. Cynthia by preference (and I go along with this line of reasoning) will take a wraparound harbor any day. This is a very comfortable feeling, to know that no matter which way the wind blows we are protected; that when an unexpected swell makes up outside it is not going to penetrate to our anchorage. But wrap-around is not enough. One wants a happy combination of depths, good holding ground, freedom from insects, perhaps solitude, a pleasant and

varied outlook, clean water for swimming. We search the chart
for possibilities and as like as not are fooled. The outlook and
the prospects for swimming may be almost self-evident, but the
insects and the solitude we will find out about only after we
are settled in. So let me touch on anchoring.

For depth we prefer something between two and five fathoms,
although I know many of our friends look for deeper water
than this. Our choice is based on the simple fact that our chain
locker holds conveniently about 100 feet of chain, and while
we carry over twice that length, the excess is stowed where it
will not clog the inner end of the hawsepipe. Chain has a way
of piling up on itself in a steep, narrow peak, like a tropical ant-
hill, and as you bring up an anchor, unless the chain locker
is accessible and your crew includes a midget who enjoys guiding muddy chain into a better stowage pattern, you find that it
has ceased to feed down the hawsepipe at just about the moment your anchor breaks its grip on the bottom, leaving you
with a drifting boat, a dragging anchor, and muddy hands,

while you yell at your wife above the shrilling wind to try to hold the boat where it is.

"Well, give her a little power! Hell, not that much power!— Don't let her fall off yet!"

And so on. The fact is, you have to yell at someone and there's no use yelling at the wind. You know perfectly well you couldn't hold the boat in position with no steerageway yourself either.

With only 100 feet of chain easily available we theoretically should anchor in not more than 20 feet of water in order to have scope equal to five times the depth, but we often find our anchor holding nicely in 30 feet if the bottom is good. The long catenary of the chain is a fine shock absorber, and we can, in extremis, work out from deep stowage as much more chain as we want.

The anchor on the end of this chain is a local Seattle anchor, a 65-pound Forfjord, selected because its design conformed to the shape of our bow, which is fitted with a roller chock at the stem head. The shank of the Forfjord comes in over the roller chock and passes the balance point. The anchor falls then into position with its flukes outboard straddling the stem and dropping their load of mud overboard. We carry an electric windlass, and to raise the anchor I simply step on the deck button, keeping one eye on the hawsepipe deck opening under the windlass, in case of a pile-up of chain, and the other overside to see when we are straight up and down. With the passage of time our procedure for getting under way has become more standardized. The engine will be on, not because I am afraid to sail away from an anchorage (in fact, everyone should practice getting off under sail against that day the engine fails to start), but because it is thought better not to draw the heavy load of the electric windlass without the alternator doing its bit. The rudder is put amidships. The chain is brought taut, and I relax a moment from the effort of stepping on the button to let the weight of the chain start to draw us ahead; once the boat has some forward way, she continues fairly readily, and we try to keep the slack coming in over the windlass so that we don't override the bight of chain and then get blown off sideways. When the anchor breaks the ground, I yell, "Off the bottom," although unless we are in a tight spot, nothing yet needs to be done. This will be followed soon by my yell of "On the surface," at which point Cynthia knows we can proceed without dragging anchor chain across our bottom. Of course if Cynthia is in the galley doing the wash up, there isn't much point in yelling, but that is a calm-weather situation anyway, and we are all relaxed. In case the chain has piled up under the hawsepipe (and it invariably does) I have rigged a short piece of oak in the chain locker at the foot of the hawsepipe, held to the bulkhead by shockcord, and controlled by a flexible cable leading through a sheave to and through the forward cowl ventilator. A yank on this upsets the pile of chain, and we can continue without interruption. It is very ingenious. Occasionally it works.

For holding ground we like best of all a bottom of clean white sand, a frequent find, but of course indicating the fact that wave action occurs under some circumstances. An utterly protected spot will probably produce a mud bottom, usually good holding, but a bit dirtier to contend with and producing less colorful water. Some mud is like soft butter, and one must beware of anchoring in this if the wind is going to pick up. A good example is Porto Longo on Sapienza Island, just off the Peloponnesus, where the bottom is said to be strewn with the bones of ships which dragged anchor and were dashed on the rocky sides by sudden winds. We visited this harbor to snorkel over the wrecks ourselves, and were driven out by the gusting wind, unable to make our own anchors hold in the soup-like mud. Grass is found through much of the Mediterranean and is less reliable to anchor on than sand; a Danforth, whose holding power we find unbeatable in sand or good mud, becomes a sleigh in grass. One good bunch of grass roots hooked between its flukes, and all holding power is gone. Here the Forfjord is preferable, with its weight and widely spread flukes, but Irving Johnson told me that the old-fashioned kedge or Herreshoff anchor, whose fluke can bite deep down, had served him better in grass than any modern anchor. I have never been shipmates with a CQR or plow anchor and have heard varying reports on its efficiency in grass.

We carry three anchors, the 65-pound Forfjord on chain, a 20-pound Danforth and a 35-pound Danforth, with 200 feet of nylon for each. We also have a few fathoms of chain for each, but I gave up using it long ago. If the botton is clean, we will have anchored with all chain in the first place, as we will also have done if there is coral or sharp rock about (or unfriendly natives, too, who might cut an anchor line in the night), and if it is mud I prefer to clean no chain at all. Scientific proof to the contrary, we can distinguish little difference in holding power if we have enough scope out. It bears repeating that plenty of scope is the key to safe anchoring and that we have dragged just as often because of too little scope as because of poor holding ground. Indeed, I recall a windy day when we had anchored in Koroni to have lunch, after which I rowed ashore through the chop to pick up ice, while Cynthia and our guests stretched themselves out for a nap. Because of other boats around us we had anchored on rather shorter scope than the approved, and when I came back to the dinghy with 100 pounds of ice I was surprised to note how far out into the bay we had anchored. And the more I rowed, the farther it seemed. Fortunately a man in a rowboat can move faster than a boat can drag anchor, and eventually I came up with *Cynthia R*, now almost at sea, her crew snoring loudly.

There are more techniques to mooring a boat than simply to drop an anchor; on very frequent occasions we set two. If the wind is up to Force 5 or more we are very likely to drag a single anchor. *Cynthia R*, in common with a great many modern boats of high bow and cut-away forefoot, and in common with most power cruisers, tends to sail back and forth at anchor, particularly in gusty winds, and as the chain or line fetches up on its anchor, first one way, then the other, it tends to work it slowly through the bottom until it picks up a clump of grass or plastic or streamlines itself with clay and loses its grip. With two anchors set well apart the boat will still present first one side and then the other to the wind, but cannot sail off in wild swoops, for as soon as she starts to travel she fetches up on the far anchor, and always with the same angle of pull at the anchor, hopefully setting it ever deeper.

If we know we are going to set two anchors on arrival, I will usually plant the little Danforth first, and as it goes down try to crab sideways across the wind until at least 100 feet of scope is out, then drop the Forfjord on chain, and fall back on both, adjusting scope so that each takes equal although alternate strain. If we are already lying to chain when the wind comes up, I may put the little Danforth in the dinghy, flake down the anchor line in the bottom so that it will run free, and row off at a desirable angle. It is better to have the line pay out from the dinghy than from on deck, as towing 100 feet or more of hawser

to windward in choppy water can be strenuous work, and it will pay out better when flaked down—that is, in a continuous figure-8 coil—than from a simple round coal. Of course, in the anxiety and haste of the moment you may find that you have flaked it down with the anchor end on top so that it pays out from the bottom, and you have to start all over again.

This is not the only way to set two anchors. One can always turn on the power and motor up to the spot where he thinks the second anchor should go down, but I find it almost impossible under the circumstances which prevail at such a moment to estimate the correct place to let go (unless we have buoyed the first anchor and can see its location) and one tends to risk breaking the first anchor loose while planting the second, so this easy method is reserved for those days when the rising wind is too stiff to row against.

Two anchors are used in other ways. Quite often in calm air a roll may set into a bay, and this is the general case when one is anchored off an open beach, even in a good lee, as anyone who has sailed down the Lesser Antilles has learned. Here an anchor dropped astern, or carried out astern, will keep a boat from perversely lying in the trough, and a roll which might keep you awake all night, clinging to your bunk and listening to the pieces of china in the galley and the bottles in the medicine cabinet clink against each other, and a loose screw roll back and forth in the bilge, is converted into an almost unnoticeable lift and fall. If this is expected we will circle close to the beach, drop a light anchor astern as we head out again, pay out all its scope, then drop our bower and fall back, bow to the swell. The scope astern in this case is not too material if the anchor has once dug in. In fact a light grapnel has proved sufficient here, and we often drop that on a series of docking lines tied together, most of which we recover and untie as we fall back. Then, should that bugaboo of a sudden onshore wind catch you at anchor, you are in a good position to buoy that aft anchor, cast it off, and proceed safely to sea. The truth is, this has never happened to us, but it is one of those things we like to worry about when anchored off an open beach after we have finished worrying about everything else.

Still another two-anchor mooring is known as the Bahamas method, particularly useful for anchoring in narrow channels where the current ebbs and flows, characteristic of the Bahama Cays. Here both anchors are dropped from the bow, the first on the fly, paying out full scope, then letting go the second, and hauling in half the scope on the first. The boat will now lie in one position, merely turning end for end as the tide turns. That is, it will if the wind doesn't blow too hard. We lay this way once in Warderick Wells, when a west wind of such strength blew in that, even with the current rushing by, our counter was actually overhanging the coral on the edge of the channel. Our third anchor was dug out of the engine room and rowed to a sand bank across the channel where, at low tide, it sat ludicrously on dry land, holding us just clear of danger, while we hoped no second boat would come sweeping through the channel on the tide, to trip over our line.

In heavy wind a line ashore, if possible, can be very comforting, and in Greek waters, where furious gusts are a standard experience in harbor, we have often not dared to leave our boat for a walk until we have two anchors down plus a line around a tree or to a chain around a rock. Or in Port Kaio, near Cape Matapan, to the rusty bow of a sunken freighter. It was here that our dinghy was half filled with water on a cloudless night, simply from wind-driven spray right in the landlocked cove. And we well remember one night lying in the little cove under Cape Sidhero on the northeast tip of Crete. The inner basin is too shoal to swing in, so one must lie in the restricted entrance channel between the cliffs, opening southeast, anchored fore and aft to prevent being set into the rocks on either side. It was a calm evening and we had, in fact, rowed an anchor line to the boll of a pine tree on the beach, and we were enjoying a pre-dinner drink when I idly tuned in to the evening forecast. In those days the Greeks were giving an evening forecast in Greek, English, French, and German, a plan unfortunately later abandoned. I thought I understood the Greek to mention "Northwest, Force 7," hardly credible on this quiet evening, but sure enough, it came through Force 7 in each language in turn. I set down my glass and carried out the two Danforths, one on either

quarter, planting them in the knee-deep water of the inner basin. Before the job was done the wind was already whistling, and all night long it shook the masts and buffeted us toward first one side and then the other of our narrow slot, and without the anchors spread to windward we would have been on the rocks of either side in turn. But it was a glorious night, the scudding wavelets under the full moon tripping over each other in their haste to be blown out to sea, while our four-way moor held us securely a few feet from the rocky edges.

The Scandinavian method of mooring is a variation of these; here amongst these steep granite shores and in a nearly tideless sea one drops a stern anchor and eases the bow over a convenient outcropping of glaciated rock, stepping off with one or more lines. If there are trees, one takes a wrap around a convenient birch or pine, but amongst the outer skerries, swept bare by the winter storms, one carries a couple of pitons and a hammer and gets a quick belay in the nearest secure crevice in the

granite. Our pitons are our lightest anchors, and, as with all anchors, a steady pull is more secure than a working motion, so it is wise to provide a good straddle on two bow lines and then to set up on the stern anchor until all is in a state of slight tension.

A nice anchoring job is not finished when the anchors are down and holding. If there is any wind or sea a chain will grind back and forth in its roller chock, or grate across the bobstay of a bowsprit design, and a dry nylon rode under tension will squeak and groan as its strands come and go through the chock or around a cleat or bitt, or against each other. A length of some sort of chafe guard is helpful here, and while it no doubt adds to the life of the line, it probably adds even more to your own life by allowing you a good night's sleep. We find most of our friends now simply using plastic tube, and if the plastic squeaks, a few drops of liquid detergent are indicated. A good soaking with water is better than nothing with a groaning line. If the chain threatens to make bothersome noises I will now shackle a short length of docking line to a link of chain just outboard of the chock, belay it, and then pay out slack on the chain until the line takes all the load. If you use this method, however, be sure the shackle pin threads are greased and not set up too tightly, and that you can put your hands on the pliers in the dark, because you just may have to bring that anchor up in a hurry.

Cynthia and I had come down the chain of the Dodecanese alone, stopping not at the tourist islands, Patmos, Leros, and Kos, but at the seldom visited islands of Gaidhero, Arki, Lipsos, Arkangelos, and Levitha, and at the unprotected concrete pier of Nisiros. Evening after evening we had faced the question of only semi-secure anchorages with twin anchors or warps ashore. Most of the time the *meltemi* had blown with some degree of vigor, covering each anchorage with whitecaps, and on our return from Levitha, which lies some 20 miles out in the Aegean, we had confronted the first gale warning in months, broadcast, as you might guess, after we were safely in harbor. It had been a great sail, but the kind which is even more fun if it is someone else's boat, and apparently more fun for men than women. Finally after a rolling night in the open bay of Tilos, Cynthia announced she had had enough. "I want a landlocked anchorage that we know, where we can get the anchor down and have a good night's sleep." I had thought to continue past a couple of other as yet unvisited islands with questionable harbors, and then double the southwest point of Rhodes, but being unable to guarantee that night's sleep, and sensing mutiny in the air, I gave over. We had a fine reach to Symi and came in to Port Pedhi, a commodious deep bay on its leeward side, where we anchored close under the beach in gusty winds. It was about 3 A.M. when I came awake, sensing something amiss. Maybe it was the goat bells. At any rate, a glance out the companionway revealed high cliffs looming directly over our stern, pale in the moonlight. I hit the starting button as I came on deck (isn't it nice to hear an engine start sometimes) and while Cynthia took the wheel I unscrewed the greased shackle pin and then began grinding in the anchor, which came up bearing about the biggest meadow of grass I have even seen on one anchor.

I was in no position to say, "I told you so," or make any other such husbandly remark, because I had picked the spot to let go in the first place and judged that we were holding. About all anyone could say was, "Who wants to sleep on a beautiful night like this?"

Why all this talk about anchoring and mooring anyway? Simply because on the average coastwise cruising one spends probably seven-eighths of one's time in port, and who can enjoy his shore explorations, his meals, or his lovemaking if the anchor is dragging?

Good harbors of themselves do not make good cruising, and a look at where cruising people like to go brings out other possibilities. There was an evening gam where the subject of the favorite cruising ground came up, and among the many places mentioned which we have never seen were the Aleutian Islands, that string of storm-swept volcanic islands which spans a distance equal to that from New York to the head of Lake Superior, where it was the lure of the north, the aura of mystery surrounding such a remote and uninhabited area, not the harbors, not the weather, which tugged at our speaker's heart. Another voted without qualification for the Polynesian Islands, a more understandable choice to us who don't seek Aleutian weather for fun, but again the harbors had little to do with it. The anchorages of the Marquesas are all rolling ports and subject to squalls. Tahiti's Papeete is a noisy modern city, and so on. No, it was the people this man loved, the gentle, generous, easygoing, laughter-loving, but innately dignified Polynesians. Another man voted for the inland passage from Puget Sound to Alaska, a distance equal to that from Savannah to Portsmouth, New Hampshire, where almost endless choices of alternate channels, fjords, and inlets provide a lifetime of possibilities. The Virgin Islands, the Baltic, the Lesser Antilles, Maine, Greece, and Dalmatia were nominated. One man, who had cruised the South Pacific, the Cape Horn Archipelago, and the Atlantic coast of South America to the West Indies and Florida, named the coasts of Argentina and Brazil his favorite because of the pleasant reception these people had given him everywhere. As the conversation developed we realized that those men who were caught up in the tumble of our normal world, who spent most of their waking hours in dueling with other people, were the ones who dreamed of solitude, of that lonely anchorage where they could drop the hook and lie for days in utter seclusion, while those of us who had already dropped out, temporarily or permanently, were judging cruising grounds in part, at least, by the quality of the personal contact we could expect.

Well, let us be thankful that we have differing objectives in cruising. What a mess the Mediterranean would be if every cruising man wanted to explore ancient ruins, or the South Pacific if hula girls came first. (Frankly, I'm not worried about overcrowding the Aleutians.)

But no one nominated those areas close to our big cities where necessity forces most of us to sail. No one suggested the shores of Lake Michigan (where we learned to define a harbor as "two breakwaters and a pile of coal") or Long Island Sound (which had some pleasant harbors before the days when you could walk across them on the decks of the moored boats), or the inhospitable coast of California. I could have put in a good word for the North Channel and Georgian Bay, and I assume the reason no one mentioned the Great Barrier Reef was that no one that evening had been there. And there are those people who urge the coast of East Africa on me, but I have never learned why.

This has wandered from the subject for a purpose, and that is to admit that there is more to cruising than good harbors, but still, when cruising men get together over a drink, harbors form as big a part of conversation as any other topic. So I should like to offer some reflections on harbors on a regional basis, regions where it is practical to expect the average reader might some day cruise himself, on his own or in a chartered boat. These are generalizations, to be sure, and as such subject to exceptions and attack on the part of those who really know each area, but this is how it will come over to the visitor.

I said earlier that a Lake Michigan harbor was "two breakwaters and a pile of coal", a generalization I might have applied to all the U.S. shores of the Great Lakes, but it isn't really true. There have been a few improvements on the west shore of Like Michigan, where this really was the case a couple of decades ago, and the east shore tended always to offer small lakes connected by dredged channels to Michigan, which serve as harbors. But it is still a far cry from the romance we dream of. Nevertheless, close at hand (close by world cruising standards) are the uncharted, island-studded bays of the Canadian shores of Lake Huron, the North Channel–Georgian Bay coast, slightly more extensive than the coast of Maine, where one could wander literally for weeks, navigating from the spreaders and mooring in the Baltic fashion.

On our own East Coast we can start with Maine—after all, many of our great sailors did start there—where the beauty of the wooded islands and rocky shored passages can lead to an isolated cove or to a white painted village nestled beneath its white church steeple. A couple of points bear remembering as one picks a harbor in Maine, centering around rocks, tide, fog, and mud. If it is clear weather when you enter, chances are it will be foggy when you want to get out. On entering, get your bearings or courses and distances along the safest deepwater channel to the first buoy outside, where normal piloting can take over. Note the tidal stream and decide whether it will set across this channel. Rocks are everywhere on the coast of Maine, sometimes with a pattern, often scattered at random, sometimes miles out to sea, but at least they are all charted, unlike the rocks of Georgian Bay or the Baltic or the coral heads of the Bahamas. Your harbor choice should offer you swinging room clear of rocks at every stage of tide and wind and scope. And don't overlook that tide; it may run from 10 feet to over 20 feet, depending where you are on the coast, and if you anchor near high water, will you be afloat at low? Or if you anchor at low water, have you put out enough scope for high? Will that weedy ledge which protects you now be fifteen feet beneath the surface in six hours? The bottom will probably be mud, very likely some of the stickiest, gummiest, greasy clay you have ever seen. Be prepared for a real scrubbing job as chain and anchor come up. But don't forget, as it goes down, that this dirty mud is covered with generations of old lobster pots, rubber tires, containers and plastic sheet, items an anchor just loves to bite into, but which, at the moment of truth, turn out to have less holding power than you had counted on. Back down well on your anchor when you plant it; give it a chance to tell you right then: "I'm dragging".

These remarks about Maine apply equally well to Nova Scotia, with an added warning that along the southwest coast, from Cape Sable to the Bay of Fundy, the current runs like fury. That bay extends over 100 miles from Grand Manan to Chignecto Head, averaging 30 to 40 miles in width, and its surface must rise and fall an average of 25 feet at spring tides, a 25-foot change over 3,500 square miles of water every six hours! And it still has to flood another 40 miles of Chignecto Bay and nearly 80 miles of Minas Basin, where the tidal range builds up to 50 feet. Long ago I beat into Petit Pass in the Digby Islands in a 21-foot sloop with no engine, having crossed from Grand Manan, then swung around before the wind to come into the boat moorage area. We were now sailing north, back toward the Bay of Fundy, at close to hull speed, wing and wing, a bone in our teeth, but the tide was ebbing and to our horror we were being swept rapidly south toward open St. Mary Bay. Even if we had had an engine I doubt we could have held our own. But we crabbed across, sweeping backward past the moored fishermen, spotted a mooring buoy coming up astern of us, and crash landed backwards, getting a line to it as it bobbed along our side, to spend a delightful three days here, while the diaphone on Boar's Head grunted into the fog. But I should think it folly to expect the average yacht's anchor to hold in the island passages west of Cape Sable.

We once ran with the tide through Cordero Channel ("encumbered with islets and not without dangers," the ever-cheerful *Pilot* informs us) into the Yuculta Rapids, which are accorded a maximum velocity of 6 to 7 knots, but I can assure you I would be reluctant to do it again. It is in these passages that a yawning, whirlpool may suddenly open beside you, and a friend of mine was caught on the rim of such a one, his auxiliary engine at full speed just holding him on the edge. "What should we do? What should we do?" his wife yelled in panic. "Get the camera up and take a picture of it," he said, and she wouldn't speak to him for the rest of the day.

Slack water in these passages is brief. We have stood on the shores of Boat Pass, an entrance to Winter Cove (if you are not too mindful of the *Pilot*'s encouraging "can be used only with local knowledge") and timed the duration of slack water at 30 seconds, by watching a piece of driftwood enter the channel on the last of the ebb, pause, and retrace its route as the flood set in.

And it is time for me to retrace my way to the New England coast, from which I have wandered.

Between Maine and Sandy Hook the harbors are so well known that I will pass them by, but when one turns south from the latter a new situation develops, long stretches of harborless beach, broken by a few inlets hazardous to enter at the very moment you want them. I will leave to others the technique of running an inlet in surf and current and will stand offshore to come in again at Cape May; not that the Delaware Bay is great cruising, but it is a convenient approach to the lovely Chesapeake. And I would add that we found the Cohansey River on the east shore of Delaware Bay a convenient overnight spot, if you don't mind being alone in the marshes. In fact this is one of the finest aspects of a cruise on the Intracoastal Waterway, which follows the Chesapeake, that is, the opportunity to turn aside from the dredged channels, far from the towns on the route, to lie at anchor in some nameless channel, often surrounded by the life of the marshes, the traffic of the waterway at a distance. As silence falls after the noise of anchoring and securing on deck, as the sun lowers, this life begins warily to accept your presence. Migrating ducks settle for the evening, a wader peeks through the marsh grass at you, fish jump in the sunset, if you are lucky a flight of roseate spoonbills will straggle by, or a skimmer graze the surface, his lower mandible cutting the smooth water as he scoops up dinner. Perhaps a curious four-footed creature shambles out on a dead log to regard you with beady eyes. We have seen porpoise in these narrow channels, half out of water, fighting, playing, or I suspect, making love. Turtles may share the dead log or swim by. Once a harmless water snake came up on the anchor chain at night, to coil down in the main sheet, emerging over my bare toes the next day when I was sitting at the wheel. I will confess I was a bit shocked, not then knowing this was the harmless kind. But we have never seen a moccasin. If you don't care for this sort of thing, you may tie up at the frequent marinas instead, but you may still have visitors. Three times we have had rats come on board to raid our garbage, and since the only opening we had left unscreened was the ventilator to the forepeak, the rat's approach pattern to our garbage took it up Cynthia's or my bare legs in the bunk. So back to the marshes. At night one has the unbroken sky in all directions. Depths in these byways and meanders are often not those shown on the chart; I would assume that diversion of the currents and silting after the waterway was dredged has deepened some and caused others to shoal, so caution and leadline or fathometer are indicated.

Another less pleasant form of life prevalent throughout all our east coast are the insects: mosquitoes and midges. Every boat opening should have its screen, and because a screen cuts the air flow in half, an exhaust fan is a great help too. Since no screen will keep out the midges, I have one suggestion for using repellent before you douse it on, always unpleasant on a hot and humid night: spray it first, from inside pointed out, over all the screens. This may deter the midge from entering even where he is able, and allow you to sleep in a clean skin, unless the midge's appetite and your own attractiveness thwart even this method.

Crossing that choppy stretch of water, the Gulf Stream, from Florida to the Bahamas, we come upon a very different harbor pattern. Here in the Bahamas the water is spread thin, and the main problem is finding a protected spot with more than 6 feet of depth. Island after island (and we are talking about a fair distance, because these islands laid out on our northeastern coast would reach from Cape May to Nova Scotia) has an apparently landlocked bay or lagoon, but when the chart is examined it proves to be nearly dry at low water, or with three or four feet at best, or with its entrance so blocked by sand bores or rock as to be inaccessible. We based for a winter at Rock Sound, a truly land-locked bay, but with a fetch of over a mile any time the wind hauled from the usual easterly slant, when we would be forced to crawl around the shallows here and there and find a spot as close to the new windward shore as depth and holding ground allowed. Since the Bahamas are composed of a windlaid sandstone, there are areas where the bottom looks just like sand, but turns out to be smooth sandstone, where you can hear the anchor ring as it hits.

On leaving Rock Sound one had a two-and-one-half-hour run over shoals and between sand bores, with several course changes, before reaching the royal-blue water of Exuma Sound. The courses were mostly based on bearings and distances from a beacon outside Rock Sound, which had unfortunately been carried away in a hurricane two years earlier and never replaced. A dozen channels between sand bores lead off to the west here, and only one does not dead end in the horseshoe of sand characteristic of these current-washed channels, so picking the right one acquired some importance. The only other nearby protection was in the dredged basin of Davis Harbor, opening into Exuma Sound through an entrance channel which accepted our draft from two hours before high water until two hours after, provided no sea was running. Some 40 miles up the coast of Eleuthera is Hatchet Bay, another protected lagoon entered by an artificial cut 100 feet wide through the surrounding cliffs. While Hatchet Bay provided all-around protection, it was running low on supplies when we were there, because the usual supply ship from Florida had missed this channel at night and run head on into the cliffs, the ship being on auto pilot and the skipper's alarm clock having failed to go off in time.

But the typical Bahamas anchorage in settled weather will be in the lee of a cay, whose creamy beach of fine sand continues under the water to provide secure holding, while to leeward the open horizon subtends nearly 180 degrees. And in unsettled weather it will be a rather narrow and current-swept channel between overlapping cays, the wind and tide contending for mastery over your boat, the waves sucking at the undercut cliffs nearby. The rewards are not on shore, but in the water; the richest array of water colors in our cruising experience, exquisite undersea gardens to be visited with mask and fins, cool, clear grottoes two or three fathoms down where the spiny lobster can be speared, days spent romping along in the royal blue, mile-deep waters between the banks, the Northeast Trades filling your sails.

If we work our way against these trades a long way, we can cross to the Windward and Leeward Islands of the Lesser Antilles, beginning with the Virgins, and here we begin to run into a different type of anchorage, the open lee of a big island. In the Bahamas the Trade Wind seas really don't penetrate the narrow cuts; the leeward side of a cay is reasonably calm in normal weather. It just isn't normal enough of the winter to count on it. But in the Antilles it is rare to have a winter norther penetrate, and the ocean swells roll unrestricted through the wide passages between the islands, to curve around and set in from northwest and southwest onto the exposed anchorages and modest bays. Rolling ports, these are, suggesting a stern anchor to hold one's head to the swell.

Some anchorages lie behind a barrier reef on which the sea spends its strength, as is the case at the St. Croix Yacht Club on Teague Bay, or at Christiansted, itself. As summer draws in, the yachtsman takes note of the nearest hurricane hole, a hurricane being no respecter of prevailing winds or the modest protection of coral reefs, and locates a wrap-around spot with mangrove roots on its edges, where boats can lace themselves into safety, if a hurricane should actually head that way.

Far to the east of the American shores we come to the Old World of Europe, and if we have touched at the Azores en route we have already had a taste of a Western European harbor, with its massive breakwaters, carrying roads, and railroads and traveling cranes on its inner side. This, you will find, is typical of the entire West Basin of the Mediterranean. Most harbors of Spain and North Africa and Italy are of this type, while southern France seems to be one giant marina after another. There can be only a handful of natural harbors left on the Riviera. Corsica's magnificent west coast is thought by some to be a fine cruising ground, but we, after two weeks there, concluded that there was probably only one safe, natural, all-weather harbor on the whole coast. The northeast shoulder of Sardinia offers a few coves and bays, but their security may be judged from their emptiness, the yachts of the Beautiful People being crowded three deep into the few artificial harbors.

No, too many cruising people have sampled the West Basin of the Med and come away disenchanted. And not enough have continued to the larger East Basin, to the multitude of islands and coves of the Adriatic, the Ionian, the Aegean, and the Turkish coast, to counterbalance their impressions. I don't know what to say about these areas except that the variety and number of anchorages is so great that there is literally something for everybody, from the Riviera atmosphere to the most primitive.

Of the Channel ports of France and England, where one enters through a lock gate at high water and then lies afloat while the approaches outside go dry, I can say nothing, having never had the courage to sail that coast, although in the Bay of Fundy I have lain in their poor cousins, the same port without the lock gate, where everything goes dry, and on Bornholm in the Baltic we have moored in the inner basin of the little fishing harbor of Allinge, behind lock gates, this time not to hold in the tide, of which there is none, but to hold out the surge when the winter northers blow down the Baltic.

So here we are in the Baltic, where along the northern shores and across the span between Stockholm and Finland the islands and rocks are so thick that it has been described as "stone soup." Lake Ontario may have its Thousand Islands, and Georgian Bay its Thirty Thousand Islands, but the Baltic claims One Hundred Fifty Thousand Islands. There's nothing like it in the world. Harbors, of course, are just everywhere, as so many passages are just too narrow and too intricate for any sea to build up. We have already moored to those rolling granite shores in this chapter, but I have one more word of advice on gunk-holing the Baltic. It was all recently glaciated, and the northern faces of the rocks and islands are rounded and polished by the ice, while the southern faces are broken into jagged steps, as masses of granite were pulled away. So it is best to hit a rock on its northern face (and hit a rock you will if you cruise the Baltic), and the way to assure this proper approach to striking is always to head south in the Baltic.

Geographers in describing various harbor forms always include the crater harbor, the flooded center of a partially submerged volcano, and I have no doubt that, if you sail to the Aleutian Islands or the South Pacific you will sooner or later arrive in one. My only experience with this form of harbor occurred in the Azores. After several days in Punta Delgado's dirty harbor, where we had been so pleasantly entertained by the American consul and the Canadian consul, and the officers of the Canadian oceanographic vessel, it was clear I had to put to sea again in order to give my young crew a much-needed rest. Now close off the south coast of Sao Miguel and a few miles to the east of Punta Delgado, a small volcano rises from the sea, Ilha Vila Franca, described in the *Pilot* as enclosing a basin "with a depth of 6 fathoms and a narrow entrance on the northeastern side." What a fine spot for a full night's sleep for all hands before that long run to Gibraltar! So after taking the latest conquests of my crew for a brief sail and setting them ashore again, we slipped quietly away and by late afternoon were off the crater. We found the entrance to be about 20 feet wide, between flat shelves of rock, alternately submerged by the oily swell and then lifting above the channel while water cascaded off on all sides. With the crew forward with boathooks and the fathometer reading no bottom we straightened out in line with the entrance and moved slowly in. "Narrow, but deep," I thought, as we ghosted into clear water inside, the fathometer still showing no bottom, at which point one of the men called back, "Say, skipper, it looks pretty shallow at this end." I lifted my eyes from the fathometer to notice that we were no longer moving; I left the wheel and looked down over the side. "Looks pretty shallow at this end, too," I reported.

So there we were, hard aground in the crater of a volcano in the middle of the Atlantic ocean. I don't believe even Columbus managed that much. And where had we gone wrong? I had failed to turn the transducer transfer switch from the recording unit in the navigating cabin to the flasher visible from the wheel, and below we had a nice trace of the bottom coming up to meet us. And more, not only is there no 6 fathoms in that crater; there is about 0.6 fathom; this depth is correctly shown on Portuguese charts and in the Portuguese *Pilot*, as we later determined while visiting the International Hydrographic Bureau in Monaco. Only the U.S. information is wrong.

Somehow we worked ourselves around, gunned ourselves off the flat-shingle bottom, avoided the rocky sides again by six inches, and said, "What the hell, it's only a thousand miles to Gibraltar. Let's go!"

III

Wind

And now the storm-blast came, and he
Was tyrannous and strong:
He struck with his o'ertaking wings
And chased us south along.
    Coleridge,
      "The Rime of the Ancient Mariner"

There are bad winds and good winds, and what readers most like to read about and sailors to yarn about are the bad winds. As Kipling reported from Fultah Fisher's Boarding House: "And regally they spat and smoked, and fearsomely they lied." That's us sailors, all right.

The Trade Wind of the Caribbean and of the low latitudes in much of the Atlantic must be counted one of the truly good winds of the world. How else explain the old sailor's prayer, "God grant me time enough to make one more passage in the Northeast Trades." This doesn't mean they don't blow pretty hard for a small boat most of the time, but with a steadiness and reliability which are a joy to any who have lived with the fickle breezes of many centers of sailing.

At the other end of the spectrum is the Mediterranean, about which most sailors seem ready to repeat the refrain, "There's either too much wind or none at all." I could argue the point, having had some splendid sailing there, but I can't deny that winds are erratic. The mountainous terrain, complex shoreline, and many basins of water lead to unpredictable weather phenomena, and it is in truth subject to several respected winds.

Some winds blow close to the surface, and with these an island forms a lee, it often being quite flat under the land. But other winds blow in depth, with greater velocity aloft, and even a fairly high island standing in its path serves only to trip and tumble the swift wind down its leeward side in gusts of greater velocity than the wind outside in the open. Such a wind is the *meltemi* of the Aegean, the summer wind which can keep a cruising yacht in port for days or even weeks.

The heat of the Middle Eastern deserts creates a permanent summer low over the Levant, as the heated air expands and rises, causing a drift of cooler air from the steppes of Eastern Europe to flow south and replace it. When a high lies over this part of the continent the drift is reinforced to a strong flow which, meeting the barrier of the Balkan mountains to the west and the mountains of Asia Minor to the east, is concentrated into a rushing mass of air down the comparatively narrow channel of the Aegean Sea. This can blow with such persistence and fury that cruising yachtsmen follow the simple rule of staying out of the central Aegean during July and August, although the peripheral shores are still acceptable cruising, often under shortened sail.

The *mistral* of the western basin is somewhat akin. The cooler, denser air associated with a high pressure pattern over northern France finds an outlet down the valley of the Rhone, where it blows with legendary force, to fan out over the Mediterranean Sea as a westerly along the Riviera, as a northeaster in the Balearics.

The *bora* of the Adriatic is again the product of a cold air mass to the north, which may build up behind the wall of the Dinaric Alps until, like rising water behind a dam, it overspills the top and descends with increasing speed through the less dense air of the warm sea, whose surface it flings over the nearby islands. The northeast faces of these islands are devoid of vegetation in places, all killed by the wind and salt, while in places where the narrow channels lie between steep shores there are stone bollards hewn into the bed rock on the southwest faces, so that ships caught in the *bora* can make fast until it has blown over.

"Aren't you frightened when it's stormy?" is one of the questions we are most frequently asked, to which we reply with emphasis: "You bet! Of course we are!"

"Well, what do you do when a storm comes? How do you heave to?"

And here is the remarkable fact. In some 40,000 miles of cruising we have never had to heave to. Only once have we carried a storm trisail, and then more to test it than out of necessity. The storm jib has never been up at sea. All this reflects not only the play of fortune plus a devout cowardice on our part, plus the leisure to indulge it (we can call it careful planning, but this means being able to afford the time to await good conditions), but it also reflects the comparative rarity of encountering truly heavy weather at sea. Don't be misled that one can venture out with impunity. And you who are more experienced than I, don't think I underrate the weather. The above is cited rather as an interesting statistic.

Time was when I thought the smoky sou'wester of a New England summer was heavy weather, and so it was in that 21-foot sloop with no power, in which we had made our first passage. On our third night at sea, returning from Nova Scotia, I was sleeping soundly when Dick, at the helm, had called me on deck to double reef, and after struggling into boots and oilskins I looked at my watch.

"Hey," I yelled, "What's the idea calling me up now? I'm not supposed to come on watch until midnight."

"You're nuts," Dick said. "For ten minutes while you got dressed you've been firing questions at me about the wind and sea conditions. You doing all that in your sleep?"

And the truth was, yes, I was. Apparently I had responded automaton-like to his "All hands," and never properly woke up until I had pulled on my boots.

It was glorious sailing, double reefed, through the full-moon night, but by the first watch, when I was again in my leeward bunk, things were getting nastier. The cast-iron sash weights

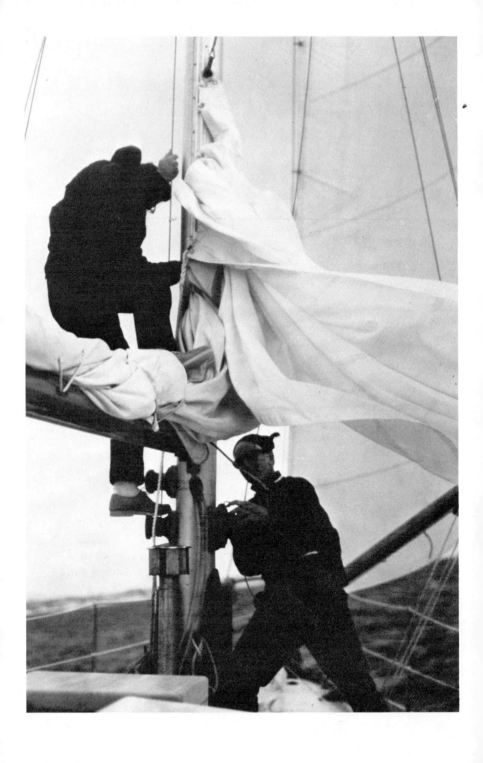

used for inside ballast were rolling and clanking in the bilge, while rusty bilge water washed up the side of the boat with every roll where, because there was no ceiling on the topsides, it had saturated my bedding and occasionally struck the underside of the deck with such force as to spray down over my head.

By daylight it was thick fog, seas were breaking across the cabin trunk from time to time, the dinghy astern was awash and towing nose in the air, a couple of slides had parted company from the main, and the leeward spreader had ripped from the mast and was dangling from the slack upper shroud. (It had been screwed into the wood, not through-bolted.) We were converging on those hungry fingers of rock which reach out to sea on the coast of Maine, position unknown, no engine, and afraid that if we had to tack or jibe with no upper shroud we risked taking out the mast. Today I hope that I would get right to work bypassing the turnbuckle on that loose shroud and eliminating the slack, and then maybe heave to on the other tack, forereaching into open water, until visibility improved, but I can't say with any certainty even now that it would really have been safer. As it was, the visibility did improve to about one mile—maybe we had sailed ourselves to better conditions—and just as we had identified the horn on Manana Island, already drawing astern to windward, we sighted a wooded point ahead, one of the islands off Port Clyde where we were soon gratefully at anchor. While it had seemed rough to us, it was not abnormal summer weather for the Gulf of Maine. I suspect the wind was never much above the top of Force 5.

But let's look at some episodes which verge on being storms at sea. No, let's look first at the first storm we encountered in the *Cynthia R*. It hit us the night after we had taken delivery of this new boat from the builder and we were not at sea at all. If I look at Page 1 of my first of many volumes of logbooks from this boat, I find it begins as follows: "The writing of the log of the *Cynthia R* begins almost forty-eight hours late, lying in Christmas Cove, with gusts shaking and rolling the boat and blowing the tops off the wavelets 100 yards from shore. Small craft warnings at 30 knots have been changed to easterly gale warnings at 50 knots and then later to 60 knots; we have dragged anchor three times and after the last time picked up a husky-looking mooring." The day is the twenty-fifth of May, 1967, although it was only later that we learned it was the coldest twenty-fifth of May on record, that several inches of snow had fallen inland, that Mt. Washington reported blinding snow with 75-knot winds, that Marblehead reported damage in excess of that of the hurricane of 1938, that boats up to 50 feet were reported sunk along the coast, and that we had experienced the sixth highest tide since records were started in 1720. Christmas Cove is as tiny and protected a spot as any sailor could ask for and, in late May, empty of any boat except ours. A strange mooring is never the best thing to hang onto, but our dragging anchor had been bringing up an assortment of rotting lobster pots and plastic sheet and immense quantities of mud, and it didn't seem the best thing to hang onto either. By noon I began to mistrust the heavy manila pennant, probably an inch and a quarter in diameter, but with a winter's weathering behind it, and was casting increasingly frequent glances at the hungry ledge in the harbor mouth, directly under our stern, so I put one of our new five-eighths-inch nylon docking lines into the dinghy and hauled myself along the manila to the mooring (blowing too hard to row now) and rigged this as a standby. I was just coming down the companionway in dripping oilskins when a report like a gun went off; the manila had parted and we fell back on the nylon, impressed by too close a brush.

By evening the roadway which forms the eastern shore of Christmas Cove was under water, and we sat up late that night, huddled over a wood fire in the cabin fireplace, until at 0200 there were indications of moderating wind and falling water.

Since then many a blow has passed over us, and mercifully most have found us, as that one did, in port. But there are still lessons to be learned, or perhaps I should say a pattern to develop.

One of the nicest instruments to have found its way on board our boat, which is not particularly instrument oriented, is the clinometer. This simple gadget, whose steel ball or bubble or pointer shows the angle of heel, has prevented more family bickering than anything except sailing single handed. On prior boats, as the wind picked up, a conversation rather like this would generally take place:

"It's getting pretty breezy, isn't it?"

"Yes, just what we've been waiting for."

Pause.

"Shouldn't we be thinking about shortening sail?"

"Why? She's just sailing on her lines now."

Pause.

"There goes the rail under."

"We just rolled it under. You've got to stop confusing rolling with too much wind."

"It's a lot easier to shorten before it's blowing too hard."

"Look here! It's good sailing for the first time. Now let's just enjoy it."

"There goes the whole deck under."

So it went. But now, with the simple little pointer or bubble or ball and the architect's information that a 22-degree angle of heel is optimum for this boat, we seldom come to annoyance over this. True, we can still argue over the difference between being rolled down by a sea and the angle of heel, but in general any time we are around that 22-degree mark Cynthia can use the same psychology as the mother who says: "The clock says it's time to go to bed." (And I might add, it works equally well when applied in reverse for the treatment of edgy wives.)

So we have come to that angle of heel, and with it a marked weather helm. Our first step is to drop the mizzen, and on this boat at least, with the mizzen boom inboard and at chest height, it is so easy to furl or to raise the mizzen that we need never hesitate. The helm is eased, and we straighten up enough to quiet the ship's company for the moment.

But if the wind continues to increase, passing from the bottom of Force 5, where we may have dropped the mizzen, to the bottom of Force 6, then with a sigh I must admit more drastic measures are necessary. I know I will have a bit of a struggle and wet feet, but it is time to reef the main. Ours is roller reefing and out comes the handle and, nowadays, the safety harness. I lurch forward to the mainmast base, let go the gooseneck downhaul, wind up one roll, thus lifting the boom some 18 inches

Beaufort Scale
with Corresponding Sea State Codes

Beaufort number	Wind speed knots	mph	meters per second	km per hour	Seaman's term	World Meteorological Organization (1964)	Estimating wind speed — Effects observed at sea	Effects observed on land	Hydrographic Office — Term and height of waves, in feet	Code	World Meteorological Organization — Term and height of waves, in feet	Code
0	under 1	under 1	0.0–0.2	under 1	Calm	Calm	Sea like mirror.	Calm; smoke rises vertically.	Calm, 0	0	Calm, glassy, 0	0
1	1–3	1–3	0.3–1.5	1–5	Light air	Light air	Ripples with appearance of scales; no foam crests.	Smoke drift indicates wind direction; vanes do not move.	Smooth, less than 1	1	Calm, rippled, 0–⅓	1
2	4–6	4–7	1.6–3.3	6–11	Light breeze	Light breeze	Small wavelets; crests of glassy appearance, not breaking.	Wind felt on face; leaves rustle; vanes begin to move.	Slight, 1–3	2	Smooth, wavelets, ⅓–1⅔	2
3	7–10	8–12	3.4–5.4	12–19	Gentle breeze	Gentle breeze	Large wavelets; crests begin to break; scattered whitecaps.	Leaves, small twigs in constant motion; light flags extended.	Moderate, 3–5	3	Slight, 2–4	3
4	11–16	13–18	5.5–7.9	20–28	Moderate breeze	Moderate breeze	Small waves, becoming longer; numerous whitecaps.	Dust, leaves, and loose paper raised up; small branches move.	Rough, 5–8	4	Moderate, 4–8	4
5	17–21	19–24	8.0–10.7	29–38	Fresh breeze	Fresh breeze	Moderate waves, taking longer form; many whitecaps; some spray.	Small trees in leaf begin to sway.			Rough, 8–13	5
6	22–27	25–31	10.8–13.8	39–49	Strong breeze	Strong breeze	Larger waves forming; whitecaps everywhere; more spray.	Larger branches of trees in motion; whistling heard in wires.	Very rough, 8–12	5		
7	28–33	32–38	13.9–17.1	50–61	Moderate gale	Near gale	Sea heaps up; white foam from breaking waves begins to be blown in streaks.	Whole trees in motion; resistance felt in walking against wind.				
8	34–40	39–46	17.2–20.7	62–74	Fresh gale	Gale	Moderately high waves of greater length; edges of crests begin to break into spindrift; foam is blown in well-marked streaks.	Twigs and small branches broken off trees; progress generally impeded.			Very rough, 13–20	6
9	41–47	47–54	20.8–24.4	75–88	Strong gale	Strong gale	High waves; sea begins to roll; dense streaks of foam; spray may reduce visibility.	Slight structural damage occurs; slate blown from roofs.	High, 12–20	6		
10	48–55	55–63	24.5–28.4	89–102	Whole gale	Storm	Very high waves with overhanging crests; sea takes white appearance as foam is blown in very dense streaks; rolling is heavy and visibility reduced.	Seldom experienced on land; trees broken or uprooted; considerable structural damage occurs.	Very high, 20–40	7	High, 20–30	7
11	56–63	64–72	28.5–32.6	103–117	Storm	Violent storm	Exceptionally high waves; sea covered with white foam patches; visibility still more reduced.	Very rarely experienced on land; usually accompanied by widespread damage.	Mountainous, 40 and higher	8	Very high, 30–45	8
12	64–71	73–82	32.7–36.9	118–133	Hurricane	Hurricane	Air filled with foam; sea completely white with driving spray; visibility greatly reduced.		Confused	9	Phenomenal, over 45	9
13	72–80	83–92	37.0–41.4	134–149								
14	81–89	93–103	41.5–46.1	150–166								
15	90–99	104–114	46.2–50.9	167–183								
16	100–108	115–125	51.0–56.0	184–201								
17	109–118	126–136	56.1–61.2	202–220								

Note: Since January 1, 1955, weather map symbols have been based upon wind speed in knots, at five-knot intervals, rather than upon Beaufort number.

Courtesy of Bowditch/American Practical Navigator

on its track, slack off 18 inches of halliard to lower it, cast off
the jackline from the lower slides, taken another turn (perhaps
yelling aft not to let the main sheet wind up on the boom, a
request usually answered by "What did you say?"), and repeat
the whole performance four, five, or six times. Five rolls is all I
usually seem to get before a thick ruff of boltrope is wound
around the gooseneck, but we are now close to being double
reefed, and, with mizzen furled, the boat seldom asks for more.
When the wind is up, the difference in speed is hardly detect-
able. It may not be necessary to mention that in reefing under
way we have slacked the main sheet to take much of the strain
out of the sail, without letting it luff to the point of tearing the
battens out of their pockets.

If I were to start over I might have gone to jiffy reefing. I have
never been shipmates with it, but reports are so favorable that
it must have something going for it. Roller reefing very definitely has something going against it if you lubricate the worm
gear too well. I have on occasion done all this work, set up taut
on halliard and downhaul, worked my way aft to trim in, only
to have it unroll itself a turn when the strain comes on it.

I haven't mentioned the jib. We carry both a genoa and a
self-tending club jib, and if we have expected a beat to windward we would be under club jib anyway. But if under genoa,
we may have to move down to club jib as the wind builds up.
Mind you, this sort of change down doesn't happen often, a few
times in a season at most, perhaps as often as a racing crew
shifts jibs in the course of a single race.

But we are not a racing crew. We are just a not-very-young
couple trying to get from here to there in as much comfort and
safety as is compatible with small-boat sailing; night is approaching, we are reaching at seven knots in a slowly rising wind, and
it is time for the change. *Cynthia R* has a single headstay, and
we keep the bagged club jib hanked on at all times. Now we run
off before the wind to ease the strain and motion, strip the bag
off the club jib, fasten the clew to the jib outhaul, drop the
genoa on deck and bundle it down a hatch, snap the halliard to
the club jib, and up it goes. Or up it should go if we haven't
made the classic error of letting the halliard roll itself around a

spreader while slack. If we have two hands forward, the whole operation can be done in two or three minutes. Whether we have chosen to reef the main first depends on circumstances.

You will have noticed that I mentioned a jib club outhaul. Since the luff of the sail is farther from the clew end of the club when down then when set, one must either outhaul it on the club after raising it or have an ample jackline, which permits the boltrope on the lower luff to move aft when slack, and a good solid hoop encircling the club with integral rings for clew and sheet. This is simpler, stronger, cheaper, and more foolproof, and avoids the potentially dangerous job of outhauling against a thrashing club, and I really ought to switch over. Also, if I were starting over, I think I would go to double headstays. There seem to be snaphooks on the market today which remove the old bugaboo of having a snap pick up both stays at once, making it impossible to lower.

So that's what may be happening on deck as the wind builds up. But what about below decks? If we have our wits about us, Cynthia will long ago have pulled the oilskins out. She used to ask me, "Do you want your rainy gear yet?" and I, who don't like the encumbrance, would probably say: "Let's hold off a while and see." Now she is more inclined just to bring it up and say: "I'll hold the wheel while you get yours on," thus not forcing me to prove my manliness by answering any queries.

But we still play games with our guests. "Would you like to put your oilskins on now or after you're soaked?" we ask, and the poor guest, still warm and dry, looks at these oilskins and says: "I'm fine; if it gets wet I'll just sit over here." Little does he know that we aren't thinking of that errant bit of spray which may lip over the windward rail, but a skipper finds he has to push his guests around so much anyway that he is reluctant to do it when it isn't absolutely necessary. And we may not

know for sure that we *will* get wet. But then, when that first
sea happens to burst like an explosion under the turn of the
windward bilge, and suddenly everybody and everything, including that spot "over there" where the guest thought he
would stay dry, is streaming inch-deep suds, it is such mean pleasure to see the look of incredulity, consternation, and the sheepish
grin of awareness. No, we shouldn't really do it. It may be hot
in the sun, but being soaking wet is cold, and even under foul-
weather gear one wants warm, dry clothes when the wind is up.

We will also have checked stowage. I will have worked
through the cabins: our own shelves, the head, the galley, moving or chocking anything left loose. I will have surreptitiously
invaded the privacy of the guest stateroom aft, looking for
cameras left loose, glasses of water, bottles of pills, books lying
around, or anything nestled in the clothes hammocks which
may now start hammering against the ship's side. I will have
checked the lugs on all portholes to make sure they are tight.
The "chockers" are passed up to the man at the wheel. The
dining table is folded shut, so no one will be thrown against
its open leaf and snap the hinges, and the fiddles are put in
place so we can set down stray objects in safety. Hatches are
dogged down, and the drop boards for the companionway are
set up. A quick peek into the bilge to make sure we are dry
enough there and a peek under the toilet lid to check on water
level are reassuring.

Something we should do more of and don't is have snack
food ready. From the stomach's point of view, neither Cynthia
nor I is a great sailor, and the prospect of preparing any food
in rough conditions, in a now-airless cabin, and feeling a little
nervous to boot, is unappealing. But I remain convinced that
nibbling is a good prevention, that nourishment, as long as one's
body will accept it, is an important part of winning any prolonged battle with the weather, and that if one's stomach is to
go down in humiliating defeat (as mine has done at one time
or another on every size ship afloat), "pumping an empty bilge,"
as they say, is far the worst of it. So we should have something
ready and stowed where a quick duck below, when the weather
is worse, can produce some acceptable food. As it is, I usually

emerge with a box of salted crackers, a jar of peanut butter, and a knife, and try to shield these with my body as I pass nourishment to the watch with salty fingers.

Adlard Coles, in his excellent book *Heavy Weather Sailing*, includes in the final chapter a section entitled "Preparations for a Gale," and its repetition is so worthwhile that we have, with his kind permission, inserted it here. This list can be edited and supplemented for your own boat; each will have its peculiarities of configuration, stowage, and equipment to consider. I carry a copy of this list, edited for the *Cynthia R*, on board at all times. Now—if we could only discipline ourselves to use it!

PREPARATIONS FOR A GALE *

The following affords a list of things to be done if strong winds develop into a gale and one gets caught out in it. Some of these will have been done already, but the list may be useful as a reminder.

1. Don safety harness or lifelines.
2. Shut off or bung the exhaust pipe.
3. Close petrol cocks, both if there are two.
4. Open cockpit drain cocks.
5. Close all other skin cocks.
6. See that cockpit lockers are shut and watertight. If there is an engine hatch in the cockpit, see that it is screwed down.
7. Put storm sails in a quickly accessible position, such as in a quarter berth, or, if necessary, set them. Stow spare headsails below, not on deck.
8. Secure all deck gear and spinnaker poles. Rubber shock cord is not enough to hold the poles in their chocks and extra lashings are necessary.
9. Secure dinghy or raft with extra lashings.
10. Shut hatches. Turn ventilator cowls to leeward and if thought necessary screw down ventilator covers, or stuff the vents with cloth or socks. Scuttles on the lee side should be kept open as long as possible to give ventilation and only closed under extreme conditions.
11. Check that slide fastenings (shackles or stainless steel wire) are in good order. This should have been done in

* K. Adlard Coles, *Heavy Weather Sailing*, Revised and Enlarged (Clinton Corners, N.Y.: John De Graff, 1975).

harbour, but is sometimes overlooked. Also check that
shackles are ready for the storm jib at the head and tack
to secure to the stay in addition to hanks.

12. See that no loose tools are left on deck or loose in the
cockpit, and that winch handles are properly secured.

13. Hoist radar reflector.

14. Put stopper in hawse pipe if this has not already been
done. Where this has an opening for the chain link, stop
it with waste or cloth to prevent leakage round the chain.

15. Place foghorn in accessible position from the cockpit.

Work Below

a. Mark position on the chart, bring log up to date, note
barometer reading.

b. Distribute sea-sick pills (at least an hour before the gale is
expected) to any members of the crew who are likely to
need them. It is useless to leave pills until the emergency
arises and they should be kept in a known and readily available position so that nobody has to ask for them.

c. Stow everything securely, especially cooking utensils and
provisions, so that they cannot be thrown about or rattle.

d. Check that bilge pumps are not choked.

e. Check that the crew knows the position of the storm
screens or panels to go over windows and where the nails
or screws to secure them are stored. Screens are only required in exceptional gales.

f. Check that navigation lights and anchor or masthead light
are in proper working order. If oil lights, see that they are
full (but not too full) and check that there is enough
paraffin or calor gas for the stove, as anything in the nature
of filling lamps or changing a gas cylinder during a gale is
unpleasant.

g. See that warps are conveniently accessible for streaming if
necessary, and that they are free to uncoil.

h. Check that no member of the crew has forgotten the position of flares, fire extinguishers and first aid.

i. Place dry biscuits, cake, sweets, sugar and snacks in a position where they are readily available. Prepare soup or hot
food and put into thermos if time permits.

j. Put boxes of matches in a dry place or polythene bag, as if these are left lying around they will become damp owing to condensation and will not strike.

k. Put polythene sheeting or waterproof over quarter berths if spray can reach them when the campanion doors are opened, or on any berths over which deck leaks can develop.

l. Before nightfall put white flares in a polythene bag in a position handy for exhibiting in event of a ship approaching close on a collision course and unable to identify the yacht's lights in the seas and spray. Red flares can be left in their usual place, provided the crew knows where they are in case of emergency.

Now let's see how all these logical formulae work out in action. It is midnight. We are approaching Calvi on the northwest corner of Corsica after a 100-mile run from Port Cros; we are under genoa and full main, heading east by south at seven knots with a brisk southwest wind on the quarter, the flashing light on Cape Revellata already visible. Clouds are drifting across the stars; it is the dark of the moon. The mizzen has been handed hours ago to ease the helm. Another couple with their two sturdy sons, sailors all, he a past commodore of the Seattle Corinthians, are with us, and I have just turned over the watch to him. We have compared notes; all is well and under control; and I slip below to get a bit of a doze on the cabin floor before closing the harbor in the night. Fifteen minutes later I am called on deck. The wind has suddenly backed to the south, putting the apparent wind well forward of the beam, and is rising rapidly. Time to drop the main and set the mizzen, is the verdict, as we are clearly overpowered; the wives are sent to dig out the safety harnesses, which turn out to be in a bag at the bottom of the sailbin. (You see, one keeps on learning. Better to have them available in a hurry, isn't it?) By the time two of us have struggled into them and forward and brought down a thrashing mainsail in the dark, there is no thought of adding the mizzen. The helm is easy, and we are continuing at seven knots under genoa alone, the bows illuminated in red and green spray in a continuous cloud around the pulpit. It is about then that we find our safety harnesses snapped to each other, not to the rigging. Oh well, if one has to go, it's nice to go in the company of a past commodore.

The story ends with a couple of knockdowns under the walls of the citadel of Calvi as we lower the genoa at 0200 and grope into the bay to anchor on clean sand, and with (this time) hot chocolate for all, as the wind shakes the mast.

A sudden squall is a different matter. One seldom knows how hard this may blow, and it is our practice to drop the main as the squall approaches. If it is vicious, jib and mizzen are quite enough; if not, it will soon be over anyway.

Many years ago one such black squall bore down on us in Long Island Sound. We were then sailing a heavy Atkin ketch, and this weekend we had taken Cynthia's father off for an overnight. He was an experienced sailor himself, but of the monkey-wrench variety, which meant he was accustomed to handling his boat from under cover. We had dropped the main on time and headed off to take the wind astern. As the writhing cloud arched over our heads and the sound of approaching wind became audible, he opened a black umbrella and stood up to face the wind, which promptly pushed him forward to the base of the mizzen mast, pinned him there, and then, with great deliberation, slowly folded his umbrella for him, breaking each metal rib. Not inside out, mind you, but just a slow crushing, leaving him still pinned to the mast, holding his closed umbrella pointed against the wind like a lance. What does the wind blow to do this? I have no idea, although I'm glad it doesn't last forever.

More lately we were alone, Cynthia and I, off the tip of the Istrian Peninsula in the northern end of the Adriatic, heading for Pula to pick up guests. A *sirocco*, the moist southeast wind, had blown us nearly there under a canopy of cloud, when an emerging blackness in the west heralded a squall approaching from the direction of Venice. Could we press on to harbor before it hit? Optimistically I hoped we could, and thus held full sail until it was nearly upon us, and the harbor mouth still a mile or two away. At this point even the optimist had to agree that it would blow, and I now sprang forward to lower the main on the run, something Cynthia had been suggesting for the last quarter-hour. My timing was thirty seconds off; between lowering the main and the chance to get a couple of stops around it, the squall hit abeam with such ferocity that I never thought to look at the clinometer. Under jib and mizzen we were probably laid over 45 degrees and pinned there while a mixture of lashing rain and salt water in equal parts swept up our windward side in a sheet arching across the house top and disappearing to leeward, while the mainsail flogged grotesquely in this mist. We must have looked very much like the old paintings of sailing vessels caught in hurricanes. Why do we never get pictures at a time like this? Normally one might bear off and let her scud in such a squall, but we had the sawtooth rocks of this rugged shore a few hundred yards to leeward, and no choice but to hold on until visibility improved to show us we were off the harbor entrance.

Episodes like this are more fun in retrospect than at the moment, but they do serve to build confidence in one's boat. If the rigging and the engine are well cared for, they will take care of you long after you are ready to call it quits.

Some blows turn out to be just good sails, and one such seems to occur regularly on a passage across the bottom of the boot of Italy as one comes to the Golfo di Squillace, the Gulf of Squalls. Here a saddle in the 5,000-foot chain of mountains which runs down the toe of Italy serves as the only aperture through which the northwest winds in the Tyrrhenian Sea can escape into this part of the Ionian, and this they do with a vengeance. At this same place the shore recedes in a broad bight, giving one the illusion of setting out into open sea on the forty-five mile run between Capes Colonna and Stilo. The wind fans out from the gap in the mountains so that whichever way one is going he is met upon entering the gulf by a dismaying array of steep seas and whitecaps which force him below his course. But if he grits his teeth and slogs into it for a few miles, he notices that it is slowly fairing, and soon he can ease sheets, very often ending in a glorious reach or run through tumbling seas to the farther cape.

Wind action of this type is prevalent in many places, and our own home waters of the Pacific Northwest spring to mind. How many times have we set out from Nanaimo, northbound across the Strait of Georgia, into a wind and sea which has kept a fleet of motor yachts held up for days? We can expect to be miserably uncomfortable for the first five miles and enjoy great sailing from there on.

The west wind blows bravely into the Strait of Juan de Fuca almost every clear summer day, to fan out as a norther into the reaches of Puget Sound to the south and as a southeaster up the lovely sounds between the Gulf Islands of British Columbia. But all the air must move through the Strait, a gap between the Olympic Mountains and those of Vancouver Island. We were coming east in this strait on the Vancouver Island shore in one of our earlier boats, a 29-foot sloop, on our first experience with this stretch of water. With a gentle wind dead aft I had set the working jib on the forestay and the genoa flying, its tack at the end of our bowsprit. As happens when running off before it, the slow increase in wind has the insidious effect of bringing first contentment, then elation, then the sudden realization that one has bitten off more than he can chew. In this case, as increasing speed sucked our transom under water, which now flowed quietly forward along the deck and out the freeing ports, I looked at that iron-taut genoa, fastened only at peak, tack, and clew, and had to admit that no matter which of the three I slacked away, I could be in trouble, and the last thing I wanted was a genoa wrapped around my keel. Nature took charge before I had made up my mind; an extra-heavy roll collapsed the sail, which refilled with a wrenching jerk and neatly split the length of a seam, leaving so little drawing that it now became manageable. And split seams can be repaired. But I don't set my genoa flying in a breeze of wind any more.

Speaking of this boat reminds me that I should include in a chapter on wind some mention of the day we broke our mast. With my children and their high-school friends as crew, we had spent the night becalmed in a race, withdrawn in the morning, when it was clear we could not finish before time ran out, and motored home. As we were crossing Lake Washington to our home, a sudden wind came up at last, and I let the young set sail the boat while I caught a nap. But soon it was apparent that this was not napping weather; I just had my feet on the cabin sole when the mast let go at the spreaders, the genoa went under the boat, that part of the main from spreader to clew still drawing. In my sleepy state I hit the starting button, put the engine in gear, and, you guessed it, wrapped a large ball of genoa tightly around the prop. You may well wonder why we didn't clear the mess first, and so do I. Probably the fact that we were only a mile off the east shore of the lake, which is pretty solidly bulkheaded with heavy rock, and that the squally southwest wind was setting us onto this shore, made me want to turn her head around before doing anything else. Now the lower half of the main, which could not be lowered, continued to sail us toward shore, the genoa was irrevocably around our bottom, the engine useless, and we could not gather way to tack in the chop. How stupid can one get? By great good fortune, I believe, we managed to build up enough way to fall off, despite the loss of our headsail, wore ship, headed for a cove a few miles down the lake, where we could round in and anchor, most of this lake being too deep to anchor in, and where we could then go overboard to free the prop, and up the mast to take care of the main. And so, ingloriously, we motored home.

To analyze this accident, we noted that the break in the painted, solid-wood mast revealed that at this point the grain ran diagonally down from the after to the forward face of the mast. It would still have taken the load, as it had been doing for fifteen years of cruising and racing, had I not cast off the forestay, a three-quarter stay, in order to handle the genoa easily in tacking. Without the lower forestay and with all the load of the genoa on the headstay, the masthead was pulled forward and the mast itself bowed back.

Earlier I said we had only once been under storm sails in our boat, but I did have this experience while making an April passage with a friend from Seattle to San Diego. This is an inhospitable coast; harbors are far apart and almost all have bars across their mouths, so at the very moment you might want one, it becomes dangerous of access. The boat was a sturdy and powerful steel ketch with several passages already to her and her skipper's credit, the *Eleuthera* with Earl Schenck in command, and it was when he said he planned to stand 200 miles offshore before turning south and not to close land above Point Conception, California, that I decided to cast in my lot. Four of us made up the crew: Earl; his family doctor, Bill Watts; Bill's son John; and myself.

In the event we picked up gentle westerlies 150 miles off and took a southerly course; ran through a bleak stretch of head wind, cold rain, and spray our third night out; and then, with morning, came into glorious sunshine and fair-weather clouds, together with the northwest wind, the trade wind of the Pacific coast. All sail was set with twin spinnakers forward, each about the size of a large staysail, and we surged happily on our way. At noon the mizzen was lowered. Early in the afternoon it was time to furl the main. By late afternoon the skipper decided to drop the port twin, and in the lowering sun we commenced surfing down the faces of ever-increasing waves. The sky was now a hard cloudless blue, the seas beginning to streak with foam, and from the wheel I was able to report to the skipper that the speedometer had gone full circle and up to three knots on its second time around. "That's it," he said, and we fell to muzzling that last sail. For a short time we tried lying ahull, which was miserable, and running off under bare poles, which proved sluggish (although a light displacement boat might have scudded nicely). In the end we followed the doctor's advice and ran up the trisail. Instantly everything was under control, our progress adequate, and our motion, even running off before it, not too bad.

By midnight, when I came on watch again, the wind had increased. We all tend to overestimate wind velocities, and I suspect most of the reports of high winds we get from yachtsmen come from reading an anemometer recording from the masthead at the moment the boat is pitching forward while sailing to windward. But this wind was being officially recorded now at 50 knots at Point Reyes, which was fifty miles to the east of our DR position. A 12-foot-diameter toy nylon parachute, left by John in its paper bag in a corner of the cockpit well when chow had been called, had passed unobserved in the darkness, out of which from time to time a louder whoosh or roar above the general level of noise would herald a breaking crest coming up astern. Not long after straddling the wheelbox and clipping my safety harness to whatever was handy, one of these crests came bursting over our port quarter, filling the well with sizzling salt water, the bag disintegrated and the parachute quickly clogged all the drains. The harness prevented me from leaning far enough down to drag it free, so I contented myself with computing the weight of water, perhaps a dozen cubic feet, we had added to our load, and decided it was no more than a cockpit full of people, and far less troublesome. In due course the wheel was relieved, the cockpit freed of its impedimenta: it drained, other waves broke and filled it and it drained again, until that became the pattern of the night and

succeeding morning. One heard them coming from behind, steadied down on course, ready to wrestle the ship to one side or the other as she might be thrown, and then, if the crest were directly astern, we would leap forward with a splendid feeling of acceleration and the foaming crest would pass harmlessly on either side. But when the crest was off a bit to one side it would burst over everything. By daylight the seas were majestic, but more inspiring of awe than of fear. At one time a great aircraft carrier loomed up, passed close under our stern, and then turned to parallel our course, filling a sizeable segment of the horizon when viewed from a crest, while from the troughs not even her control tower was visible.

(I would like to add here that four years later John, by that time a college student, was one of my transatlantic crew, and that the good doctor and I have subsequently sailed together in the Bahamas, the Baltic, and the Mediterranean, including our own worst blow, which I shall soon come to.)

But back to the Pacific—by afternoon on that day we added a staysail; the next day we were under full sail again. Winds don't blow forever.

Things get wet below at a time like this, and I like to cite the example of my camera, in its case, in a drawer under my bunk, well removed from the cabin skylight, which was dogged down, covered with its canvas cover, the lashings of which snugged into a groove in the skylight coaming, and the whole covered with the inverted dinghy. After the storm that camera had droplets of salt water on it. Dressing under that skylight had made one feel the proverbial yachtsman standing in a cold shower while he tears up his money.

The most dramatic example I have experienced of this ability of water to blow through a closed cabin came in the hurricane of 1944. No, I wasn't caught at sea; that Atkin ketch was afloat in the narrow landlocked slip leading to the old mill at Roslyn, Long Island, and had to fend for herself, which she did quite well. Now, that boat was gasoline powered, the engine under a solid bridge deck with an off-center access hatch. But when I got to her the next day to check things out, I found the bowl of the distributor brim full of water, under its snapped-down cap and despite the seemingly invulnerable position of the engine.

While that blow had been well forecast, we cannot always take forecasts too seriously. It happens that I am writing these paragraphs on a late May day in the harbor of Katakolon, Greece, having started out at 0830 on a flat, calm, and cloudless morning with a forecast valid for the next twelve hours of light variables, Force 2 to 4, and calm sea. Our destination, and the next protection on this coast, was Pylos, the sandy Pylos of Nestor in the *Odyssey*, which lies 50 miles south by east across a broad bight.

As we rounded the breakwater (Cynthia and I were alone at the moment), we came into a swell from dead ahead, not the long ocean swell from a storm a thousand miles away, but a steeper one, the kind that means there is wind from that direction not too far ahead. The barometer had been falling slowly for twenty-four hours, a break in the usual fair-weather pattern of diurnal variation.

"Well, what do you think?" I asked. "There's wind ahead somewhere."

"Yes, but with a good forecast, why don't we go on for 30 minutes and see if the swell builds up?"

"OK, maybe it will die away. But it looks like a warning all right."

By 0900 the seas were definitely higher and steeper, we were beginning to plunge a bit; at 0915 a catspaw on the water hardened into a ruffling wind from the southeast. "Who's going to be right?" we wondered. "Shall we lose a day's progress because the first light variable is from dead ahead? Am I a man or a mouse?" And I answered the question by putting the helm over and doing a 180, motoring back to the pier at Katakolon, where all was serene, glassy calm under a hot sun. It was 1010, and I was a mouse. At 1030 the flags were standing stiffly out; by 1100 the bay outside was full of whitecaps, spray was leaping high above the 15-foot seawall to windward, and I was, at least, a very smug mouse. The wind surely was Force 5 gusting to 6, yet the noon forecast came on the air for light variables, 2 to 4. I was thinking of the story of the old seacook on

the spoon-bowed schooner yacht of long ago, who was on duty
serving a hot luncheon to the guests in the salon, while they
beat through The Race, with the wind against the tide. Finally
he braced himself in the galley door, tattooed arms akimbo,
and announced to the company, "Only damned fools and
yachtsmen beat to windward."

We often laugh at the Italian forecasts, which seem to tell
one only the existing or perhaps the prior day's weather. In 1974
we left Sardinia for Ponza, a run of 170 miles due east, with
fair weather and light southwesters forecast. And for the
first sixteen hours this was so, although a long swell from the
northwest bespoke wind spilling off the mountains of Corsica
far behind us. At midnight the shift came, an arch of cloud
swept over, the wind went west and slowly strengthened. By
morning we were taking a series of long tacks downwind; by
noon, with Ponza in sight, we were surfing down the cresting
seas, the fishboats dipping out of sight in the troughs, and the
radio was still forecasting light southwesters. At 1500, with two
anchors safely down on Ponza's clean sand, the radio caught on
and came out with "Avviso! Burrasca in corso." ("Notice! Gale
in progress.")

And that same year the Italian radio did it to us again. We
had sailed from Crotone to cross the Gulf of Taranto, 70 miles
from the toe to the heel of Italy, to Santa Maria de Leuca, a
long day's run. One of our guests at this time made a good case
of not really liking wild adventures at sea (although she has
had her full share with us over the years and is a good sport
about it), and we had promised her a good night's sleep at
Leuca. The little harbor had been miserable the last time I had
been there, but had been improved in the meantime. What I
didn't know was that it had never been protected from the west,
but with our forecast of light southerlies that should not have
mattered. But again there was that disturbing swell from the
west, and since the seas could hardly have come over the toe of
Italy, it had to be generated by some pretty good wind somewhere up the gulf. We sailed pleasantly on until, with Leuca
a couple of miles off at 1800, three things happened: a band of
cloud scudded out of the west, obscuring the lowering sun;

the wind suddenly hauled to west and freshened; and the Italian radio gave their evening forecast: "Avviso! Burrasca di nordovest in corso nel Golfo di Taranto." Through the binoculars we could see the wildly careening spars in Leuca, clearly no place for us. The first harbor of Greece lay another 70 miles to the east. But 20 miles up the heel, on its eastern shore, lies the little old port of Otranto, and although we had never been there and it meant a nighttime arrival in windy conditions, our choice was easy. We spun around the heel, and in its lee shortened down from full sail to working jib and main, thus beginning one of our grandest short sails, driving fast in calm water with the sun setting behind the hills and turning the menacing clouds into an Italian sunset. Apparently we reached Otranto on the wings of the gale, because even as we were anchoring in the darkness there was much hurried shifting of rafted boats around us.

And yet again! This time the Greek weather service. We had discharged our last guests for the season at Samos and were returning in easy stages alone to Rhodes for winter layup. It was September, and the *meltemi* season in the Aegean was dying away, when I said, "Let's sail out to Levitha. It's only 20 miles off, a beam reach, and I have a hunch there's a harbor there. And if there isn't, we have time to get back to Leros before dark." There is no detailed chart to reveal whether there is or isn't a harbor, and our guidebook was silent.

Cynthia demurred: "I've had enough of Aegean wind for one season. It just isn't sensible to go out in the middle when we don't have to."

So we compromised by my promising that when we got to Levitha I would not keep going to the next island and the next. We did have a glorious sail, and there was a deep and landlocked harbor on Levitha's southern side, a creek or cove running east-west between shores high enough so that the wind blew over the top where we got an anchor down and a line to shore. Only one family lives on this barren island in a pleasant compound well back from the water, complete with many buildings and its own chapel, and visits were exchanged, in which the subject of the wind and its effect on their lives seemed uppermost. So with fair weather forecasts we spent a reasonably pleasant night until early morning gusts woke us, shaking our mast and sending us this way and that against our mooring lines.

Daylight brought no change in the forecasts for moderate north winds, Force 4 to 5, but even in our cove we could tell the wind had picked up outside, so we rolled four rolls into the main, left the mizzen in stops, set the club jib, and departed for Leros, the wind just forward of the beam. It was great sailing, a bit of spray, the boat balanced and driving hard, the peaks of Leros looking like separate islands over the horizon in the clear autumnal air. But soon it strengthened, the sea rose to a jumble of breaking crests about 10 feet high; wave after wave burst over us, we were laid over 40 degrees, and I saw the bow wave breaking into the jib, a rather remarkable sight, considering that the foot of the jib clears the foredeck by some three feet. The barograph, whose trace seldom even registers rough weather, threw ink up and down the chart. The dinghy was trailing its stem in the water, the only time I have seen this since we installed higher davits. All in all it was quite a dusting for a Force 4 to 5 forecast, and we were not surprised, after making the harbor of Leros and snuggling up to the quay, to hear the forecast change to gale warnings, actually the first gale warnings we had heard all season, and to hear that the harbormaster had orders to let no boats sail. We had estimated a good Force 7 outside, and a charter boat at Siros radioed that she was hanging on in harbor in Force 9 conditions. But thrilling sailing—especially if it had been someone else's boat and gear.

"And someone else's wife," Cynthia adds.

Anyway, you get the point: a forecast of fair weather doesn't always mean the weather will be good. The rising swell and falling glass mustn't be ignored. A Greek merchant captain from one of the Ionian islands told me he paid no attention to forecasts; he trusted only the barometer. Nor should local knowledge be ignored. A man who spends his life on a small fishing vessel gets an uncanny sense of local weather. Or perhaps, as one told me, he knows which way the wind will blow by the direction in which his cat faces to wash her paws.

Nor does a forecast of bad weather always bring doom. Probably the worst forecast we ever heard was made when we were on the island of Bornholm in the Baltic. This was the infamous Whitsunday Bank Holiday of 1972, and we had planned a 60-mile run to Karlshamn to enter Sweden. The early BBC forecast began: "There are warnings of gales in all sea areas," and went on through that romantic-sounding list which fills so many sailors with nostalgia: Viking, Forties, Cromarty, Forth, Tyne, and so on. The North Sea was to be southwest 7 to gale 8. Western waters were to be gale 8 to strong gale 9, while northern areas were to have southwest strong gale 9, hauling northwest and becoming storm 10. "Have a pleasant day on the water," the announcer finished in his clipped English. By rights all this weather should have come pouring over us within the next twenty-four hours, and facing a 60-mile run to an unknown harbor on a lee shore, we prudently waited in port, although the English sailors ran their scheduled races in the Channel. Stout fellows, good for them! And the weather never came to us at all. Cynthia and I made the run alone the following day in conditions so pleasant that we could take our lunch below while the ship sailed herself.

Except for the brief fury of thundersqualls, the strongest winds we have experienced in our 40,000 or so miles in our own boats seem to have been off the three peninsulas which form the southern coast of the Greek Peloponnesus. These are high but broken land, and to their north lies the entire body of the peninsula with its many mountain ranges deflecting the winds around these points, or tripping higher-altitude winds down to sea level. Our expression "a Greek lee," that strip of water which ought to be calm in the lee of high points and islands, but which in fact is whipped to a fury of driving clouds of spray, whirlwinds of spray, little waterspouts of spray, is nowhere better seen than off Capes Matapan and Mala. With a wind coming off a beach a hundred yards to windward we have had spray blown over the house top. And it seems not to matter whether the wind is east or west.

The worst of these found us in the Messenian Gulf, which lies to the west of Cape Matapan, the central peninsula and the southernmost tip of mainland Greece. This cape is a continuation of the Taygetus mountains, still snowclad in May of 1970, as we set out on the 15-mile crossing of the gulf, eastbound. Bill Watts, the good doctor mentioned earlier, and his equally good wife, were our crew. It was midafternoon and no air stirred, although a steep chop remained (we thought) from some east wind of the morning. Five miles out vagrant puffs began to come in from northeast and southeast, and we set working jib and mizzen; we might have set the main as well, except that we weren't sure it would last long enough to bother. By now, motorsailing into the slop, we were beginning to take green water over the bow, but the windward shore was only a few miles away, and we plugged ahead to gain its shelter. However, it was not shelter we gained. Down the steep cliffs ahead was pouring an invisible waterfall of air, hitting the sea at its base with the same effect as a true waterfall. A misty cloud of white water and spray could now be seen between us and shore, with a sea so short and steep that soon every wave was not only breaking over our bow, but sweeping back, up and over the housetop, to create its own little Niagara at the forward end of the bridge deck. Despite generous drains our cockpit cushions were afloat. Under club jib and mizzen, both aluff, we were laid over to the point where the contents of the man-overboard kit, lashed to the lifeline, were washed out, and the jacket and strobe light struggled behind us briefly on their lanyard and then were lost. The dinghy in tow was being tossed bodily into the air until blue sky was visible under it. It was next to impossible to look to windward, but despite averted faces and compressed lips the bitter salt was driven deep into our throats. The heavy bronze jib outhaul track, throughbolted through the club was bent in a 45-degree arc, the throughbolts with their washers and nuts being pulled deep into the solid spruce spar. What was it blowing? We all tend to exaggerate, but I would settle for 60 knots.

Only one bay was within reach before nightfall, that of Limenion on the shores of the Deep Mani, and here we took refuge. It was here that, lying to two anchors well bedded into the white sand as close to the windward beach as we could approach, the gusts off the shore were hurling spray over the housetop. And below we had again experienced the phenomenon that, despite battened hatches and closed ports, every bunk was wet from end to end. Only after a stiff drink and a shaking out of sheets to dry and a rough toweling of our saturated selves did we turn our attention to our position. We were alone at the eastern head of this deep bay, which was the continuation of a valley in the barren mountains down which the wind roared and battered at the few terraces of olive trees. On shore were a dozen dreary stone houses, while up the hillside glowered the deserted ramparts of some mighty fortress of the past. And what kind of people might we expect to find to welcome us on this desolate and forsaken coast?

Let us turn our attention to the guide books and read about these people, who were now one hundred yards to windward of us.

IV

People

In the district of Mani, the southern province of the
Morea, there is a regularly organized system of absolute and general piracy. . . . All flags are equally
their prey, and the life or death of the captured crew
is merely a matter of convenience.

Captain Beaufort, 1812

The most savage looking animals I ever saw.
Captain Stewart, 1807

Woe betide, if ever for her sins, a sailing ship
chances on these shores, be she French, Spanish,
English, Turk or Muscovite, be she large or small,
everyone wants his share. They have neither shame
before man nor fear of God; they have neither compassion for the poor nor pity for strangers. Such are
their rawness and beastlike madness that they bear
no likeness to humankind.

Niphakos c. 1788

Famous pirates by sea, pestilent robbers by land.
George Wheeler, 1675

Such were the descriptions of the inhabitants of the Mani, the
coast which afforded the only available shelter from the breeze
of wind last described, and you can imagine that it was with a
certain amount of interest that we awaited the authorities after

clawing down sail off the bay of Limenion and motoring to its very head, where we had cuddled close up to the beach under a cluster of improverished stone houses. But no one came out that evening, which was prudent, as he would surely have blown out to sea.

It was midmorning before the first boat put out, manned by a blond youth, representing the harbor, and his sister, Theodora, in black, their father being dead. A living from the Mani is difficult under the best of circumstances, and for widows and orphans it must be a bleak outlook indeed. Who will earn their livelihood? Who will furnish a dowry? But such thoughts did not depress the lively and charming Theodora. Despite bare feet splotched with dung and tar, she was an irresistible combination of eager girl and gracious lady, and would not allow us to take her picture until she had borrowed Cynthia's comb to straighten her windblown black hair. When we in turn visited ashore and met her mother, drawing water at the well, we were again in the presence of a lovely woman. I hope I shall never be too old to recall the picture of Theodora disappearing into the olive trees to bring home the cows, waving goodbye in that manner of Greeks and of royalty, palm inward, which seems half a farewell and half a beckon onward. So much for the rumors of the fierce Maniots. Whatever the rough life of the Mani may bring you, Theodora, we wish you well.

This bit of sentiment is to illustrate that, whatever the joys of blue water may be, one of the greatest pleasures of cruising comes from the amalgam of human contact. At home we are thrown together for the most part with people whose lifestyles and outlooks are not very different from each other's or from our own. The world of cruising offers its share of stereotypes, to be sure; the ubiquitous little men who come running to catch your lines, hoping for a cigarette; the American expatriate who sees in the flag the chance of a new drinking companion; these, like the weather, we learn to accept or to avoid. But apart from them we find our lives immeasurably enriched by the variety of contact. And I am afraid it is variety that the roving sailor gets, rather than depth of friendship and understanding. First of all, we are much on the move. It has not been our habit to lie long days in port, and a day or two or three of contact hardly brings out the innermost thoughts. Then there is the language barrier. Perhaps we can handle the question of supplies and of dealing with authorities in Swedish, German, French, Spanish, Italian, Greek, or Turkish; but a conversation? Hopeless. And even if one can put the words together, the intent may be lost. In a most remote cove on one of the Ionian Islands, with half a dozen houses on shore, we were exchanging a few words with a very attractive young woman who seemed brighter and more responsive than most and showed some interest in the sociology of these lonely spots, when with some struggle I finally sorted out enough Greek to ask, "In a small village like this, how does a young woman get a husband?" She threw back her shoulders and with flashing eyes replied, "I *have* a husband." End of research; quick retreat to boat before the husband comes home and is informed that I am propositioning his wife. Yes, communication is tough all over.

Some contacts endure for years, although in only brief and scattered episodes, as opportunity allows. John Kampiotis is a contented man. He is the hereditary port pilot of the Port of Katakolon, which is the stop for cruise ships on the visit to Olympia, and since it consists of one long straight pier jutting at right angles from the shore into a wide and unobstructed bay, quite free of other traffic, the task of piloting the cruise ships is not heavily demanding. We first met him in 1970, when we came in past this pier to lie along the waterfront at its base. Fortunately he waved me to the very spot I had picked, so we were happy with each other to begin with. John, it appears, is a first rate raconteur and philosopher, his only problem being a certain lack of ability to distinguish amongst the various languages he has picked up piloting ships of all nations, and his rapid-fire conversation is a lingua franca, English, French, German, Italian, and Greek words tumbling together in every sentence. An agile mind gets the gist, and the gist, as he took us to his home a block inland, and to his garden, which climbs the hill behind his home, was that life was sweet. When a ship moved in or out he did his day's work, collected his fee (and no doubt some refreshment), and then came home to sit in his garden, to eat his own fruit and to drink a little wine from his own grapes; or to sit in the *taverna* with his friends over an *ouzo* or a coffee. What more could a man ask? We were welcome to our wandering ways; his sons, scattered on merchant ships throughout the world, were welcome to theirs. For his part, the world comes to him; he welcomes it with multi-lingual gusto, and in the evening he sits gratefully in his garden. And we, who enjoyed it with him, came away loaded with fruit and flowers and wine.

Another evening found us tied to the quay at Pigadia on windy Karpathos, windy because any wind that blows seems to pour through this slot between Crete and Rhodes, and it seemed unlikely that we could put out in the morning. I was sitting on deck having a last look around before turning in when

a foursome, linked arm in arm, came singing down the quay, to stop by the boat and hail me in English.

The first pleasantries being aside, I asked, "What does one do here when the wind blows?"

"That's easy," one of the girls replied at once. "You come up into the mountains and drink wine with us."

And the next day, with spray leaping the seawall as expected, we found that they had arranged a taxi and given the instructions, and at midday we were in fact sitting on the steps of a little chapel 1,000 feet above the wine-dark sea, passing the bottle of homemade wine from person to person, not forgetting our taxi driver. It turned out our new friends actually resided in Rhodesia.

"And what do you do in Rhodesia?" I asked.

"We make money," she said, "and then we come back home to be happy."

In the Aegean world of bleak, goat-nibbled islands, one might wonder why the Greeks want to come home to be happy, but still they do, from all the world to which their diaspora has led them, but mostly, it would seem, from the English-speaking world of the Antipodes and America and Africa. With their savings or their social security or their union pensions they live on a scale satisfyingly above what they might have achieved by staying home. But the readjustment is an uneasy one. The stultifying life of sitting endlessly at the little tables of the *tavernas* in a world of perpetual unemployment after the thrust and drive and progress of a more northern world gets to them. And their success breeds envy, not admiration, among those who stayed at home. Many realize that they have no home at all, neither here nor there, and their lives are now tragedies.

Some still have their foreign adventures ahead of them, and their tragedies. One windy afternoon we blew into the windy harbor of Tristoma on the north end of windy Karpathos,

shedding fragments of battens from our mainsail, Arthur Fairley, retired Dean of the Maine Maritime Academy, at the helm. *Tristoma* means *Three Mouths* in Greek, and there are three narrow cuts in the entrance to this landlocked bay; but Tristoma sounds sad, and indeed it is, the remnants of its inhabitants living crouched with their goats amongst the ruins of a village which lies along a rocky beach so heavily encrusted with tar that it seems to be paved with soft asphalt. A couple of Greek sponge boats lay tied to the windward shore, and after three or four tries we finally got two anchors to hold toward this end of the bay, whereupon Eleanor Fairley and I rowed the hundred yards to shore for a look around. As we clambered up the rocks I sensed an unbelievable shift of wind on my face, and looking back could see *Cynthia R* just beginning to reverse her stance to a 180-degree change in the wind. We jumped back into the dinghy, and before we were back on board she was already dragging both anchors toward the shore which five minutes earlier had been our protection. Just like that. Cynthia already had the engine on; we brought up the anchors and moved to the western end of the bay, to be caught in a blast which lifted the surface off the water and sent it in a cloud of salt mist up and over the bleak hill to the north. By now the spongers had moored in the slight lee of a point of rock so small we had not even noticed it, and waved us in. Dropping an anchor off the point and throwing a shore line to them, we were soon secure, while the new wind settled into the northwest with vigor enough to hurl spray over our rock right in the harbor. Here we sat for the next two days, with the spongers as our neighbors. They were good spongers (in fact they sponged a bottle of Johnny Walker from me) and used their time to clean, sun cure, and bale a boatload of sponges, two or three of which found their way to us in recompense for the whiskey. Considering the price of sponges in the tourist market and the fact that I had bought the whiskey in bond, it was a fair trade all around.

But I am wandering from the point, which is that one of the sponge divers, who had a few words of English, confided in me that he was about to give up sponge diving and move to Gary,

Indiana, where his uncle ran a Greek restaurant and the streets were paved with gold. I asked him if he had ever been in Gary, Indiana.

"No," he said.

"I have been there," I said. "It is cold in winter."

"I don't like cold," he said.

"The air is full of smoke," I told him.

"That's not so nice, but," with a gleam in his eye, "there's lots of money there."

I looked at him and I looked at the blue Aegean and the white horses of Poseidon and the cloudless sky and his caique, and thought of Gary, Indiana, which, unlike him, I have seen, and I sighed.

A more sophisticated Greek was Elias Krallis, dealer for the Scott Paper company, among other things, for all of Greece. Paper goods in the form of towels, napkins, and tissue, are a priority item in stocking a boat, and I had his name from our local manager at home, since Malta, in the sterling area, did not have paper towels commensurate with our holders. (In fact in the sterling bloc one does not buy paper towels at the supermarket; one buys kitchen rolls at the ironmonger's. Communication is tough in any language.)

We had had a difficult day in Athens, going from place to place as each address in turn proved out of date, as was that of Mr. Krallis's office, necessitating another ten blocks of walking in the heat. So it was with some misgiving that Cynthia and I stepped from the elevator into his outer office and informed the secretary in faltering Greek that we were from an American sailboat. She disappeared, and at once a smiling young man emerged.

"You must be Mr. Carter," he said in perfect English. "And this would be Mrs. Carter. Come on into my office and we will have coffee and then take care of your supplies."

Somebody knew us! We felt as if we were at home. What a great feeling that is after a day of frustration in a foreign land. Later in our visit to Greece we had his family on board the boat, two darling girls and a wife who had been to college at Colby in Maine, not far from where the *Cynthia R* had been built; and they in turn took us to dinner. But I have always thought of this as the time we bought a roll of toilet tissue and were invited to dinner. We still exchange visits as we pass through Athens and exchange cards when we don't; the little girls are growing up and, I suppose, will soon be married.

The Greek tradition of hospitality to the stranger is legendary. Do you remember that episode in Book III of the *Odyssey*, when young Telemachus has come to sandy Pylos to seek information about his father from old Nestor? Telemachus and his ship's company find Nestor with his tribe feasting on the beach, and although the visitors are utter strangers, they are at once invited to join the feast, plied with food and wine, and only "when they had put aside their desire for eating and drinking" does old Nestor say: "Strangers, who are you? From where do you come sailing over the watery ways?"

One afternoon we came into Kastos, an island of the Ionian seldom visited because the cruising guides do not credit it with a harbor, although in fact it has a small excuse for one, and were walking through the tiny village on the mule path which passes for a street. (There were no cars and no electricity here.) In front of the solitary store two women sat, and as we approached chairs were brought from inside and we were commanded to sit down. Mini-glasses of *ouzo*, spoonfuls of jam, and glasses of water were thrust upon us, and after we had eaten and drunk the storekeeper said: "Now tell us who you are and where you come from."

This is uncanny; it sends the shivers down one's spine, to think it possible that any tradition could survive 3,000 years of Balkan turmoil; one would think it mere coincidence, except that this sort of hospitality to the stranger, this almost sacred obligation to the stranger, is repeated in the remoter parts of

Greece wherever one may be. The Greeks are often not very nice to each other (and this, too, appears to have been a part of their history for 3,000 years), and I will come to times when they were not very nice to us, but they are usually a surprise and a joy in out-of-the-way places.

It has been more difficult for us to come to grips with the matter in Turkey. There seem to be cultural differences to which we have not adjusted, and the language barrier becomes almost absolute. A visiting yacht in Turkey seems to be utterly without privacy; we feel as if the stranger were being treated rather as if he were an exhibit in a zoo. No sooner is the anchor down than small Turkish craft appear as if from nowhere, some for trade, some just curious. You may want to coil down your lines or relax with a cool drink, but instead you find that on the port side a gift of eggs or shells or gray-looking yogurt is being thrust upon you, the prelude to bargaining for fish or lobster or rugs or antiquities (a typical Turkish rowboat may produce each of these in turn), while to starboard little boys are working their way, bare feet covered with the tar of the Mediterranean beaches, slowly over your toe rail and onto your clean decks. If you shoo them away, the very best you can hope for is that they will hang onto your railing and stare through your portholes while you cook, eat, undress, bathe, and go to bed, communicating by sign language, when they catch your eye, that they would like a cigarette, or a pair of shoes, or maybe your fountain pen.

When you are in Turkey you are in the Near East, the home ground of the shrewd trader, and you had better believe, when that shy and sweet Turkish lass in baggy pants so picturesquely standing to her oars, and so modestly holding off a boat length from you, starts to bargain, she is going to best you in barter. It happened to us in a cove outside Kaş; the fulsome maid, the baggy pants, the sweet smile on her plump cheeks, the proffered gift of half a dozen eggs from the solitary farm on shore, offered with greatest diffidence. We were novices then at Turkey, and did not realize that our sweet miss was not going to leave us until she had Cynthia's finest scarf from Paris in return for her eggs.

The next morning found her patiently sitting on shore (her father had gone off with the rowboat) offering a chicken, perhaps the one who had produced the eggs, in an equally seductive manner, but I was afraid to ask what she would want in return.

As we have become slightly more at home in Turkey we have overcome our first instinctive fears of the intrusions. In a most isolated cove on the Gulf of Mandalya we anchored off a pair of black tents, home base for a couple of goatherding families. At this moment we had on board identical twins, who were no doubt in their bikinis as we had come in, and for some reason girls attract boys. It was almost bedtime when the two boys appeared from the night, paddling in the hollowed-log drinking trough of the goats, and clambering into our dinghy they made their way over the stern, seeming to hide something on deck as they did. We were all nervous, especially as calls and whistlings were exchanged with reinforcements on the invisible shore, but they seemed in good spirits, not bent upon murder and rape, and by and by Cynthia came up and gave them an unmistakable farewell greeting in Turkish and they got the idea, and I rowed them off to their drifting log. On deck we found their mysterious weapons were a gift of fresh goat's milk and cheese, and it was this they had come out in the night to bring us.

By day these same boys crept along the shore with a casting net and bagged a dozen small fish, which they brought as another gift. Nice kids—I think.

These brief notes on Turkey should not be taken as generalizations. We have been sailing there in the most primitive places, and the local people have no exposure to the big world outside as do the Greeks we talked of above.

Mifsud is a Maltese workman, and when I think Maltese I think of Mifsud. Like most Maltese he is built four square, short and powerful. He works quietly away at such jobs as scraping and painting and polishing and lifting anchors, jobs not particularly conducive to deep conversation. A few years of religious schooling followed by many years in the British Navy have also conditioned him not to speak out too freely in the

presence of his fellows. But it has been our privilege to be alone
with Mifsud on a couple of occasions when there was nothing
for any of us to do but wait, and this at a period of great
interest in Maltese politics, the early years of the Labor Government. We found that a few well chosen questions and a glass
of wine left us hanging on the words of a character whom
Hemingway would have been proud to create.

"Mifsud," I had asked, "Does the church keep its power
under the Labor government?"

"All right, I tell you, sir. I tell you the truth. I tell you so you
can understand me." And the sincerity of his tone was un-
deniable. "When I was young, when you walk down the street,
if you see a priest and he doesn't like the way you look at him,
he says to the nearest policeman, 'Arrest that man,' and you
are arrested and you have nothing to say. Don't misunderstand
me, sir. I love Jesus Christ. I have two great loves in this world;
my first love is Jesus Christ and my second love is the British
Navy. But sometimes the priests, they go too far, so now the
government says to them, 'You stay with the Church and don't
try to run everything.'"

"And your family, do they really live better now?"

"All right, when I am small we are ten children in the family.
My father has a *dghajsa* (the gondola-like rowboat which served
as a water taxi in Malta Harbor), and many days he would come
home from twelve hours work with 23 cents in wages. It is true,
meat was only 18 cents a pound, but it is not good to feed ten
children on only 23 cents. I leave school after third stage and
work; my father could not buy the books. But now see my
children, they have eight, twelve years of school, and the government gives them the books."

Eloquence which should have made Mifsud a politician, had
he had more guile, could hold our rapt attention until the
yacht-yard workmen returned from their lunch of bread covered
with tomato paste and waved us into the slip for hoisting, and
Mifsud was again the silent workman.

It is a humbling and perhaps beneficial experience to us
Americans to see the value attached to small things in other
and less fortunate cultures. Some years ago, before it was as

popular a tourist island as it has become today, while our boat lay in the harbor on the north end of Virgin Gorda in the British Virgins, we climbed a hillside trail to visit the local schoolhouse, a one-room building for all ages, with a unisex privy in back by way of plumbing, and a small crate on the wall for a bookcase, covered sadly with a padlocked chicken-wire door to protect the half-dozen old books. In those days school appropriation money was flooding into our school district at home, and we were interested in its use.

"What," I asked the schoolmaster, a dignified black in a dark suit, white shirt, and necktie, "would you do, if you had more money to spend on the school?"

I thought he might double the size of his one-crate library, or build a second privy for the girls (women's lib had not yet arrived), or a partition between the upper and lower classes. But no.

"If we had more money," he said softly, "well, last year we were given a phonograph, and we have only one record for it. If we had more money, I would buy another record."

By way of contrast to southern waters, let us switch to a rocky uninhabited cove on the Swedish coast below Stockholm, where we were coming in for a Swedish-style mooring, anchor astern and bow approaching the rocks, where a guest was to leap ashore with a line to take around a nearby birch. It was our first such mooring with these guests, and I was busy with controls and stern line, while our guest called the closing distance and Cynthia from below called up the rapidly shoaling depths from the fathometer. Meanwhile a man in an outboard circled around asking questions, to which I might not have been civil in replying except that he looked like the kind of person we would like to know. After securing I sat on the rail and we fell into conversation. He was in international law, it turned out, and this being the summer of the Nixon-McGovern campaigns I naturally asked the going opinion in his circles of the choice we faced.

"Of course people differ," he replied. "If you were to ask me I would say you must vote for Nixon, but if you were to ask my brother, he would say you have no choice but McGovern.

I hesitate to mention my brother's name, but it is Olaf Palme."

We had, by chance, chosen the property of the Prime Minister's brother, Claus, to moor to.

"But don't let that bother you. Come, jump in my boat, all of you, and we will go around the point to my place and we will have a sauna and swim."

And soon we were all sitting with him in his sauna, talking of ambassadors and presidents and the problems of the world and the impossibility of finding qualified domestic help.

Chance plays little part in meeting a port pilot when entering his port, or a property owner, if you happen to choose his property to moor to, but other worthwhile contacts may come about almost entirely by chance. We were lying in Göteborg's yacht harbor of Långedrag, stern to the pier, one sunny day in 1972 (that summer the sun shone daily in Scandinavia) while I serviced the diesel and the batteries, unshaven, smeared with oil, and wearing my battery-service tee shirt, eaten through with acid, when I became aware of Cynthia talking across to someone on the pier.

"Yes," she was saying, "You might have seen us in the Baltic; we just came across on the Göta Canal."

"Ask them on board," I called from the cabin floor, always ready for an excuse to knock off engine work, and crawled out to find the main cabin brightened by two lovely women, who turned out to be mother and daughter, and the daughter's Finnish friend, who had lately been sailing in the Baltic. It appeared that Veiko claimed he had seen the *Cynthia R* in the Åland Islands, and his friends believed he couldn't possibly recognize her now on the other side of Sweden.

"But I think he could," I said to Lena, the mother, polishing the apple. "I hope I would recognize you on the other side of the world."

And Veiko could, as a comparison of dates and places proved, and as any sailor will admit.

Conversation led to names. "I wonder if you know—oh, it's foolish to think you would know him—but we have a friend who used to live in America, a sailor, Gus Eriksén," Lena said, naming the one American we really did know in all of Sweden.

Gus had been commodore of our club in Seattle, had later moved back to Sweden and had been most helpful to us when we were getting bids on boat building in Swedish yards. When we asked them to sign our guest book Lena spotted Claus Palme's name up the page (or did I just happen to point it out?). "Why that's one of Hogay's good friends," she exclaimed. Hogay turns out to be the Swedish pronunciation of H. G., her husband, whom she now insisted we must meet. (I felt we were sailing under false colors if she thought we were more than passing acquaintances of Herr Palme, but I wasn't about to break the spell.)

Fortune has not thrown us in Veiko's path again yet, but we hope we can count Hogay and Lena and Josephine as friends for life. Lena, in addition to being a wife and mother, had her own hallmark as a silversmith, did painting and sculpture, sang in the Göteborg opera company, spoke half a dozen languages, and was a gourmet cook. (It is about at this point that our housewife friends at home cry "Stop!") Hogay was a lawyer and ombudsman for one of the world's big shipbuilding companies. Josephine, still at her studies, spoke English so well that I assumed it was her major, until she said she considered it her weak subject, being more proficient in French, Spanish, and German. Then which of these was her major? None of them; her major was medieval Spanish. But right now she was taking Finnish as well. Ah, Veiko!

And I haven't even mentioned that they were all accomplished sailors. Lena and Hogay have sailed with us in Norway, and we have enjoyed delightful meals at their home, where Josephine, after dinner, sitting at the piano in a red velvet dress in a room which glowed like an Old Masters painting, played Bartók into the night.

If the recital of shoreside contacts so far seems confined to Greece and Sweden, it is not because we have lacked them elsewhere, but perhaps because we have spent more time or been more at leisure in those two countries. But dipping into our recollections of a few weeks on the Norwegian coast, I am reminded that nearly every family seems to have a blond and beautiful daughter who has been studying English for years in school and who serves as a welcome interpreter. And Norwegians, whose lives are based on the northern sea and who have therefore a lively and intelligent interest in boats and an appreciation and understanding of our problems, were as a group the most sympathetic of all our contacts.

I picture the evening we took shelter in the little harbor of Sirevaag, south of the open stretch off Jaeren. We came in alongside a fishing vessel at a private landing, and I went to the house above to ask permission to lie there for the night (translated by the blond and beautiful daughter, of course) and returned to the boat bearing an invitation to join the Skansen family for the evening coffee, cake, and cognac, which turned into a feast. Mr. Skansen, the owner of the fishing vessel, usually spent several days at a time on the fishing grounds in the northern limits of the North Sea, running out to the westward until he intercepted a certain beat on the Stavanger consol; he showed me how to pick this up on our own portable radio.

The evening of Midsummer Day found us putting into the harbor of Fosnavåg, north of Statlandet, on the shores of the Norwegian Sea above the North Sea, and I started a bit of a walk around the harbor by way of stretching my legs and building up an appetite. Within a few hundred yards I had been picked up by a repatriated Norwegian American who insisted on my joining his family for a bowl of the special dish eaten by Norwegians on this occasion, a sort of porridge made, so far as I could tell, of library paste, milk, and melted butter, liberally sprinkled with cinnamon sugar. Now the Swedes celebrate Midsummer Night by dancing around a sort of maypole, and a year earlier we had joined them, waltzing on the greensward in our oilskins to the music of three ancient fiddlers, whose violins were protected from the rain by umbrellas. But the Norwegians on Midsummer Night build huge bonfires on every point of the rocky coast, consisting sometimes of elaborate structures of hundreds of used and oily herring barrels, while all of us who have boats mill around in the twilight bays watching the fun and dodging the other boats, which may be manned by crews in any stage of inebriation. Perhaps the bland and greasy traditional Midsummer Day dish is designed to soothe stomachs still coping with the pagan wassail of the night before: otherwise it must represent an acquired taste.

While in Norway we put in for supplies at Måløy, just south of Statlandet, and there I fell into conversation with a young man who was teaching his little boy the way of a sailing dinghy. It turned out that he owned the local fish-packing plant, and he gladly opened it up; ran out a fresh-water hose for us to fill tanks, and helped with ice. In the cabin, after securing from this operation, and enjoying a beer, he suggested we should backtrack a few miles to the island of Selje to see the ruins of the monastery of St. Sunniva, the legends of which are gathered in Sigrid Undset's *Sagas of the Saints*. The true history has been lost, apparently because a widow of the ranking clergyman expected her husband's successor to take her, along with his new post, and when he had other plans she burned all the records in a fit of pique, a point worth mentioning as long as we are talking about people.

We made this back trip, a most worthwhile excursion, and on returning from our shore walk to the brooding loneliness of the old towers, we were visited by a young naval architect, Herr Nygård, and his wife and family, who had come over from the mainland by small outboard because "Yours is the most beautiful boat I have ever seen anchored in our bay." Now there's a person who needs no Dale Carnegie course.

That's the way it goes in Norway. The very next evening we lay under a solitary farm at Hovdenvåg on the island of Hovden, and were soon befriended by the family Strömmen (two blond and beautiful daughters speaking English this time) and invited to the farm in the morning for beer, cake, and coffee. Grandfather Strömmen had moved to this island 69 years ago at age four, when Great Grandfather Strömmen had built the farm. Father Strömmen is the lighthouse keeper, an easy job in summer, when it never gets dark, and not too difficult in winter when it scarcely gets light. And since the farm chores diminish then, he doubles as a rug weaver. The girls go to school by school boat, which stops at every landing, morning and evening, throughout the long dark winters.

At Kviturvikpollen, the location of the Bergen Yacht Club, a few days later, the Commodore, A. K. Egger, drove us and our dirty laundry into the city in his Mercedes, found a laundry for us, and helped us arrange a rental car. The Norwegians have an empathy with us sailors from a small boat on broad waters, perhaps deriving from a folk memory of the voyages they made in similar boats a thousand years ago. (When we visited the Viking ship museum at Roskilde we found the merchant ship, which was thought typical of the ships which carried the Viking emigrants and their cattle to Greenland, to be almost identical in dimensions to the *Cynthia R*, although lacking the ballast keel and decking.)

A last word on the general friendliness of the Norwegians was our experience at Larvik, the birthplace and home of Colin Archer. I had undertaken on behalf of my friend Carl Vilas to see what references existed in the library there, while *Cynthia R* lay in front of the summer home of the Maartmanns in the next bay to the west. Berit Maartmann had lent us her car and called the Larvik library to explain in Norwegian our project. So upon arrival at Larvik all references were assembled. While asking some questions at the desk, the librarian appealed to the next man in line for help in explanation, and on hearing my mission, he said: "Well, Colin Archer's grandson is my best friend. He lives just up the street in the old Archer house. Come along and we'll find him."

And soon we were sitting under the big trees on the sweeping lawn, looking down Larvikfjord, talking with Lektor Justus Henry Archer, the grandson and a physics teacher, a great-grandson, who is a computer technician, and a great-great granddaughter, who was engaged in changing her doll's diapers. With tea on the lawn, the Victorian house behind us, its six generations of the Archer family in our minds, and quiet conversation, we were suddenly back in the ambience of the nineteenth century.

Shoreside contacts are varied indeed, but contacts with other yachtsmen are, in their way, more exciting. Although we have done a fair amount of sailing ourselves, we are small fry in comparison with those people who quietly take off for places which make our most remote discoveries seem to be in our back yard.

Here are Tim and Pauline, who, in *Curlew*, an 80-year-old Bristol Quay punt, a 28-foot gaff-headed cutter, had sailed from England to Greece and Cyprus. We had met them briefly in Malta in the spring, but now in the fall encountered them in the Ionian, whence they were to return to Malta a few days ahead of us. Two days later we came in to anchor at Othonoi, our favorite jumping-off place on leaving Greece for the Adriatic or Italy if the wind is not southerly, and found *Curlew* there, awaiting a wind to sail to Syracuse, and we had them aboard for dinner. Another two days found us together again in Crotone, where we both stopped to wait for persistent gale warnings to the west to be lifted. Killing time there, we all went out for a sail on *Curlew* (there were seven of us on this 28-footer), setting the three headsails on a pole bowsprit, the gaff main, and the gaff topsail, while Pauline made fresh scones on the two-burner paraffin stove. Since then, engineless and toiletless, they have sailed via the Canaries and the Cape Verdes to the Caribbean, on to the west coast of Central America, and were last heard from in Hawaii, debating whether to head for Alaska or the South Pacific.

In the windy lee of Cat Island in the Bahamas is a small sloop with two Australian boys, Andy and Bob of the *Carronade*, a 30-foot double ender. They are three years out of Australia, via Hawaii, Cailfornia, Tahiti, Cape Horn (actually cruising amongst the Cape Horn islands), the East Coast of South America, and the West Indies. They had tried to enter the Bahamas at Columbus's San Salvador but had been forced out to sea by a chance westerly and now were snuggled in the shallows under Cat Island, the northeast trades again blowing so hard that the authorities would not come off to the boat, the bay too shallow to approach the village, and no dinghy. After two days they had put their papers in a waterproof cannister and swum ashore, to walk into the customs house in dripping trunks and say: "We've just arrived in the Bahama Islands."

On the island of Ponza off Italy are Bruce and Leslie, young Australians also, heading from England to Greece in a 25-foot sloop. We ran into them, quite literally, one night when a stray easterly blew into our usual anchorage at Ponza, making it untenable, and forcing us to seek refuge after dark in the tiny basin behind the breakwater, where boats were already moored in tandem out from the breakwater's inner quay. Dropping the anchor in the dark, amongst many others, we backed down on this little sloop, where Bruce did a seamanlike job of making all fast to the boats astern of him, which in turn were moored to the quay. We were rewarding them with a beer when the fishing fleet across the narrow harbor began to move out for their night's fishing, lifting all the small boats' anchors as they brought up their own and. spreading havoc amongst us moored yachts. Life is like that in an Italian harbor.

Two weeks later we overhauled Bruce and Leslie at sea, running in light airs for Cape Palinuro south of Capri, *Cynthia R* flying her quadrilateral spinnaker. (It was quadrilateral now because we had blown out the top third in Norway and it was unworthy of further repair, only the wire luffs remaining aloft, but I am sure if we flew it in a race and happened to win, we would start a new fad.) Then we didn't see Bruce and Leslie again until the following spring in Malta.

"The Med is just like a little village," the English say. "Sooner or later you run into everyone you know."

Well, Leslie came on board and rather diffidently gave us two beautifully composed color prints of *Cynthia R* under her four-cornered spinnaker, shots we would never in the world have been able to get for ourselves, and which she had enlarged herself during the winter and carried for months on the chance they would somewhere cross paths with the *Cynthia R* again.

Fine, brave young people, these, who dot the oceans of the world, living on a shoestring, working at odd jobs when the money runs low, but with a sense of values so different from the standard that they must look with compassion on the rest of us whose sailing is incidental to a frenetic search for security. And when they do something for us, and I am sure they do more for us than we for them, I hope they know how much their thoughtfuless is appreciated.

And out in the wild Aegean are Pierre and Anne Marie, crossing this stormy sea in the *meltemi* season on a 20-foot Tornado catamaran, a dacron trampoline for a cabin, its edge for plumbing, balancing their boat with dual trapezes from the masthead (the Olympic rules allow only one, but then we cruising people, you see, put safety first). By night they would sail the boat onto a beach, leap ashore as did Ulysses' crew, and pull the boat well up onto the beach so that they could sleep in dryness on the trampoline. Pierre is Swiss-French, Anne Marie Chilean-Swiss-French, both then seniors in mathematics and filled with the exuberance of youth. They stopped by our boat in Rhodes to ask if we had any Turkish charts they could copy, since they would now like to top the adventure by crossing on to Turkey.

Of course I had to ask the obvious questions (I flipped a cat once myself, during a North American championship, when I put back to pick up my skipper, who had gone over while jibing around the leeward mark; but I had a committee boat to pick me up after the race was over, and there are no committee boats in the Aegean Sea) but Pierre had the strategy figured out for every contingency: flares in case of capsizing, emergency water, ideas for a jury rig, a miniature fiberglass repair kit. Their stowage allowed room for a one-burner Primus and a bag of rice, their staple food; two light sleeping bags; toothbrushes, and mountaineers' compasses around their necks.

"What do you miss most when you're living like this?" I asked.

Would it be privacy, a dry bed, an armchair?

"Easy," Pierre answered. "I miss most a steak dinner with wine in tall stemmed glasses."

So when they got back from Turkey (and they did, you see) we had found a place in Rhodes which served a chewable steak and wine in tall stemmed glasses to toast their voyage. Isn't it great to see the younger generation more able and daring at facing their dreams than we! Good for them! And when they are creaky with age, maybe they will treat some youngster who has crossed the Aegean on a surf sailer.

But in 1976 their daring outdid the ability of their little catamaran. In an attempt to repeat the voyage and then go on, they were caught in the center of the Cyclades in a Force 7 to 8 *meltemi.* Northeast of Naxos, scudding under jib alone—but let Pierre tell it: "I saw it coming from far away, for it was much higher than the others. I said to Anne Marie: 'Hold tight, a big one coming.' The wave hit us three quarters on the stern—we were pushed, submerged, slipping, trying to resist, in the water, the Tornado overhead falling on us quickly. Anne Marie was caught under water by the trampoline—I grabbed her by the hair and pulled savagely—we climbed on and put our life vests on. Also freed the watertight bags and put them on board out of the water. The waves were so big that I thought we had a chance to flip the boat back. But we didn't succeed. Decided to take the mast away and sail reversed to Naxos. Rigged the boom as a mast, jib and a little main up, mast as a rudder. The boat would not luff, would not be anything else than a raft. We got close to the shore, never reached it. The wind blew too much from the northwest. In the afternoon I flashed to the villages with the distress mirror, but, anyway, no caique could have put to sea with those waves. As night fell we decided to go to shore and not spend the night on the boat for the danger of exposure, waves, etc. We tried to go between the Koufo Islands, but we were drifting towards a cliff, and so we altered course towards low-lying coast. Saw a boat and sent flares, but the shore was too close, shallowing fast, breakers, so we got ready for disembarkation."

When they hit, the hulls broke apart at once; our two friends were tossed up on the rocks by the waves and in the morning were befriended by a goatherd and eventually returned to civilization. The goatherd's compatriots looted what they could of the wreck, and now Pierre writes, "Now I want a monohull, heavy, slow, safe, with which I can still sail with Force 8 blowing."

To turn the clock backwards, though, the older people have had their moments, too. In 1976 we found ourselves in company with Humphrey and Mary Barton in several harbors. Hum was in his mid seventies himself and had just completed his twentieth crossing of the Atlantic, many of these trips having been made in little *Rose Rambler.*

And I notice in my log from 1973, under date of July 8,

when we were proceeding south on the inside passages of the
west coast of Norway, the following entry: "Raised full sail as
we entered Bömlafjord and altered course to southwest, bringing the wind abeam for a splendid reach. Ahead of us was a
little open double-ender, with Viking ship lines and a square
sail, a *seksrøming* style, and we gave chase, overtaking her in
about 45 minutes." Later we picked up the newspaper article
and read about the crew, whom we had met only with a wave
and a hail, before altering course down some other lead amongst
the islands. The article was entitled, in translation: "Seventy-
seven year old man in year's longest rowing tour." Although we
had caught them under sail, they had rowed most of the way

around the coast of Norway in their "six-oar," which is what "*seksrøming*" implies. One of Aksel Eide's crew, younger than Aksel, we gathered, had rowed alone from Norway to the Shetland Islands four years earlier. We are still sorry that we had not pursued them into harbor, brought them on board, warmed them with *akvavit*, and started them spinning yarns. One of our crew spoke Norwegian and could have translated.

But here is Peter Edwards, now in his mid eighties, whose yarns we have not missed, still sailing the Mediterranean in his 32-foot *Selamat* aided by his younger friend, Wendy, who not only does a large share of the work, but the cooking and navigating as well. Peter was a rubber planter in Malaya when World War II broke out, and his services were accepted by the Royal Navy, which stationed him in Singapore. When the Japanese were knocking at the back door, Peter's commanding admiral said something like, "Well, Peter, it rather looks as if it's every man for himself. What do you expect to do?"

"Oh, I thought I might just take off in my Six Meter and sail out of it," Peter rejoined.

"Mind if I come along?"

"Come along? Now I can't have an admiral as crew on a Six Meter. Who'd give the orders?"

"Oh, just treat me as an ordinary seaman for this trip; you give the orders."

About now it is time to fill Peter's glass again.

"I don't drink much," Peter says, "I just drink often. So there we were, swimming out to our mooring. No boats around, you know, and we got to her and the sails were missing, locked up in the clubhouse, I suspect. Pitch dark, you know. And I said, 'Well, old Reggie's sails are on his boat. He's not going to be wanting them for a bit. I'll just nip over and pick them up.' So I swam over and found the sail bags and swam back, towing them, shells falling all around me, you know. And we bent the sails and caught a bit of night breeze and made it into the Strait of Malacca, and there it fell calm and in the morning the current had drifted us right back into Singapore harbor, with the shells all around us again. But when the day breeze made up we were off for Sumatra. And here we found a group of Royal Navy seamen stranded on the beach, their ship had been shot out from under them and the officers lost, so we ordered them to fall in with us and we marched them right across Sumatra to the Dutch port on the other side and we marched into the office of the Dutch administrator and said, 'Here we are. What are you going to do for us?' And of course there was nothing he could do, but while we were waiting in came the captain of a little English tramp steamer, and he said, 'My Malay crew has just all deserted and you have to find me a new crew.' So I said, 'Here we are, both officers and crew for your ship,' so we put the lot of us on board and we sailed right away, right through the Japanese Navy, to Australia."

Back in Malaya after the war Peter revived the plantation, weathered the Emergency by always going unarmed. "No point in killing me if I didn't have any gun for them to get." And in due course he retired, had his little *Selamat* built and shipped to Suez, and sailed her engineless from there to England. For the past many years he has cruised the eastern Mediterranean, and there are probably few ports he has not seen. We have run into him in half a dozen, and I can picture his head emerging from *Selamat*'s companionway, eyes blinking in the Greek sunlight, rather turtle-like, and calling, "Drinks at six o'clock." Nothing more needs saying then. And it used to be a homecoming to arrive in Malta for spring outfitting and have Peter greet Cynthia with a kiss and a "So nice to see you again, my dear," although we secretly suspect that Wendy may just have told him, "Here come Bob and Cynthia Carter," and Peter may have said, "Who in the devil are they?"

One meets a lot of people in the course of many years of cruising, and the stories about them could go on and on, but for a change of pace let's talk about a sailor of a different degree of competence, whom we encountered one fall in the broad and shallow bay of Gouvia on the island of Corfu. Four boats were lying in the southern part of that bay one evening in early October: a tiny sloop flying the Egyptian flag, an 80-foot cruiser with Norwegian colors, a boxy 40-foot ketch with a mother and 10-year-old son on board, and ourselves. We had talked with them before, and it is an integral part of the story to point out that the Widow Jones was young enough and attractive enough and her situation appealing enough that Cynthia and the Norwegian wife conceived an immediate coolness. It seemed clear that thunderstorms were headed our way (I refer to the weather now, not our wives), and before dark we set a second anchor. Still, when the wind hit at 0100 I sat in the companionway for a time, watching our bearings, and observing the Norwegian drag rapidly northwards. I was considering whether he would hear a danger blast from our air horn when he appeared to fetch up, and I figured he had been veering scope or setting another anchor himself. The other boats were riding well, and I turned in again with that "let it blow" feeling.

Morning revealed a different scene. The Norwegian was now reanchored well to windward of us, having dragged again until he hit the mud, and the Widow Jones was well up on the rock ballasting of a tiny pier used by local boats. Two caiques and a knot of Greeks on shore were trying to help her, but the water level was down several inches, and the expanse of bottom revealed to the air gave that look of being solidly on. I rowed over to find a thoroughly upset young woman. Being on the rocks was a new and devastating experience and probably the end of everything, although the now-sunny and placid bay offered no further danger. The caiques had given up, saying that at noon the water would rise again and she would come off. I was dubious about this, although they were proven to be right, but by linking all our spare line together we were able to put a splice over her forward bitt, bring it up taut over our stern with the jib sheet winch and set up hard on our own anchor chain; then we sat back to wait. A fresh north wind now came to add its weight to these forces, and the water did come up. The Norwegian and the Egyptian came to her aid, laying out a kedge and raising her jib and main to heel her over, and then stationed themselves forward and outboard, and when flotation was within an inch or two of the normal waterline we slowly added power on the *Cynthia R*. At slow cruising speed nothing happened; at medium speed her boat took a lurch and the boy's bicycle plunged off the after deck into the salt water. Work was suspended while this was fished out with a boathook, we took up the slack of stretched lines, and then on with the power again until, at 1500 rpm, the widow's boat turned on her heel and slid neatly into deeper water.

Not much more left to do, you might think, other than to retrieve and coil down several hundred feet of cable and accept a glass of wine from the Widow Jones, but in doing this, she enlisted my aid again. They had no bread and couldn't get ashore to buy any because their oars had blown off the deck in the night and disappeared. Could we lend them some bread and a pair of oars? This was done, and led to the next request. On shore she had a car, but the battery was dead; would I care to give her a push? Here gallantry faded; the rescue at sea of an attractive widow has an element of romance which I found lacking in pushing a car with a dead battery.

We have not seen the Widow Jones since we sailed from that port, although we have seen the boat laid up with a For Sale sign, but the episode gave rise to lengthy philosophical debate as to whether a woman so little prepared for the sea should place herself in a position of dependence on the charitableness of others to keep going, or whether, on the other hand, the individual has the right to take whatever chances with the elements and with the good will of mankind he or she may choose. To no one's surprise, perhaps, the opinions fall into a distinctly sexist pattern. Males are likely to laud her courage and independence. The most charitable opinion I have heard a female express is that she was, after all, making certain males feel very gallant and masculine, by needing their rescue.

"But, Cynthia," I say, "there's not a single one of her problems that I haven't sometime created for myself in a cruising career. These things happen."

"Yes," says Cynthia, "but they don't all happen at once on the very same day."

People are not the same in the mass as they are as individuals, and that this is so may not be for the better. In time of peace one is more apt to deal with people as individuals, and we have been fortunate to be cruising in Europe in a time of peace. Only a couple of wars between Israel and her neighbors; the bloody expulsion of the Palestinians from Jordan, including skirmishes with Syria, followed by their expulsion from Syria; the overthrow of the Cyprus government followed by the

Turkish invasion; the prolonged civil war in Lebanon; the overthrow of the colonels in Greece; the repeated threats of war between Greece and Turkey have occurred within a few hundred miles during the few years we have sailed here. Truly a period of peace, as these have had little impact on the sailor or on the tourist unless he steps into the middle of it.

But in 1976 that is what we did. Now, everyone in Greece knows that the Cyprus debacle was sponsored by the Americans. Just what we stood to gain by the overthrow of a friendly government whose territory in a crucial area was guaranteed neutrality may be a bit difficult for you and me to grasp, but it is quite clear to the Greeks. The Americans, so goes the story, wanted bases closer to Israel in order to support that country in her next round of war, and since the government of Cyprus was bound by treaty not to open its soil to such use, we had to engineer its overthrow. Obvious, isn't it? Well, it seems obvious to the Greeks, whose own officers in the employ of the Cypriot army were the ones who actually pulled the coup and installed a bully boy who had threatened to exterminate the Turkish minority. You and I may think that when it backfired they found an easy scapegoat in the Americans, because they had assumed the U.S. Navy would block its ally, Turkey, from "protecting" the Turkish population of Cyprus. When we did not, and the British did not, the Greeks felt that their best friends had betrayed them. They might have thanked us for sparking the downfall of the colonels, their then-dictatorial regime, but they did not. While our own newspapers were praising their wise selection of their new leader, his government was cranking out anti-American propaganda on the radio and in the press.

Until 1976 all this had had little direct impact upon us lone sailors. The Greeks we encountered everywhere on shore remained personally as hospitable to us strangers as ever, and perhaps glad of an American ear to listen to their grievances, which they discussed freely as being the result of our misguided government policies; and we in turn could be personally sympathetic, knowing that almost every family had relatives in Cyprus whose children had been napalmed and their homes destroyed, without commending the attempt to overthrow a friendly government by either the CIA (their view) or their own officers (our view). Once in the small port of Lixurion some boys of high-school or perhaps university age had come to us and asked us not to fly the American flag in their port, and one by one almost all the officials of the town came down to apologize. "They are teaching them to be communists in school. They do not speak for us." It had all been very touching, particularly since our reason for coming to the little port had been to bring some small gifts from America to a family there who had befriended us a year before when our boat was in a bit of trouble. Perhaps word got back to these youths somehow that the problems of international politics are not as simplistic as they had imagined.

But back to 1976 and the twenty-fourth of May. We were lying in the yacht harbor of Rhodes, which was crammed with boats of a dozen different flags, at a time when the Greek parliament was debating a bill to ban strikes by public employees and the reaction of the government employees was to call a two-day strike. So the streets were filled that morning with crowds of young adults in a holiday mood and ready to show their muscle. With an uncanny aptitude for wrong timing the U.S. Navy chose that day to try out the first visit of a major warship since the Cyprus war. At dawn, our carrier No. 66 and two escorts came to anchor off the city, and as the first launch arrived at the end of the breakwater, the crowd which had been in front of the government buildings headed there to repel the invaders.

"I think we ought to take in the American flag," Cynthia advised.

"Gosh, I hate to do that without being asked to," I said, "right here in full view of the whole town."

"But you know what they're like. It's just going to get us in trouble."

"I'll think about it, but I'm reluctant to do it out of pure apprehension."

A letter, written to our club back home in the course of the day, might just as well pick up the story:

May 24, 1976
All day long the crowd has surged back and forth along the quay to hassle any spot where a launch from the carrier would come in to

negotiate. From our cabin top we have had a fair view of what goes on: the first trip of a launch, the crowd on the quay, the American officer jumping ashore and talking with police, and then the return of the launch to the carrier. All day liberty boats have backed and filled off her stern, but no shore parties have appeared. We were still debating whether or not to take in our American flag, which practically overhangs the quay, when the decision was made for us. A group of young men came running up pointing at the flag and shouting, "Get out! Get out!" This poses a moral dilemma: Shall I let pride force me into a confrontation, which may be just what they want, but is no means what Cynthia wants, or shall I be a coward and take down my country's colors? Cynthia solved the problem neatly by saying, "You mean angry people are coming; it is not safe to have the American flag?" "Yes, yes, get it out," they said. "Well, thank you so much for warning us, and now we will take it down," Cynthia said, shaking hands with their leaders, while I rolled up the flag with deliberate neatness, trying to prove I wasn't panicked, while they ran on to remove, roll up, and toss into the cockpit the flag of the one other American boat on the quay. No other hostility has been shown us so far, but the day is not over. To prevent anyone casting us off, I carried a chain around a a ring and back to the boat and hauled off the quay far enough to be out of reach, although if they get ugly they can throw rocks, as they were doing at the carrier's launches, in which case we have no option but to slip our lines and move to another island. For the most part I have turned my back on the demonstrators and scrubbed teak.

May 25, 1976

You lucky guys now have a sequel to yesterday's report, because when Cynthia and I walked up the quay to the post office this morning we found a large crowd in front and up the steps. School had been let out, and a hundred or more school girls in their blue uniforms had run that way, still carrying their books, along with their male classmates, all chanting something about the Americans. The mechanic who had worked on my engine went by, stopped to shake hands and ask if we were OK, then hurried on to the anti-American demonstration. At the post office we found the crowd eyeball to eyeball with a phalanx of about 100 police in white helmets, gas masks, and with plastic shields. We decided we would sit this one out, that mailing a letter to the Corinthians was hardly worth fighting a mob, so went back a block to the public market to visit the tailor who is making up a pair of pants for me. An ambulance was driving up to the crowd. We were in the tailor shop when the shooting started—tear gas—and the crowd came charging back down the street and quay. "Now we have a tear-gas problem," Cynthia said to the tailor. "No Turkish problem, American problem," the tailor responded. Communication is tough all over. A tear-gas shell exploded under the tailor's window, which we closed just as the first fumes came in. He finished up his measuring, and we started across the market toward the boat, a full block, all open inside the vendors' stalls, headed for the gate nearest the boat, when it suddenly erupted in tear gas, cannisters rocketing across the pavement at us. So we made an end run around the market, our eyes smarting a bit, and found the boat unmolested, so hauled off from the quay again beyond reach.

While writing this the crowd formed up right here, tear gas has been used, and a couple of cannisters kicked into the harbor two boats from ours. The light breeze is off the water, so no gas has come below. By now it is siesta time, so maybe there will be no more riots until after they had had their naps. Cynthia has opened a tube of Norwegian caviar, because if we must be capitalist imperialists, we might as well eat caviar as the tear gas explodes around us.

10:00 P.M.

We were right. Everything was quiet from 1 to 5. Then the crowd came out again. We were going for our laundry when the police charged down again and we had to abort that mission—more gas. At 8 P.M. we were having another couple on board for a drink and since everything seemed quiet I stepped across to the market to buy something and instantly all of Rhodes erupted again, running crowds and tear gas everywhere. I got back to the boat choking and weeping a bit and we closed up until it blew away. By now the streets are covered with broken glass, overturned litter cans, and the remains of bonfires. The Americans seem forgotten, and it is now political. The radio mentions riots in Athens with one dead and many injured. And only two years ago their prime minister was a hero when he replaced the junta of colonels. If I don't add another page, you'll know I made it to the post office without being gassed. Well, it's different from going around the buoys.

On the third morning when I looked to seaward, the American navy had disappeared in the night, and a giant Soviet cruise ship, the *Maxim Gorki*, was at anchor preparing to set her tourists ashore. Everything was quiet, everyone was as good as gold, the streets were being swept up, and we said: "Thank heavens the Soviets have arrived to protect us." Because it was gossip among the yachts that the demonstration was leftist inspired and that the leaders now had orders to knock it off. Soviet tourists must not see that labor elsewhere has the privilege of striking.

And at our next Greek port the harbor master said, "Why do you not have the American flag up? We like to see flags. It is good for tourism."

The whole thing was maddening and funny and sad, just like people. That American carrier was one of the few things standing between the Greeks and a Russian takeover. But history may repeat itself, because it was this very inability to live with themselves and their neighbors which caused the Hellenistic Greeks to open the doors to the Romans 2,200 years ago, and when the Romans came in, they, like the Russians, came to stay. I am glad to have cruised these waters before they are closed, before a request for permission produces that unarguable Communist reply: "It is impossible."

V

Guests

There are many unsanctified martyrs;
For starters I give you the Carters.
　　They welcome each guest
　　With unqualified zest,
But are even more blessed by departers.
　　　Barbara Fiske—a guest
　　　Dedication in a book of limericks

Guests are really people, too, even if we don't always treat them
as such, and this chapter is addressed to each and every reader
who may at any time be a guest or charterer on some other
skipper's boat.

You, gentle guest, as you stand on the quay with your happy
family about you, see a sleek yacht in sparkling water. A weary
and expensive trip lies behind you, and you are ready to leap
on board, put up the sails and go. Visions fill your mind of a
glorious reach, enlivened by a dash of salt spray, a refreshing
swim at the next port, steak and French wine for dinner, and
then into those clean sheets. After all, isn't this the way it
sounded in all those articles you were reading and those folders
you collected?

Now a charter skipper must be rather like a doctor. He sees
his clients stripped of all pretense, and very likely stripped of
everything else, too, but he must treat his observations as con-

fidences. Since any resemblance of characters mentioned here to living persons is strictly intentional, we shall refrain from mentioning names. Let's just say there are two sides to the argument, and an argument is just what you may get if you are unable to see the skipper's side of it, too. I've been on both sides, formerly as an occasional guest making snide remarks about my skipper's timidity and the cook's rigidity, and later as the timid skipper himself, trying to nurse his floating home through a succession of eager charterers and to keep his poor cook happy when faced with the vagaries of the affluent American appetite, on top of putting up with me.

But we have left you on the quay, wondering why the skipper is looking at you as if he had expected you next week. What he is seeing are all those suitcases with metal lugs on the bottom, the children looking glumly for a TV antenna, and, God forbid, your dear little dog that the neighbors wouldn't take in at the last minute. He knows how far you've come, how much you've spent, and that this may be the big event in your year. He also knows that storm warnings have just come over the air, that the last supply boat never made it, so that no fresh foods were in the market, that the town's only ice making machine has broken down, and that the local laundry is on strike. Further, the last guests broke a critical part of the toilet, which is now disassembled all over the cabin floor, there is an undiagnosed oil leak in the diesel, and the electric anchor windlass has just packed up and the chain must be brought in by hand each time.

But you are still standing on the quay, and the skipper, forcing a weak smile of welcome and hoping that the obvious problems will be forgiven, that the concealed ones will be overlooked, and that with the remainder he can con you into believing that "this is the way it's done," now hurriedly urges you on board, saying he will bring the suitcases. This isn't because he wants to lift the damn things around; he really hoped you would show up with duffle bags, because he knows what those lugs will do dragged across the grain of the teak.

So anyway, we have you on board at last, and soon you are off to your first idyllic anchorage in the tropic seas.

Snorkeling is a must in the limpid waters of the Bahamas and the West Indies. The entire new world which opens up to the snorkeler just shouldn't be missed. But how far should we skippers go in forewarning our guests, new to tropic waters, about the customary precautions of snorkeling?

Don't touch the sea urchins.

Don't touch the fire coral.

Scan the surface for the Portuguese man-of-war.

Never annoy a shark.

Never reach into a hole in the rocks.

Take off your jewelry.

Never swim after dark.

Keep away from coral in the surf.

Moray eels can be vicious.

Spiny lobsters are spiny.

If a barracuda follows you, he's curious. Don't panic.

If a shark follows you, he's hungry. It's OK to panic, but don't show it. Swim in a steady and purposeful manner for the boat or shore.

About now the guest says, "Well, thanks, I really prefer to go wading anyway."

So the skipper must start all over, explaining how much safer it is to go snorkeling than to go wading. The ubiquitous broken bottle causes more injury than all the denizens of the deep combined, and there is always the nasty stingray, buried in the sand, waiting to be stepped upon.

Finally the unconvinced guest is poised on the swimming ladder, mask in place, and taking a firm grip on his courage he leaps suddenly into the sea. Two things happen. The rung he has been standing on shatters and his snorkel tube fills with water. We failed to tell him that a swimming ladder is not a springboard, and we failed to tell him how to blow his tube. Coughing and gagging, he clutches for the missing rung while we hasten to drag out the spare ladder from the lazarette. A week from now our snorkeler will be cruising serenely, two fathoms down, amongst the coral heads and waving fans, but right now he wants to see nothing deeper than a tall drink.

Shall we scrub the teak cockpit sole before our guests arrive?

Of course pride dictates that we welcome our guests to a spotless ship. Even the skipper of a schooner we were on in the West Indies must have felt this way. He kept a little schipperke dog on deck, and each morning the first duty of his cook was to patrol the deck before his guests were up, picking up and chucking overboard the droppings, which we learned by sad experience might be anywhere, after which he went below to prepare breakfast. Well, we don't keep a ship's cat or dog, but somehow the teak gets grubby anyway. The first sandwich with mayonnaise, the first shred of cold chicken, the first potato chip, and you've had it. So maybe there's not much point in having it clean to begin with; they'll probably never notice anyway. Maybe better to let them help you scrub it the day after they arrive. *Then* they'll be careful with the suntan oil.

Of course suntan oil is a nuisance when it gets on the teak, but it's better than a bad case of sunburn. The skipper mustn't presume to butt into his clients' private affairs, but as a mediator with the sun he had best draw on his experience and get his guests to cover up before they might have expected to. The tropic sun can be bad business, and the cooling trade wind is its deceptive partner. So if, on your first day out, your skipper suggests after 30 minutes that you should put on your husband's old shirt and slacks, don't think he doesn't enjoy your figure, or is a religious zealot or something. He enjoys looking at your figure very much, in fact. It's just that he wants to enjoy it again, browning slowly day by day, not cooking like a sausage.

One charter skipper we knew of *was* a religious zealot. He and his wife did not approve of the demon rum, but they knew they had to provide a happy hour for their guests, so they would set out the bottles on the saloon table and then retire to the cockpit, where they would sit, glowering down the companionway, while their guests tried to have a happy hour on the road to hell. At night the guests would find religious tracts on their pillows, as the skipper fought with Satan to save them from their ways. I understand he didn't stay too long in the charter business.

Another skipper we know is an absolute teetotaler, but joins his guests with a glass of fruit juice and is just as happy as they are. If they drink too much, they aren't accepted another time. If they drink much too much, they are put ashore at the next port. He has lasted a lifetime in the business.

While we were guests on the ship with the ship's dog, the schipperke, we never blamed him for introducing fleas. Perhaps he was free of fleas, or perhaps the fleas found him preferable to us. No, it has been our own guests or ourselves who have brought fleas on board. We got to know certain islands in the Bahamas where we wouldn't set foot on shore without first spraying all hands with insect repellent. But our worst experiences have been in the Mediterranean, where shoreside scrambles in remote harbors often wind up in a barnyard environment.

Now we're all in favor of the environmentalists, but, I submit, if you would introduce them to some Mediterranean sheep pens, rich with an accumulation dating back to the Middle Ages, there is not one who would not be crying for the most potent product of modern chemistry. And when the little visitors have stowed away in your socks and then moved into the mattress and carpets and the next guests are due tomorrow, well, there's no choice. Everything in the cabin must be turned out, hung up, pulled open, ports and hatches sealed, and then a desperate rear-guard action fought with a spray can, while, holding his breath, the skipper backs out of the noxious mist and closes the cabin behind him. Bless those pollutants! On the morrow, as we show our guests to their quarters and speak the ritual hopes for comfort, they will never know just how fervently we really are hoping.

I used to maintain that if a ship was free of vermin and the skipper reasonably sober, a guest shouldn't expect greater luxuries, like edible food or a functioning head. Imagine our horror, then, at encountering our very own vermin, cockroaches. Like fair-weather friends and drinking companions, you can find these in almost any port, although ours were Greek and came on board in cartons from the grocery store. Or maybe they walked across the mooring lines at night, like rats, although in suspect ports we spray these with repellent. The skipper has two choices: he can treat the entire galley area with the same vigor with which he has just attacked the guest stateroom, or he can hope his next guests don't prowl at night, which is when the cockroaches do. Unlike the fleas, they are cooperative little animals and do their best to stay out of sight. While one may not feel exactly warm toward a cockroach, except for Don Marquis's Archie, one must still grant grudging admiration for a form of life which has come down so nearly unchanged since Paleozoic times. But like that other skipper's drunken guests, they don't belong on our boat, and having spoken a word in their praise, we proceed to exterminate them. Let us wish them well in their native habitat, but not in our galley.

It's great to have guests who want to participate in running the ship; a good sailor appreciates enthusiasm in his shipmates, and after you have worked together for a couple of weeks it can really lighten the load. Of course, then it's time for the guests to go home. Meanwhile here are a few helpful hints on being helpful:

If you want to wash the salt off the plate glass windows, remove your diamond rings first.

If the windows are plexiglass, don't wipe them at all.

If you close a porthole, dog it down. Otherwise the skipper will be fooled into thinking it is closed tightly when you get outside, and it may be over your own bunk.

Don't mistake the brake handle on the anchor windlass for the wildcat and start wrapping the chain around the handle.

When you are raising sail, don't strong-arm it. If it resists, look aloft; you may have caught a batten under a shroud, or the pennant halliard in the sheave, or maybe you didn't let go the sheet.

When you lower away, check that the bitter end of the halliard is belayed. If it isn't, it may be your turn to go aloft and retrieve it.

When you're feeling really helpful, pitch in on the dinner dishes. Do we love people who do the dishes!

And when you feel seasickness coming on, don't lie on the main cabin floor blocking the companionway ladder. That gives the skipper claustrophobia. It's perfectly OK to lean over the lee rail; you're in good company. Your skipper's probably done it many a time. Lord Nelson did it on the *Victory*; Darwin on the *Beagle*. But the doctors say you may feel better lying flat in the leeward bunk aft. That is where motion is minimal and you can drift into unconsciousness without being in the way, and wake up in port.

Standing watch under way can be a help too, provided you watch your course. Time was when I expected every guest to stand watch. I guess I had grown up in a sailing environment where one's turn at the wheel was the big moment of the day and the routine was by now a reflex. With a watch system everyone knows just when he is expected to do his part and also just when he is free to read or nap or goof off. The person off watch can pitch in and fix a meal, and we do not fall into the departmentalization of work as we do at home. Cynthia can hand, reef, and steer as efficiently as I can, if less daringly, and I can cook and wash up as daringly as Cynthia, if less efficiently. It never occurred to me that things might be differently arranged. Come to think of it, she was a liberated woman before the phrase was coined.

"But I don't want to be liberated," Cynthia wails. "I just want a cozy home on dry land and someone to take care of me."

But with guests I quickly learned that there is another world, and most of our friends inhabit it. In this world the husband, strong, but not silent, assumes the helm and calls to his wife to bring him a drink, a cup of coffee, a snack. At the end of his watch he says, "Hey, Hon, take the wheel a sec. I've got to make a visit."

And his wife says, "I couldn't ever steer this great big boat all alone. You hurry back now."

And the skipper thinks, "Well, they've come a long way to do this, and if this is the way they like it, why not?"

Actually anyone can steer the *Cynthia R.* She is a steady and forgiving sort of boat, and I find that if I can sit alongside a novice helmswoman and tell her how well she's doing, she will probably steer a good course and come back for more. But the average housewife is so accustomed to taking her orders from her husband on the one hand, and being protected against ever having to put on her oilskins and get out there and steer when it's nasty, that the idea of standing watches as an equal is a strange notion.

And later, perhaps some evening when the skipper and this guest wife are sharing a watch together, I may hear a good discourse on the tyranny of sex roles, how fate had condemned this good woman to the kitchen and nursery when she should really have been out in the world striving with men. Uncertain, coy, and hard to please, that's what they are. Why can't a woman be like—me?

But the skipper, at least this one, *would* like to know when he can take his mind off the minute-by-minute operation himself, and this is only possible when he knows an experienced sailor is taking the con. If a group of guests are passing the helm back and forth indiscriminately the skipper daren't drop his guard.

We started across Exuma Sound from Davis Harbor one day, our guests on watch, while I retired below with a two-week accumulation of business mail to tend. It was a slow passage, and when I finally came on deck to see if we were approaching Staniel Cay I was rather shocked to find the lone radio tower, which is well to the north of the cay, just abeam on the horizon. We set a new course, and it was only after passing miles of unfamiliar shore, an hour later, that I was forced to admit the existence of a second radio tower, which turned out to be on Black Point and then uncharted, far to the south of Staniel Cay, which we had never seen at all.

On another occasion, rounding a noble headland in the Land of the Midnight Sun, I carefully figured our course to pass between this headland and some offlying reefs, set the auto pilot, there being no wind, checked that it had settled down as desired, and dropped below for a nap, while a party of four guests enjoyed an early happy hour on the bridge deck. In perhaps fifteen minutes I became drowsily aware of a change of motion, lifted my head to a porthole, and saw our headland not on the starboard bow, where it should have been, but on the starboard quarter, and coming on deck found a happily chattering crowd aiming straight for the submerged reef. Someone had unknowingly kicked the auto pilot switch, and the boat had taken a slow turn to port, while our guests may have thought the sun had to hurry around in front of them if it was ever going to make it into the north by midnight.

All other problems combined pale into insignificance when compared with eating habits. If you think babies can be fussy eaters, try planning the menu for charterers. I recall a Swedish motorboat skipper who had just signed on a group of American archeologists to work on some remote peninsula of Turkey. Their contract had solved his problem by specifying steak and French wine every night.

As I've said, we have been on both sides of this, and I can well remember one departure from Antigua. The skipper had promised us a professional cook, fresh from a local restaurant, and at sailing time he was still not on board. The last line was being slacked off from around an old cannon at Nelson's Dockyard when a bearded youth in shorts and sandals and a beautiful girl with a guitar came running down the quay. For a brief flash I hoped our cook might be the girl, but it was the beard who leaped to the taffrail as the line was let go, a true pierhead jump, if ever I saw one. The guitar sailed across the widening gap of water and that was the last we ever saw of the girl. It was almost the last we saw of our cook, too. He retired below, not to the galley, but to his bunk, while we built up our appetites in the trade wind seas. Hans *had* been employed, as stated, by a restaurant, but not as a cook. He was in fact a singing waiter and a Dutch artist, and he played a mean guitar. We were soon all singing, "Oh, the cook was Dutch and behaved as such. . . ."

In the week which followed I can only remember one meal he prepared, a handsome dish of sandwiches, made in the lee of Dominica and left in the galley sink for safety as we came out into the trades, where as soon as we were laid over the breakfast dishwater backed up and inundated the lot. We would gladly have traded for sugar and glue.

On the other hand, we were equally critical then of our daily fare on a schooner, whose skipper anchored every noon in the tropic heat while the cook served the identical lunch in the unventilated dining saloon of hot soup, spam, and hardboiled eggs, for three weeks running. Dinners alternated regularly between roast beef and roast chicken, well prepared, but somewhat lacking in variety. In retrospect our sympathies are now with this skipper. Again and again we have put the question, "Are there any things you don't eat?" And the answer is always, "Oh, we eat everything." And of course you do, don't you? That is, you eat everything except—well? And you, gentle guest, may fill in your own list of exceptions.

One guest will say, "Dry cereal is fine for breakfast, but I don't want any mush."

And the next will say, "A bit of oatmeal for me, but none of that dry chicken feed."

Bacon and eggs used to be the old reliable, but nowadays, you know, everyone is on a low-cholesterol diet and expects a heart attack if he eats more than X eggs per week. The value of X is never constant. That is, unless he is on the high-cholesterol or "drinking man's" diet, in which case he will want hot meat three times a day, including those lunches which have to be thrown together at sea while beating uphill against the trades. And these people are serious about it; they are very serious. This becomes a matter of survival to them, and I think it *is* a matter of survival. It is the survival of their own identities, their own egos.

One wife came to Cynthia and said, quietly, "You know, Bill would really prefer you didn't serve all this hot bread for breakfast; he's accustomed to eating toast."

And another one: "My Bill's not a heavy eater. Really all he wants for breakfast is fruit, but he *would* like a variety of fresh fruit every morning."

And yet another: "Bill tells me he can't stand all this fruit you're serving. It's doing something to him."

It's a rare person who declines roast beef or roast chicken (or even steak and French wine), and this is probably the easy way to handle the crowd, except the beef you get and the chicken you get in remote spots more often seem bred for the bull ring or the cockfighting circuit (the original cockpit), and roasted they make good material for resoling your boots. Lamb and pork begin to receive shakes of the head at table, and try your guests on sweetbreads and tripe in France, or a proper steak and kidney pie if you've been to Malta, or smoked eel in Holland, or a meal consisting solely of eight kinds of pickled herring in Sweden, or stewed goat meat in Turkey, or a nice grilled octopus tentacle and some fried squid in Greece, if you want to test their reflexes.

You might think those four young men who crossed the Atlantic with me, 1,000 miles from land and with the resilience of youth, could have been expected to relish anything. Quite the contrary, after some days of observation, I remarked that only a menu of beef, rice, and raisins would have met general approval. But Paul popped his head up the companionway and said, "I don't eat raisins."

Liquids are just as big a problem, and with a 30-foot waterline one can stow only so many cases of liquor, wine, beer, mixers, Coke, and pop.

"Don't forget the bottled water for those who refuse to drink tank water," Cynthia reminds me.

So we lay in a good store of scotch, bourbon, gin, and rum, and of soda, ginger ale, tonic, and Coke, and our next guest is bound to drink nothing but vodka with bitter lemon. Even repeat guests are unreliable; one couple had drunk nothing but bitter lemon one year, and a year later wouldn't touch the cases we had bought for them, consuming our season's supply of soda water in one week. You have to have tried provisioning a boat for months on end in the Out Islands of the Bahamas, or down the chain of the Antilles, or in Yugoslavia or Turkey to appreciate the problem.

Each guest arrives filled with vigor, determined to milk the moment of its last drop of fun, excitement, romance, and experience. After all, there's so much to see and so little time to see it. They can't realize that the skipper and his wife have had half a season of this already and that in the 48 hours since the last guests waved goodbye they have taken care of two weeks' laundry; located ship's stores and liquids and ice in a strange town and transported and stored perhaps 500 pounds of these; serviced the diesel; repaired the toilet; fought for fuel and water;

visited the bank for money; located the post office, learned its hours, and picked up a month's accumulation of business mail; and, finally, scrubbed down the boat, inside and out and made up the bunks with those crispy fresh sheets the guests have been anticipating, meanwhile constantly protecting the boat from other boats which come backing in across the wind needing the same help we do, or who are pulling out and lifting our anchor along with theirs. The skipper and his wife are beat.

And the new guest, arriving at nine o'clock that evening, says, "Let's see; I think what we really want are a few days in the Greek Isles and then some of the French Canals. Oh, yes, and John really hopes we can stop in Yugoslavia on the way. And now—NOW—Whoop-de-doo! Let's all go dancing!"

There will be days when the guests will ask themselves how the hell they got into all this. But they really know the answer. Despite that timid skipper, that queer food, that seeping head, they are living an unforgettable moment of their lives. And they will be the envy of all their friends when they get home and can say, "Now that's the way to travel. You just put up the sails and go."

Their skipper, meanwhile, is trying to stop that leak in the head; his next guests are due tomorrow.

VI

The Narrow Seas

"The big ship, with a bound,
Clears the entry like a hound,
Keeps the passage as its inch of way
  were the wide sea's profound!"
  Browning, "Hervé Riel"

No breath stirs the mirror of the water, from whose surface
rises a pink-tinged morning mist, concealing and revealing a
castle half hidden in a grove of trees. To our port a herd of
cattle moves single file to pasture across a stone arch bridge;
to starboard a forested island comes alive with bird songs.
Cynthia R is a thousand feet above sea level and 250 miles
from the nearest salt water. It is Bastille Day again, and we are
in the heart of France, in our own Narrow Seas.

To the English and the Dutch the Narrow Seas meant the
English Channel, but to us, and I suspect to most cruising
yachtsmen, the Channel is sometimes too wide for comfort and
very often too rough. For the purposes of this chapter I mean
really narrow. From the sublimity of the open ocean let us go
to the loveliness of that Bastille Day morning in France or to
the ridiculousness of Midsummer's Day morning in Norway
when we were caught in a channel too narrow to turn around
in, with our forestay pinned to an uncharted overhead cable by
an increasing current. Read on and we will get you into that

predicament. After all, we go cruising for variety, and if we always stay away from narrow waters we are not realizing the full potential of our boats, the unique opportunity a yacht affords for getting into predicaments.

Both Cynthia and I had been exposed to narrow seas long before we built the *Cynthia R.* In fact, back in 1935 I cruised a small and engineless sloop to Halifax, in the course of which we beat through a narrows known as Crooked Channel between Green Bay and False LeHave, Nova Scotia, which, if my old log book tells the truth, narrowed to sixty feet in one place, and where my friend stood in the bow with a boat hook to push on the rocky shores in case I missed stays. We did not miss stays; we came through triumphant to sail up onto a mudbank on a falling tide at its far end. I don't approve of running aground on a falling tide; indeed one of my rules for safe navigation is: "Always run aground on a rising tide," but there we were. Upon being given a pluck off by a helpful fisherman I said something like:

"I suppose you don't have many yachts in here."

To which he replied, "Oh, yes, we do. Why, they was a yacht in here just last summer."

In later years we have always had auxiliary engines, but there is still a great deal of satisfaction in passing through some narrows under sail, and when, doing my winter homework, after moving to the Pacific Northwest, I came across the following paragraph in the British Columbia *Pilot*, describing the approaches to Seechelt Inlet:

"At a distance of about 3 miles within the entrance the inlet contracts and is there obstructed by rocks and islets . . . ; these obstructions prevent in great measure the free ingress and egress of the tides, thus causing most furious and dangerous rapids, the roar of which may be heard for several miles."

My eyes lifted from the page to stare into the fire on the hearth, but what I was seeing were the wooded islets, trembling in the rush of white water around them, hemmed in by the sheer cliffs and timbered mountains of our northwest coast, and no doubt socked in with cloud and rain, while huge drifting logs were sucked under and then tossed clear.

"Hey," I said, "There's a place we have to do under sail. No motoring there."

And I read on: "These rapids attain a rate of 10 or 12 knots and prevent any vessel, even a boat, from passing them, except for a very short period at high and low water; it will, however, be hazardous for any vessel, except for a very small one, to attempt to enter the inlet at any time, even though there is a passage, with depths of from 4 to 7 fathoms in it, between the islands and the western shore."

"Easy," I thought. "We stand in 20 minutes before slack water, flood begins, breasting the last of the ebbing current until it slacks enough to sail through. The tide itself will already be rising in case we miss stays."

And it was even easier than that when we came up to it the next summer. The sun was shining, and about an hour before slack water a pleasant following wind sprang up. We drove in wing and wing, to be forced back out by the swirls and boils of the dying ebb, but to tackle it again a few minutes later, breaking through so smoothly that our daughter, flopped on her tummy in the forepeak, never looked up from her comic book.

You'd think a fellow would quit while he was ahead, but a few years later, in the same boat, we tackled another of the famous rapids of the Northwest at the peak velocity of a spring flood, the Yaculta Rapids past Stuart Island. There are no such dire warnings about these; the *Pilot* simply mentions 7-knot currents "which run at right angles to the course of a vessel passing through the narrows," and we had been through often at slack water. This time reality was true to imagination; we swept up Cordero Channel on a cold, gloomy, lowering day, and after passing the point of no return, where the currents now exceeded the speed our two-cylinder auxiliary could attain, the rapids came in sight under an ink-black cloud on the mountains and shrouded in a local patch of fog, generated by the upwelling of icy water. The sensation of shooting rapids like this is of giant hands under the surface playing with the boat as with a toy. A great boil of water may thrust against the hull to starboard, while an invisible countercurrent a few feet down presses at the keel from port. Where the 7-knot current runs at right angles to the course, the *Pilot* fails to mention, it may run from the left here and from the right there, the interface being a narrow margin of whirlpools, so your bow may be in a 7-knot current setting north while your rudder is in a 7-knot current setting south, making it difficult to maintain an easterly course while dodging the logs and timbers. And there are real whirlpools, too, which can be quite awesome and in a small boat are to be avoided. It was a quick ride through, but I had to admit later it was a mistake to have tried it. Riding a neap tide would be permissible, but on a spring tide we were dealing with forces a bit beyond control, and we were approaching the borderline of the foolhardy. After all, no one is going to shoot the Reversing Falls at St. John, New Brunswick, without waiting for slack water. Cynthia's father took me through there long ago in his twin-screw Elco, and while we thought we had waited long enough we were still maybe 15 minutes early and gained considerable respect for what the Reversing Falls must be like at the peak.

Narrow seas include, for our purpose, the canals and rivers we have traveled, to which we had some little exposure even before beginning our venture with the *Cynthia R.* In 1945, shortly after V-J Day we took our Atkin ketch, *Blue Moon*, down the Intracoastal Waterway from New York to Miami, a real adventure for us in those days, and possibly more so than it would be today for anyone, as sections had sanded up here and there during the war and grounding was a daily occurence. Those waters were generally placid and currents moderate, so we developed a routine. On grounding I would get into the dinghy with an oar or pole and sound around on all sides, ahead and astern, to figure the easiest route off. Sometimes we had almost ridden over some ridge and it was best to gun the engine ahead; sometimes we clearly had to back off the way we had come on; other times it was clear the bow should be hauled one way or the other. Often with the engine running the boat would not budge until it received a jerk from the dinghy, adding one manpower to the forty horsepower, to break it free. And, of course, the kedge was resorted to at times.

Only once were we hung up. West of Morehead City an

afternoon sea breeze was drawing across Bogue Sound, and at 1300 I was just coiling down from raising full sail before securing the engine when we touched. The little spoils islands to the south of the dredged channel looked so dangerously close that our helmsman reflexed away from them, although in fact it was the north side of the channel he had touched; and now, already heeled over and driving under sail and power, we climbed up the north bank, three hours after high water. It is against my principles, as I have said, to run aground on a falling tide, but we were for it this time, with no recourse other than to hope the evening high would float us, which it did long after dark.

We were sailing in the channel, though, and this is one of the joys of a fall trip down the Intracoastal. The most prevalent wind in October is a moderate, clear northeaster, and one can take the long stretches of canal with the wind aft, being ready when approaching a drawbridge to spin the boat on her heel in the event the bridge fails to respond in time. The Intracoastal may get boring to those who have done it twice a year, or who make a living of delivery trips, but we found it memorably lovely under sail with its intimate views of swamp forest, of lonely white dunes, and of infinite expanses of soft green marsh grass stretching to the horizon.

We had our first experience with a lock on the Dismal Swamp Canal of the Intracoastal, exciting because it was a first, but a very ordinary, everyday lock, now that we have become sophisticated in our exposure to locks. To a great many sailors this rectangular lock with mitral gates at each end is the only type of lock known, since the average eastern sailor has no occasion to see any lock other than that of the Dismal Swamp Canal, and in the northwest the Lake Washington Ship Canal lock, which most boatmen traverse many times a year, is of the same type. Reinforced with pictures of the Panama Canal remembered from our grade-school history books, we assume all locks are of this style, but believe me, they are not.

In 1949 we took our *Carib*, drawing 4½ feet in salt water, from Port Washington, Long Island, to Chicago, and after studying the literature on the Trent Waterway, which gave the controlling depth as four feet, I decided to take that route. I came to this seemingly inconsistent conclusion because the controlling depth existed only at two places where no locks had been built and where instead the boat would be portaged by marine railway over the dam and down 60 feet to the stage below. I reasoned that a marine railway would drop into the water at a considerable angle and that if it were designed for 4 feet its outer end would admit the 4½-foot depth of our keel aft, while at the lower end we could always winch ourselves off.

So it was up the Hudson River to Albany, where we found an LST with a moveable crane to lift our mast; then through the Federal locks at Watervliet and the many locks of the New York State Barge Canal route along the Mohawk River; until at lock 17 we came upon our first variation, an overhead gate which poises above one like a guillotine blade.

After taking the side canal to Oswego, where we stepped our mast using the chain falls of a grain elevator downspout; crossing Lake Ontario to Trenton, where we lifted the mast again with a block and tackle dropped from a bridge railing; we at last entered the Trent Waterway and began our exposure to canaling in the leisurely European style with small hand-operated locks, although some of the vertical lifts were impressive. But on two places on the Trent a very different form is used, the hydraulic lift lock. This device consists of two tubs the size of the ordinary lock chamber which are lifted by the same type of hydraulic shaft we have all seen on old elevators. The two counterbalance each other, so that if one is at the upper level the other is at the lower, and both ends of the chamber have gates which fold out and down to the channel floor, moving with them the end gates of the canal channel where it terminates at top and bottom of this lift. This is a complex and expensive bit of machinery, and it could help solve one of the problems near the summit of any canal crossing a watershed, that of insufficient runoff of water to allow constant use of the locks. With the hydraulic lift lock there is only minor loss of water, while you can imagine that the drain necessary to fill a lock chamber to a depth of 65 feet, the height of the lift at Peterborough, Ontario, would place quite a load on limited water resources above. Too, it makes for a very smooth ride for the yachtsman. But a smooth ride is not usually the objective of lock tenders, and lack of water does not seem reason enough in the lake-filled country traversed by the Trent between these hydraulic locks and the summit at Balsam Lake, 841 feet above sea level. I surmise it may have been merely the answer to a high lift in one stage, perhaps an exercise in engineering. Having passed the summit we now dropped to Lake Simcoe, hardly part of the Narrow Seas, as even on a sparkling clear day we had a straight oceanic horizon to the west as we nosed out to cross the 15-mile-wide northeastern corner, coming at last to the Severn River, where the two marine railways are situated. We had now come over 600 miles from New York, Georgian Bay lay 25 miles ahead, and if we were turned back it would mean an 800-mile detour via Lakes Ontario, Erie, and Huron to reach Lake Michigan.

Our first railway went smoothly, *Carib* fitting nicely onto the car and the "cushions" being placed to support her bilges, the keel seeming to puzzle our operator.

"Many sailboats come through here?" I asked.

"Not very many," he answered, jiggling another cushion into place. "Old Dr. McKee used to bring his over sometimes, but he died ten years ago and you're about the first one since."

The second railway, however, was manned by an outpost of empire who should have been in a leather armchair in the window of a club in London. He said, "I'm frightfully sorry old chap, but I'm afraid you're hopelessly out of luck. Water's low now, y'know." But in thirty minutes he had us up and over and down 58 feet to the river below, looking as pleased as we were. And I had never played the cards up my sleeve. Had we really been unable to get on I could have discharged the mast, whose weight laid horizontally on horses was far aft; I could have tried a block and tackle from our stubby bowsprit, heaving us down and forward; I could have scrounged two inflated inner tubes and keelhauled them aft. Somehow we would have got her on that car.

One might think that once in Lake Huron, with New York now seventy-one locks and two marine railways behind us, we were finished with narrow seas, but not so. Most of the shoreline for the next 300 miles can qualify, as one skirts the Thirty Thousand Islands, explores the uncharted bays in the vicinity of Little Current, and progresses into North Channel, itself about the size and shape of Long Island Sound. As one explores into these bays, off the buoyed and charted channels, the passages amongst these lovely islets of pine and granite become narrower and narrower, until one is forced to give up conning the boat from the spreaders and admit that he has reached a dead end. From one such spot Cynthia and I set out by dinghy to survey Dog Home Pass, finding so narrow a cut between the granite islands that we had to ship oars to glide through. It has forever remained a mystery to me why any channel so narrow and so far from the charted track should be named or mentioned in the *Pilot* or *Cruising Guide*.

If I have rambled on about these waters it is because they are indeed fine cruising. You don't need to go to the Baltic to sail amongst the skerries; the North Channel country does not need to take a back seat to any place. With the mountains of the Killarney Range coming to the edge of the water, the oldest mountains in the world, mountains so old that the valleys themselves are scoured from pure granite, leaving the spines of still harder quartzite standing, and with a complex and uncharted shoreline which defies description, there is a challenge here to every explorer's imagination.

Another background in canaling was the trip in 1950 up the Fox River from Green Bay to Lake Winnebago and back. The locking system here offers nothing out of the ordinary in the way of engineering, but this river did offer the unusual basin behind the dam at Appleton, where narrowness was vertical, not horizontal. We had been waved over to the Appleton Yacht Club across the basin from the normal channel, bumping our 4½-foot draft across limestone slabs one evening, but by morning the water was down a couple of inches and it seemed that we would be there until the level came up. After several false starts and after sounding out a channel in the dinghy, I finally resorted to the "damn the ledges; full speed ahead" technique, crabbing across the swift current, only to pile up for fair too far out to get a line back to the pier. We were properly stuck, but the good nature or guilt of the club members came to our rescue, and with one motor boat pulling upstream on the main halliard until our deck was awash, while a second towed us across the current, we lurched and staggered our way back to an acceptable depth in the main channel. Given power enough, this is a fairly reliable way to float a keel boat, although it is a nightmare for me to think of the strain at the masthead, all that strain which would normally be exerted by the sail throughout the mast and rigging when sailing with deck awash is at one point and borne by one shroud.

So we were not wholly inexperienced when we faced the question of selecting a boat for our European venture, which was to include its share of rivers and canals.

Canal boats are great for canaling. Blunt ends, shallow draft, home-like quarters, and not too much power conform happily to the pattern of life on the canal, where much of one's time is spent in what we might call a holding pattern, waiting for locks, waiting for bridges, waiting for traffic. The canal boat, having a bit of grip on the water, tends to track at slow speeds and not to be blown sideways by the first puff of wind. And if she is, she can snuggle into the mud or bank and wait. The single screw is well protected.

The more modern houseboat appears to be an attractive substitute, offering the versatility of high-speed performance when away from the narrow waters of the canals, but all boats are compromises. This type of hull depends on speed for maneuverability, and it is generally illegal to get up and plane between locks. Many houseboat hulls have little grip on the water, so that the interminable holding patterns can be a constant annoyance if there is any wind.

But suppose you want to do more than go canaling? Suppose you want to cross oceans, explore tropical islands and uncharted coasts under sail—and then go canaling? You will take first things first and choose a hull and rig with which you will be content at sea, but which can still transit the inland waters you have in mind. *Cynthia R* was a compromise of five features to which we gave top priority at the time we selected her:

1. A fiberglass hull not over 40 feet.
2. An absolute maximum draft of not over 6 feet.
3. Directional stability downwind.
4. A main cabin with visibility.
5. Visibility over this main cabin from the steering station.

To comment on the reasoning behind these priorities and the advantages and disadvantages which have worked out in practice, I would start by admitting that steel offers many advantages as the construction material, chief of which is custom design, and many examples today prove that rust is not a necessary companion to this material. But plastic seems more of a sure thing than steel, with the added advantage that constant painting is eliminated, a great boon to those who prefer actual use of the boat to the maintenance work. By calling for fiberglass (more exotic materials were beyond our pocketbook) we effectively froze ourselves into picking a stock model, as in 1964 when the decision to build was taken, the one-off fiberglass hull was not economically practical. The reader has already noted that we violated the other part of our first priority by going to a 44-footer.

"The *Blue Moon* was plenty big enough for us," Cynthia would say, "and all the boat we could handle alone, and she was 38 feet over all."

"That's right, but look at it this way—while she was 38 feet over all, she had a 6-foot pole bowsprit, and every time we had to handle headsails in a blow, I was out on the end of that bowsprit. Now this Countess hull is 44 feet, but the waterline is the same as the *Blue Moon's* and the beam is the same and the foot of the sail plan is the same, and the only difference is that I can change headsails on deck inside a pulpit instead of 6 feet out on a bowsprit."

As I said earlier, precaution is Cynthia's sensitive spot, and we agreed that we ought to be able to handle this 44 feet of boat. Now we know that we could have handled 50 feet just as well at sea, but I would still feel some qualms about the crowded harbors and maneuvering in canals. An academic point, however, because if the cost of a boat varies as the cube of its linear dimension, you can see that a 50-footer is going to cost half again as much as a 44-footer, and we were already reaching for it.

We were well within our draft limit; the Countess hull was originally designed with a draft of 5 feet, 3 inches; with the extras we put into *Cynthia R,* starting with an additional 1,000 pounds of lead, we are down to 5 feet, 6 inches, and when we get into the warm fresh water of canals we may be down to 5 feet, 9 inches. And under way, especially when gunning the engine for current or maneuvering, I have no doubt we hit a 6-foot draft. At least, we keep scraping bottom in places on the French canals maintained at a controlling depth of 1.8 meters, the same as 6 feet.

For directional stability downwind we wanted a long keel, and while I can accept that a fin keel with a skeg and rudder aft may achieve this same benefit, the long, straight keel terminating in a small skeg (the lower rudder pivot), with the propeller tucked up behind the deadwood, has provided a feeling of confidence and response in the constant touch and go with the bottom. An alternate choice would be the tandem centerboard, which permits a shallower draft with the boards up, greater efficiency on the wind with the main board down, and the ability to track like an arrow with the aft board down. Or so they say. But centerboards cost money, they have been known to jam and to fall out, and, like a computer punch card, they are no good if folded or mutilated. In port they bang back and forth in their trunks as the boat rolls. At sea they can be worse. One friend of mine was hit by a whale on his way to Bermuda; the board slewed sideways so that it could not be retracted, and he had to cover the last few hundred miles sailing with his board at a considerable angle to his course. Another friend arrived at the yard of Abeking and Rasmussen outside Bremen with his centerboard trunk so full of gravel from a descent of the Rhine that it had to be drilled out with a jackhammer. In balance, we have been content with the long keel, which today looks as scarred as the glaciated granite of New England.

The deck house with its picture windows for visibility you are already familiar with, and let's admit that this, too, must create compromise. Those windows, the source of contentment for cooks and dishwashers, the frames of many a good photograph, are also the source of tremendous solar heat gain in a Turkish summer, where we use white plastic exterior covers to keep out the sun, and they are used by the curious in every port to stare through and observe our daily lives. While I do not worry about their being taken out by a boarding sea, because on ocean passages we cover them with half-inch plexiglass, I do feel some concern that in an ultimate storm the entire house could be driven from its foundation. A flush deck or low trunk cabin offers more safety, more privacy, a better platform to work upon. But we wouldn't trade.

The steering station's position was dictated by the house. If we were to see over that without getting a stiff neck, it had to be high. A midships cockpit would feel more secure and have slightly less motion in a rolling sea, and with modern designs this is all being accomplished by using a lower deck house, positioning the engine under the cockpit floor, and using the space beneath a wide molded coaming as headroom for a walk-through to the aft stateroom. But our 360-degree visibility is marvelous, and the high steering station is splendid in canal and river navigation.

At sea we use a two-bladed propeller, locked vertically behind the deadwood when under sail, but where it is feasible to change propellers before a long spell in inland waters, we will replace this with our spare three-bladed prop, as we find we can wind the engine up to its full rated rpm with less vibration. There ought to be more thrust, too, but to tell the truth, it is hard to notice the difference.

Another word about draft. If you want to cruise Europe by canal and river, you will find that France tends to be the limiting factor, for if you plan for depths in that country you will have little trouble on major routes elsewhere. Of roughly 4,500 kilometers of French canals all but 1,000 kilometers have a "theoretical depth" of 2.0 meters (6½ feet) or more, and there are an additional 2,200 kilometers of navigable rivers (in addition to those open to big-sea shipping), of which all but 500 should be open to the same draft. A draft of 5½ feet will open up the Canal du Midi between the Bay of Biscay and the Mediterranean, while 5 feet will let you cross Brittany or take the lovely Nivernais Canal in central France. It is not impossible to cross Europe with more draft; it has certainly been done with some 7-foot keels. It is just that the choice of routes becomes limited, one must stay in the commercial channels, and the trip becomes more of a delivery trip than a cruise.

Regardless of draft, you will be aground from time to time, sometimes bumping unseen rocks, more often easing into soft mud. In the rivers you may climb up onto a gravel bar left by one of the many dredges. So have in mind the techniques for getting off. A long line to a tree on the opposite bank, led through the bow chocks to the jib sheet winches, coupled with plenty of power, is usually enough, but station a man by the tree so that if a barge comes around the bend you can cast off and haul the line on board before a canal boat's propeller takes care of it for you. This implies that you can get to the opposite bank, and after a couple of such episodes we took to towing our dinghy, instead of carrying it in davits, against all advice, and found it little trouble. A big bow fender, a floating painter, and an occasional prod with a boat hook were all it wanted.

A friend of mine who has a boat with a 7-foot draft is actually considering temporarily fiberglassing some pads of styrofoam under the turn of his bilge, faired to the run of the hull, and with the masts unstepped no problem of stability would arise.

Another inflexible dimension is overhead clearance. In Europe one must plan on 11 feet, and then you may find a few inches to spare. But just as low water on the rivers can thwart your plans for draft, so high water can prejudice your overhead, and in flood stage you may again be delayed. But floods are not a summer phenomenon, and if you are canaling for pleasure you won't be doing it in winter.

An oceangoing sailboat may have its mast stepped through

the deck to the keel, and this will require lifting and restepping, which should not be a problem these days. But in designing with canals in mind it is better to step a mast on deck, if for no other reason than to shorten it by 6 feet, because in the horizontal position an overhanging spar is a dreadful nuisance in a crowded lock. And it is a simple step to house a mast in a tabernacle with a pin on which it can swivel for lowering and raising. This is the way most Dutch and many German sailboats are equipped to begin with, and because the major stress at the mast step is compression, it is not necessary to overbuild this member. Often two cheeks of oak are all one sees.

With the short masts and high bowsprits of traditional Dutch rigs, raising and lowering was simple, but with tall rigs and short bases a strut or A-frame is necessary. The strut is the more common, secured horizontally into the leading edge of the mast for handling it. When the headstay is secured to this strut instead of to the stemhead fitting, and a tackle is led to the stem, the mast can be lowered, although once down it must rest with its base in its tabernacle and the truck extending over the stern. In our own case we chose the A-frame, which is made by coupling two spinnaker poles with a cap and securing their lower ends into plates just inboard of the main upper shroud chainplates, set in the lateral plane of the mast. Again the headstay is secured to the cap, and a tackle from this to the stem, the hauling part leading to the jib sheet winches. With a three-part tackle and a 35-to-1 winch ratio we just can crank it back up. The A-frame has two advantages over the strut: the mast tends to hang from the apex of the A-frame and there is less tendency for it to sway from side to side in lowering; and once down we can use the A-frame to lift and move the mast. It is canted on aft, and a falls is dropped to a strap around the mast as near to its balance point as we can reach; then, by hauling up on the falls and cranking the A-frame up and forward, we can manhandle the spar into position on two spruce strongbacks which fit into the main and mizzen tabernacles, just spanning from bow pulpit to davits and just clearing the lowest fixed bridges. Bringing the weight of the mast forward in this way is quite important in balancing draft for these shallow channels.

Perhaps the last bit of preparation is fendering. A substantial rubstrake, although not pretty, is a useful part of design. Because lock walls and the barges you will lie alongside are dirty, round fenders will merely roll the dirt and grease along your topsides. Old tires are standard, but of course they rub off horribly, so we chose to cover ours with cheap canvas jackets made up with a grommet in the top, and tied them on simply by boring a hole through the tire and putting a figure-eight knot on the end of the lanyard. Then we carried a fender board outboard of the midship tires and let this take the bulk of scrape and chafe.

When one is so prepared, there is one more consideration in making a pleasure of canaling in even an ocean boat: plenty of time. Without exception our acquaintances who have said, "Never again!" had regarded their canaling as a delivery trip, to be put behind them as quickly as possible, and very often made in the off season, with ice, snow, and fog to contend with. Those who remember it with nostalgia as a fine part of their cruising experience are those who have taken their time and savored each mile.

There are more thorough descriptions of the inland-waterway system of Europe than I want to include here, but to save the reader a lot of time in locating these, or confusion when I mention examples from our own experience, let us take a quick look at the waterway pattern, as developed originally in isolated segments. Only now is an integrated whole projected. *Pattern* is not really the right word to use, because I always fail when I try to relate it to accepted patterns. It isn't quite a skeleton, although it does almost have a backbone with ribs, arms, and rudimentary legs.

Let us start with the Rhine and the Rhône, which together form a backbone to the system. The Rhine when ascended from the North Sea is navigable for motorships across Holland and western Germany, along the Franco-German border, and into Switzerland for a short distance above Basel. The Rhône likewise can handle motorships from the Mediterranean to Lyon, and by a northerly continuation on its tributary, the Saône, well into central France. Two routes connect the Rhine and the Rhône, although neither is yet ready for ships larger than the French *péniche*, the motor-driven barge built to fit exactly into the standard lock of the old French canal system. These are the Doubs River route, basically a canalized river linked by straight canal across the Belfort Gap to the Rhine near Mulhouse, and the Canal de l'Est, which continues north across the watershed between the Rhône-Saône drainage basin and the Moselle basin at Nancy. Here one has three choices; one can pick up the Marne-Rhine Canal to reach the Rhine at Strasbourg, one can descend the Moselle to join the Rhine at Koblenz, or one can continue north on the Canal de l'Est, crossing another watershed between the valleys of the Moselle and the Meuse, to follow the latter river past St. Mihiel and Verdun out of France and across Belgium, to find that it has become the Maas in Holland, which in turn is linked to the Rhine at Nijmegen— actually to the Waal, as that arm of the Rhine is known.

If we think of this as a backbone, we can fill in with ribs to east and west. From the Saône we could have turned west into France on the Canal du Centre or the Nivernais or the Marne-Saône Canal; at Nancy we could have gone west on the Marne-Rhine Canal; from the Meuse we could have angled back on the Ardennes Canal, or at Namur in Belgium we could have headed back into France along the Sambre route or westward into central Belgium, while at Liège we could have picked the giant Albert Canal direct to Antwerp. Once in Holland one can turn from the Maas or Waal into a veritable lacework of waterways, or one can take a short leg on the Waal-Rhine and come down the Ijssel to the inland sea of the Ijsselmeer, the old Zuider Zee, and thus to the North Sea or into the complex of canals in Friesland. Coming back upstream on the Rhine and looking east, we find two canals leading through the Ruhr area, the Wesel-Datteln Canal and the Rhine-Herne Canal, both terminating on the Dortmund-Ems Canal, which leads north itself to the Ems River and to the Mittelland Kanal, which crosses the North German plains to the Weser and Elbe Rivers and thus to Bremen, Hamburg, or Berlin (if the East Germans would let us). Farther upstream at Mainz one can turn into the River Main, already navigable to Nürnberg, or at Mannheim into the Neckar, navigable to Stuttgart.

These are the major routes used in going right across Europe; only the maps and the waterway guides can properly fill in the dozens of alternates, parallels, dead-end spurs, and interconnecting short or shallow waters, concentrated from northern France to the north tip of Holland.

The rudimentary legs of this skeleton come off the Rhône close to the Mediterranean. At Arles a canal leads southeast to the Étang de Buerre and the industrial complex around Marseille, at Port St. Louis another short spur leads to the sea (and this is the route for commercial shipping), and from the branch known as the Petit Rhône one locks into the Rhône à Sête Canal, the intracoastal waterway of southern France, which in turn leads to the Canal du Midi and the Bay of Biscay, as well as offering access to the Mediterranean at several ports en route.

Major projects are under way to enlarge and modernize the system. Everywhere in Germany when we were there channels were being deepened and widened, bridges being raised. A new link has been opened across West Germany between the Mittelland Kanal and the Elbe, bypassing the short but politically difficult arc of this route lying behind the Iron Curtain in East Germany. In France the swift Rhine has been canalized from Switzerland north to the German border, and the even swifter Rhône is almost tamed from Lyon to the sea. In 1973 we had picked up rumors that the Mulhouse link between the two was due for eventual enlargement to permit Rhine and Rhône ships to cross between the two, and in 1975 the French government officially announced its intention to proceed. But most dramatic of all is the work in progress to complete the Rhine-Main-Danube link, for when these links are open the grand design will near completion; large motorships of up to perhaps 3,000 tons will be able to cross Europe between any combination of the North Sea, the Baltic, the Mediterranean, or the Black Sea. Is this not a thrilling tribute to the enterprise of man?

Since we had crossed the Atlantic to the Mediterranean, we had no choice but to ascend the Rhône when in 1971 we turned our bow north. At that time it had been partially tamed, but not fully. Indeed, it will never be a tame trip to ascend or descend the Rhône. So we turned to the printed literature in various guides to see what we might expect.

To compare the Rhône with rivers we know, our own Tennessee, picked for the hydro project of the TVA, has a slope of 9½ inches to the mile from its head of navigation; the Columbia from its head of navigation at Priest Rapids has a slope of 12 inches and was considered scarcely navigable until it was tamed; the St. Lawrence Seaway from Lake Ontario to Montreal has a slope of 15 inches. But the Rhône has an average slope of 42 inches to the mile and until recent years was not canalized at all.

Inland Waterways of France, published in 1963, says, "The Rhône cannot properly be called a river; it is an enormous torrent. Those who presume to travel on its waters should never forget this torrential character, for the river is dangerous even to those who live on it, and very much more so to amateur mariners."

The French *Guide du Rhône* of 1968 says: "To be able to mount [this river] one should have a motor sufficiently powerful to permit of going at least 30 kilometers per hour in calm water."

Bristow's book, *Through the French Canals*, 1970, says: "Unless your craft can make a good 10 knots, it will not be safe to risk getting up under your own power."

And the latest word of caution was the August 1970, *Yachting World:* "To ascend the Rhône from the Mediterranean requires a powerful craft. Estimates of the minimum speed vary between 9 and 15 knots. One thing is certain, a small auxiliary yacht will not ascend the Rhône under her own power."

With these cheerful words in mind we asked Irving Johnson in Malta what he thought.

"Well, a few years ago," he said, "it would have been quite impossible, but today I think you can do it. You might just have to hitch a ride for some short stretch, but you might make it on your own."

As we nosed *Cynthia R* with her 8-knot hull speed into Port

St. Louis in June his was still the only encouraging voice we had heard. Indeed, as far upstream as Avignon we still ran into descending yachtsmen who assured us we could never mount under our own power the stream they had just descended. After that we stopped inquiring.

The 22 miles from Port St. Louis to Arles had been broad and sedate, and we had run at an easy cruising speed close under low, wooded banks, where the bird songs were louder than our engine noise, averaging 4 knots over the bottom. But Arles is the upstream end of the sluggish delta, and from here the Rhône was indeed a torrent, against which we fought our way for the next four days. I had thought that, as with most rivers, it would have placid sections between rapids, but this wasn't so. The Rhône hurled itself relentlessly against us and we battled for every mile. Bit by bit our engine speeds went up until we were running steadily at close to our maximum rated rpm of 2400. Every buoy not dragged completely under by the current carried a plume of spray. Often the water spilled obliquely across the channel over half submerged dikes, where we crabbed our way up in foam and swirls. Although we had averaged four knots over the bottom at cruising rpm the first day, we averaged just that at full speed the second day, less than 3 knots the third day, and less than 2½ knots, flat out, the fourth day. This was not all due to current, because the same dams and locks which made it possible for us to mount the Rhône at all created their own delays.

At that time there were six of them, the magnificent engineering project of taming the Rhône being then over half completed, and in addition to making the Rhône navigable the project was designed to produce 10 percent of France's electricity. But as we know, demand rises to consume all available energy and even when we returned this way two and a half years later, there were already both nuclear and oil-fired power plants along the river.

Each dam has a single lock with a straight lift, the highest being that at Bollène—86 feet—and the average lift being 50 feet. The lower gate for a lock so deep may rise vertically over your head, while upper gates generally retract into the founda-

tion beneath them, needing to be little higher than the depth
of water over the lock sill. The red-and-green-light system is
used, and if you have a red light you might as well tie up along
the wingwalls, where bollards are conveniently placed, because
it could be a long wait. Our longest was an hour and a half.
There is a loud hail system, but unless you can understand
French from a squawk box over the noise of your boat and with
the *mistral* blowing in your ears, you had best rely on visual
signals. Once inside the lock chamber, we were gratified to find
floating bollards and smooth walls, and although the bollards
were too far apart to get lines onto two of them, we found that
a spring line from amidships with the engine idling ahead to
keep us sprung into the side made for a pleasant enough ride
up. When a swirl would start to force us away from the lock
wall with seeming irresistible force, a burst of power would generally straighten matters out. But you can imagine that a stout
spring line is indicated. At the top the swirls die away, the
upper gate slowly disappears beneath the surface, but a safety

chain still spans the exit, only to drop away when the gate is wholly retracted, and at this the exit light changes from red to green and you are free to face the Rhône once more. All this has been programmed by the lock-tender, high in his control tower, who has preset his controls to determine which sluices will admit water and at what speed for each phase of the ascent. Then, at the touch of a button, a computer takes over and handles the entire operation. No human being has been seen from the deck of your boat. It is spooky and magnificent.

Above the dams are pool stages where the current is briefly not noticeable, having been diverted down a parallel channel to the power station, and there may be more or less a lake for some miles, narrowing into dredged channel and swifter current as one progresses upstream. In some places the old river bed is still used, but much of the completed project will use new artificial channels bypassing some of the bends and rapids of the old river, and even where the current is still fairly swift it is at least uniform, instead of being all boils and swirls.

I have mentioned the *mistral*, and in planning a trip on the Rhône in either direction one should assume its presence and be prepared for 30- to 40-knot north winds anywhere south of Tournon. These can whip spray over your boat in any wider stretch of the river.

The literature of boating on the Rhône is replete with tales of disaster. On our last and longest day before Lyon, a day of running for sixteen hours flat out, I saw our oil pressure slowly drop from its usual 25 pounds to 20, 17, 15. There are no landings here, there was no stopping or anchoring. In fact, no anchor would hold on that bottom of scoured gravel, and I agonized throughout the day, expecting from moment to moment as the hours passed to hear the sounds of a burned-out engine. With no place to stop we would have been swept instantly downstream to strand on some rocky bar, laid over and pinned by the remorseless current.

Since we had recently changed oil filters and oil, and the level was full, only such dire possibilities remained as a faulty oil pump or clogged sump screen to create loss of pressure; either of these would require removal of the engine from its bed to correct. I contemplated this throughout a long afternoon, as we ground our way up a narrowing channel, to break through at dusk into the canalized section below Lyon and tie up below the last lock, already closed for the night. The real culprit, I discovered later, seemed to be a slipping belt, and what I should really have been worrying about was a loss of water circulation if that belt broke on the Rhône. Well, that's the story of our cruising; we're always worrying about the wrong thing. But the moral is real enough: check every source of mechanical trouble before committing yourself to the swift rivers.

On all the bad stretches of the river we had shipped a pilot, three different men in all, a universally recommended procedure in which I wholly concurred. But the Rhône pilot is a dying breed, suffering from technological unemployment caused by the taming of the river, and when we returned in the fall of 1973 to go downstream we ran into problems. Sweet old M. Vial, who had been our pilot up in '71, conducted us downstream from Lyon to Andance, 38 miles, where we entered the pool stage above a new dam and carried on alone. It was all clear going now to Bollène, where we arrived our second evening in a proper *mistral*, registering up to 100 kilometers per hour at the control tower's anemometer. Here we had a talk with the lock tender, understanding that he would arrange a pilot for the morning, and that he would give us a green light to enter the lock when the pilot was there to board us.

We had tied alongside a self-propelled barge in the dusk, not noticing that we were under his cooling water exhaust, and were awakened in the morning to find we were moving back up-river, copious amounts of oily water being discharged onto our decks. This soon corrected, we tied back at the dolphins where our barge had been lying, and sure enough, halfway through breakfast, the light turned green. In fact it had become our method of changing a red light to green to sit down to a good meal. We entered the lock chamber, saw no pilot around, assumed we were to await his arrival quietly, and went back to our breakfast, only to find ourselves suddenly and quickly descending.

"Hélas!" I yelled, "Où est notre pilote?"

And the cavernous walls echoed back, "Hélas!"

The lower gate opened, and having nothing better to do we moved out and secured to a dolphin below the lock, climbed its ladder and so back up to the control tower, now 120 feet above us, where, of course, another man was on duty.

"What pilot?" he asked. "I do not know of a pilot."

"Can it be I have not well understood your companion of last evening?" I volunteered.

He looked at me suspiciously, perhaps trying to remember what woman I might have seen him with last night, and then brightened in comprehension. "Ah, that one! All the world understands him not. He speaks too fast. Me, he says one understands me not because I speak Provençal, but him, one understands him never in any language."

Thus reassured that I would be unable to understand either of them, I tried to bring the conversation back to the subject of a pilot. A few phone calls were made to a bar in a town downstream, and our locktender announced that our pilot must be bringing a ship upstream and should be here in the afternoon. Meanwhile nothing was coming downstream for us to follow, and we might as well enjoy a tour of the lock mechanism and then wait. We enjoyed our tour, although not as much as we would have had we been sure our pilot was on his way, then climbed back to the boat and were just settling down when we were hailed on the PA system and waved back up to the tower. Here we were informed that the pilot would not be working for two days; his wife was ill.

"But for what a pilot?" he asked.

"For that it is dangerous, this part of the Rhône."

"Is it that you have fear?"

"But naturally I have fear, like the soldier before the battle."

"But it is only 15 kilometers which is strong. After that it is nothing. And the water, it is a good level." He produced a fine old *Salagnac Rhône Guide* of 1960 to show the channel, and permitted me to take it to the boat and trace the pertinent sections. After my third climb to the tower to return his map and thank him with a pack of American cigarettes, we cast off at 1120 and, mustering what courage we could, turned downstream, soon to rejoin the wild Rhône. At a fast idle in order to allow time to match our maps with the shores, all changed by work in progress, and to spot the buoys ahead, which were more numerous than charted, we sluiced downstream at the rate of 17 kilometers in one hour flat, to enter the broad pool stage below, grinning and elated. A year later this thrilling ride would be no more; a new artificial channel to a new dam and lock would entirely bypass these hard kilometers.

No one had given us any word of warning about the passage from Avignon to Arles, the last remaining bit of old Rhône and all that remained between us and our winter layup at Arles. Filled with confidence after our successful run without a pilot down the stretch where everyone agreed a pilot was necessary, we relaxed for a day at Avignon and then headed blithely out of our last lock at Beaucaire, below which a dredge was busy at work with the symbol meaning to leave him to our port, and we shaped a course in this direction only to go up at once on a gravel bar, the current slurping around us. I was still sounding around with a pole, and I believe I could have handled the dinghy all right in the moderate current here, when a tug detached itself from the dredge and came up to give us a pluck off and a bit of advice on the channel below. It appears the dredge was working its way upstream toward this bar and that the entire dredging operation in this section of the river was contracted to the Dutch, all of whom spoke English, a help in our case. Somewhat chastened by this, we proceeded at 1,000 rpm, finding most of the buoys in place, and the currents and channel as shown in the *Guide*. With Arles in sight at the next bend in the river we came upon more confusion. Where the Petit Rhône branches off to the right, two dredges were working, the current very swift, and we running along the edge of a dike on the left bank and approaching a cross-over. We did a 180 in the stream and held our position while we studied the *Guide*, the altered buoys, the symbols on the dredges, and the appearance of the stream. No traffic was in sight to guide us, but the channel now seemed clear, so we turned again, started our crossing, and then, right where we would have expected the middle of the channel, there was suddenly a hump of water ahead of us, flowing up smoothly on the upstream side to cascade over it into white water below, clearly a big boulder just ahead of us, as all of us have seen in mountain streams, just under the surface. We did another 180 and more study, with remarks like this:

"We can't go any closer to the right bank than this."

"No, we're almost up on top of it now."

"But the *Guide* shows the channel right along the bank."

"Sure, but a big barge would never get through between that boulder and the bank."

"Well, do you suppose we ought to go outside it?"

"I don't see that there's any choice. There's plenty of water to the left of it." (Whoever said that was referring to breadth, not depth.)

"OK, do you agree we turn right, then?"

"Yes, we turn right." (Since we were headed upstream this took us to the left.)

We turned right, and crash! We were on the gravel again. The stones could be heard rolling and grinding under us as the current turned us sideways to the stream, heeled us over, and lifted us farther and farther onto the gravel, until at last we came to rest. I said something unprintable and the stones rolled us a bit farther up. No hope of sounding with a dinghy here; the stream rolled past us, creating a furrow from stem and stern, and we feared for the mast in its strongbacks as the toerail neared the water. The church spires of Arles, our winter layup, shone peacefully in the late October sunshine a mile away. But an extra boil of current and a grinding of rounded rock beneath us and a bit more lift of the boat above its flotation made that haven seem a thousand miles away. By and by a tug broke loose from one of the dredges, but it could not come close enough to pass a line. Then a high-powered outboard launch came over to assist; I opened the lazarette and dragged out everything stowed there until I came to a 3-inch polypropylene cable I had found many years ago on a beach in the Pacific Northwest, the kind of cable used in log towing, and which had never seen use on the *Cynthia R* before. The outboard took an end of this and attempted to carry it to the tug, but the strength of the current on the bight of line whirled them off down the river. They cast off, I reeled in, and again they tried with a better angle of attack, reaching the tug on the third attempt. With a purchase around our heavy mast tabernacle led through chocks forward the tug dragged us around and lurched us off the gravel and set us straight. The boulder had been no boulder at all. It was the mooring buoy of the dredge, far across the river, and it had been pulled under by the current, and was planted about in mid-channel. We should have gone right along it, and it would not have hurt us to go right over it, and I was so mad and tired and humiliated and scared that I never even offered these nice Dutchmen the bottle of wine or cigarettes they deserved for having saved us. You understand, they *could* have marked their damn buoy somehow, though.

So much for the Rhône.

Or is it so much for the Rhône? When a rider is thrown from a horse there is one theory that he should get right on again and thus regain his self-confidence. (Some people may think it is to show the horse who is who, but I could never believe the horse cared much.) Anyway, the Rhône didn't care a damn, but the next spring did see us back on this very stretch. I had offered to take guests up the Rhône as far as Bollène, following a peaceful cruise on the Canal du Midi, and we left Arles with a barge captain on board as pilot, I sitting beside him and constructing my own detail chart of this short, wild stretch. By now, 1974, those dredges which had been working right below the dam at Beaucaire and right above the branching of the Petit Rhône had approached each other until they were within a couple of kilometers and within plain sight. Only the short space between them remained of the original, old, wild, violent Rhône. The river had a good flow that day, and again it was flat out on the engine to creep past the buoys and dredges, even where the Rhône is "tamed." The *mistral* blew, as it ought to do, the great pool below Avignon was a mass of whitecaps, and the wind nearly blew us off the ramparts of the Palace of the Popes at Avignon, until our guests said, "Let's get out of here."

So after a day in Avignon we headed again down this same

stretch of river, no pilot on board, and we ran flat out down-stream to follow a power barge and watch the channel through his eyes. We made it unscathed. And now may we say, "So much for the Rhône!"

We are back to where this chapter started, anchored in the placid Saône, on our first crossing of Europe, and just now beginning to savor the relaxed delights of this bucolic existence. Rolling country, flat farmlands, and gentle hills toward the headwaters of the Saône were dotted with attractive villages. From Chalons-sur-Saône we detoured for a day by land to visit the Burgundy wine country and sample the best vintages directly from their own cellars. In all we spent seven easy days to cover the 200 miles, nineteen locks, and two tunnels of the Saône. Tunnels were a new experience for the *Cynthia R*, but brought no problems other than that of keeping a steady helm and a lookout on either side to comment on the distance off. With our tires and fender boards we had perhaps 18 inches of clearance on either side when in dead center of the channel, and I found that, by holding my head directly on the center-line and allowing the forward strongback supporting the main-mast to blot out the pinpoint of daylight at the far end, we scarcely strayed from the midline of the channel.

If you wonder why a river needs tunnels, it does because toward its upper end the navigable channel follows along the side of the river, separated by a low dike of grassy green, so that the water depth in the channel can be controlled regardless of low water in the river (at high stages the whole floodplain of the river is submerged), and when the river makes big bends to traverse some watergap, it was more efficient to tunnel under the low hill than to construct a channel around it. In our case we never made a transit of any of the spectacularly long early tunnels which brought fame to their French engineers. One of them is so long that it could not be driven through on line of sight, but had to be arched up and over to follow the curvature of the earth. Otherwise the water, whose surface does follow the curvature of the earth, would have filled the tunnel to its overhead at the middle.

In the evening we would stop at small towns and generally strike up conversations with local people who would come down to the landing. A yacht is not a rarity here, but most of them are rushing by on delivery trips and take little time to merge with the people. In the morning then, as always in France, I would be first up and, instead of pumping up the stove as I do in other lands, I would step ashore in the morning cool and wander into town, sniffing for that sweet scent of freshly baked bread, until out of some alley I would get the fragrance and follow it up to its source, to come back to the boat with a couple of long warm loaves tucked, unwrapped, under my arm-pit for flavor. When in France . . . !

At the village of Corre the Canal de l'Est departed from a much diminished Saône, and the next 80 miles to Nancy took six days and the transit of 104 locks, all hand operated, as we climbed and twisted our way up a wooded tributary valley out of the Mediterranean drainage basin and into the North Sea basin. We learned a sharp lesson on passing in these narrow waters on our first day: the *péniche* displaces nearly half the cross-section of water in the canal, and as it moves forward the water must pass around it at accelerated speed. I had moved us too close to a lock gate and tried to hold by letting the stem lie obliquely against the grassy bank while I idled the engine ahead. But, of course, when the barge came by, the counter-current on our keel was more than we could overcome; we were swung stern to channel and given a sound scuffing on the edge of the transom.

After this we always tried to meet a barge with way on, and would squeeze over to one side as far as possible and straighten our course before her bow came abeam. You might think the water level would hump up to flow past the barge, but it doesn't. The hump rides ahead of the barge, and as the bow draws abeam the current accelerates and the level drops by as much as a foot. Often we would be dropped into the mud to come to a dead stop, propeller still turning over, to lift off again as the barge's stern came abeam. By now I should have the helm turned to steer us into that stern, because as it slipped by we would be moving again and reaching for mid-channel before we lost steerage control through dragging our keel in the mud. And in tying to the canal bank we found we must always carry spring lines in each direction to prevent the boat from surging into shallower water while lifted by the humps. Another thing we learned soon was that it is very gauche to tie to that bank which carries the tow path, as a line across the tow path to a nearby shade tree may trip up some unwary cyclist making his way home in the dark.

At the summit of this canal there is a *bief* of several miles. A *bief* is the stretch of canal between two locks, and as our ascent steepened some of these had been only a hundred yards or so in length. Now this long one offered a moment's rest, although it started with a sharp curve through a very narrow rock cut. We had just said, "Hope nothing comes around that corner," and committed ourselves to it, when a *péniche* crept

into view. It was by far the tightest passing we had encountered, and there was not time to moor to the shore.

"Everyone aft," I hollered, assuming we would hang up, and always preferring to have my weight aft when that happens, because you can always move it forward later to get off. But the rock cut was steep right to its cliffy side. The barge's suction picked us up, and I had to gun the engine to keep steerage as we surfed down his slope of water, his steel side inches from our fender, the cliff a foot or two to starboard, and our keel eventually banging along over loose rock on the bottom. I had a peculiar *déjà vu* feeling, as I had sometimes dreamed of sailing, only to have my waterway become, in that peculiar logic of dreams, a babbling brook, down which we were plunging in our ketch. And here we were, my dream come true, and heart in mouth. How dull life would be without contrast.

At Epinal we had crossed the Moselle River on a beautiful stone arch bridge or aqueduct, idling along in calm water with the swirling river 50 feet below, and now, on leaving Nancy, we crossed again on an equally attractive bridge to start the climb up and out of the Moselle Valley and to tunnel under the watershed into the valley of the Meuse, taking another week to the Belgian border, 170 miles, seventy-six locks, and five tunnels away.

In all, then, what with a lay day here and there, we had consumed three weeks to cover our route from Lyon to the Belgian border, and I think to move any faster would be a mistake. One could really double this time and not feel that there was a day wasted if one is interested in savoring rural France. In retrospect we remember these days in the canals as among our most scenic of the season. The canal, once out of the canalized river, is generally raised above the valley floor, often following the first contours of the hillside, where one has a sweep of view across the fertile fields, although the reason for placement of the canals was not to give the barges a view, but to conserve the flat agricultural land for its better purpose. The tow paths may be shaded by stately trees; in the background rise wooded hills; tantalizing glimpses of distant church spires, farm villages, and *châteaux* come and go.

With rare exception the lock tenders were pleasant; we carried to them the news of coming barges, or they might tell us of one ahead in the channel; from many we could buy fresh vegetables and eggs. We have even exchanged Christmas cards with one handsome matron who came from her kitchen in wooden *sabots* to handle her side of the lock, and who wrote that she hoped she would have the pleasure of conducting us once again through her Lock No. 17. (Locks are numbered downwards from each watershed in each direction.) These were small locks of the standard size, just holding one *péniche* with inches of clearance, if she puts her enormous rudder hard over to one side. The locking procedure has been repeated in many accounts, but, to be brief, one comes to an open lock gate, enters gently, and backs down alongside, clambering quickly up the recessed steel rungs of a ladder, with bow and stern lines in hand. This is no trick when the average lift is 9 feet, but in the deeper locks, and if the water is restless, it requires speed and skill. With boat made fast, one seizes a handle for the crank that closes his side of the lock gate, while the lock tender, the *éclusier*, swings shut on the other side. Each then walks forward and with another crank begins to open the four sluices in the upper gates. These are, in effect, heavy gate valves; they are a century old, and there is a good head of pressure against them. It is not light work. On board someone is taking in slack forward, and if lines are kept taut the boat should ride smoothly up the lock wall, but stray eddies will snatch at the keel and the hollow sockets of missing blocks of masonry at the fenders. It is not all rest on board, either. This is the moment at which those on shore, standing on the catwalk of the upper lock gate, exchange formal pleasantries and information about the canal and traffic; they accept the offered cigarette and tuck it behind the ear, and then it is time to lean on the crank to swing open the upper gate. Extraordinary how even a fraction of an inch of differential in water level makes this almost impossible. Stepping back on board and pushing the bow slightly out, we give a momentary burst of power and then idle out through the open gate with a "Je vous remercie, m'sieu," to the *éclusier*, who is leaning on a crank—thinking of what? Probably not of the rich Americans in their yacht who are fools enough to do this for pleasure. More likely of the bread and wine and soup soon to be served up for lunch, or of his wife, with whom he will then have his brief siesta.

For the locks shut down at the lunch hour, and woe betide the ugly American who comes between a Frenchman and his food. Once or twice we inadvertently did this, although we know better, and were given rude treatment. And on occasion we would come to a lock where the *éclusier* was enjoying too much siesta after perhaps an extra carafe of wine with his lunch. Closed gates at the approach to a lock may mean that there is a barge transiting the lock, in which case one must hang well back to give room for maneuvering with way on, but it may just mean that the gates are closed, the lock half filled, as it is usually left in a state of rest. After waiting a suitable time and looking for signs of life with the binoculars, we will now nose our overhanging bow into the canal bank and let someone drop to the grass and walk ahead. Soon we may see

him or her opening lower sluices to empty the chamber, opening the gate on one side, walking around the lock to open the
gate on the other side, then motioning us to come. We enter,
tie up, close gates, close sluices, walk forward, and there, under
a shade tree, is the *éclusier* in the blue trousers, underwear top,
and black beret, sound asleep in the grass. "Beaux rêves, mon
ami." Life can be slow and sweet in rural France.

The barges always had a wave for a passing yacht. Unlike
the large corporate-owned barges and motorships of the Rhône
and Rhine, these French and Belgian and Dutch *péniches* are
family affairs, handled by a man and wife, the children in a
playpen on the hatch covers, the family Renault or VW slung
up forward. One, appropriately named *Ile d'Amour*, had a baby
in every window of the small house aft. On Bastille Day, where
we came in, no locks operate, and we shared a short *bief* with
a *péniche*, *La Science*, carrying a load of maize north to Germany. The man and his flashing-eyed wife had both been born
on barges, although long after *La Science* had been built in
1926, and their two boys, ages six and seven, were growing up on
board, except that during the school year the children of most
barge families are in a special school for this group. M. and
Mme. Barbe had covered most of the canals of France, carrying
from 250 to 400 tons of salt, sugar, potash, grain, or flour. (But
only four times upon the Rhône, which they cannot ascend if
loaded.)

One day we stopped for lunch immediately beyond an
extremely low drawbridge in a small town dominated by a fine
old *château* of mellow stone, and some of us walked up to its
wrought-iron gates, where I observed that those to the farmyard
were open. *Farmyard* is not the right word; it was almost a
courtyard, flanked by stone barns, a fountain in its center, and
a narrow-gauge railway leading across its stone pavement from
one of the storage buildings. We were contemplating this scene
from an unfamiliar world when an elderly gentleman in shirt-
sleeves stepped from the main building. I assumed he was a
caretaker, but when my faltering French had either informed
him that we were Americans, or had baffled him completely, he
sent out his daughter, who spoke English, to check on us, and

this resulted in a tour of the estate and a conversation in the drawing room with the master and mistress. He had not been a caretaker at all, but an impoverished aristocrat, who had been military attaché in Belgrade during much of World War II and had returned to an altered world. Now, with the aid of wife and daughter, he was trying to restore a building that must once have boasted thirty servants. His *château* itself had been used as a German officers' quarters throughout the war, and when I asked if the place had been looted by the retreating armies he almost bristled.

"Ah, no, no! The German officers were correct, absolutely correct," he said, with that peculiar affinity of the aristocracy for their own caste, the officer caste, which transcends petty nationalism. "But I am pleased to show my home to Americans, because if the Americans had not saved us, I would have no home to show."

And as we begged leave to go—we had many miles to cover yet that day—he pressed upon us a bottle of the region's brandy, Mirabelle, distilled from his own plums, which had descended from those planted by the marquis who had built this *château* in the days of Louis XV:

Back on board to cast off we had a hurried visit from the bridge tender, his wife, and their little girl, the father arriving with an unlabeled bottel under his arm, from which he proceeded to pour us all copious drinks. This, too, was Mirabelle, it developed, fiery stuff, which after a few toasts provided us with the courage to continue down the canal into a black thunderstorm.

Pastured cattle, horses galloping beside the canal, red-tiled villages seen through the groves, tunnels under ancient fortifications, everywhere the ubiquitous French fisherman, his line in the canal, his wife under a beach umbrella up the bank. These are flashes of memory of central France.

At the Belgian border the Meuse becomes a proper river with water skiers and pleasure boats on its broad back and high hills on either side, but still eighteen locks to descend as we traversed the 70 miles to Holland. Locks along this stretch are very like those we had become used to in France, although on a larger

scale, and some were electrically operated. But it was only as we came to the Dutch border and were ready to lock down to the Dutch Maas that we hit something new. By now we were sharing a huge lock chamber with a dozen barges and motorships, and having made fast, I sauntered off to see what lay ahead and to present papers. To my horror, I found we were about to descend 46 feet. This new high lift lock had replaced three previous locks. The lock tender was demanding three francs; I had no money in my pockets; my crew were sitting idly on board with little thought that their world was about to drop out from under them, leaving the *Cynthia R* suspended on her docking lines. So, trying to make my voice sound as if I were speaking Flemish, I said I would send up the three francs and dashed madly the hundred yards back to our end of the lock and dragged out long anchor lines to double around the bollards. And in the nick of time, as we were just starting down. And then we sat there feeling like fools. These were floating bollards and came right down with us. Always worrying about the wrong thing. What we should have been worrying about as the enormous gates behind us grew taller and taller and leaked ever more copious amounts of spray upon us, until we were enveloped in a mist, and the work boat of the barge besides us filled and swamped, was the still of the lock gate, upon which our keel or rudder would have hung up had we not inched forward as we came down. And thus we came to the Dutch border.

We were now running into a new form of lock gate, and this is a good place to pause and describe the ingenuity with which various locking problems have been faced. We have already seen the typical mitered gate; the vertical lift gate, either flat or curved; the submerging gate, and the hydraulic lift lock whose gates hinge out and down onto the channel bed. The submerging gate may be either a plane or curved surface, dropping vertically in its shaft, or it may take the form of a giant half-cylinder, turning on a horizontal axis at the level of the channel bottom into its own basin beneath the channel of the lock chamber, the advantage of this last being a self-clearing action which prevents debris from fouling the gate movement. And we know these gates may be hand cranked or electrically powered or hydraulically powered (one ingenious French *éclusier* had rigged an electric power-drill motor and worm drive to operate his hand crank for him), but in this large lock we found the lower gate suspended by cable and pulley from overhead railway cars. When the chamber had emptied the gate was lifted a few inches clear of its seat and then retracted to one side as the cars moved slowly along their railway. In the old Canal du Midi, actually the earliest major canal to be built in France, the lock chambers are not rectangular, but lozenge-shaped in plan; the early engineers of this canal were appalled by the collapse of a straight wall under construction and from then on all locks were built with the principle of an arch laid over on its side, making a rather pleasant fit for a sailboat, but less effective for a slab-sided barge, and of course demanding more water to fill it. At Agde on this canal there is a unique circular lock, the diameter of the chamber being exactly equal to the length of a barge, because here a branch canal takes off to the old port of Narbonne. All three entrances lie at different water levels, and a canal boat making a transit may have to rotate her position 90 degress to take the desired exit, like a railroad car on a turntable. Also on this Canal du Midi (and remember it was all engineered 300 years ago when there was precious little experience or precedent in canal building) is a ladder of seven locks, the upper gate of each one of which is the lower gate of the next chamber, thus climbing a steep hillside out of a river valley.

On the enormous Kiel Canal in Germany, at each end of which are two lock chambers, each capable of holding half a dozen oceangoing vessels at a time, the gates also retract laterally, although in this case they must be running on some unseen track beneath, as they do not first lift from their seat, and it is interesting to speculate how such a seat or track could possibly be made watertight. In Belgium the new approach to the Albert Canal near Antwerp is via a steel tub lock chamber, large enough to hold an oceangoing ship, which rides up an inclined railway to the level of the canal above. The modern bypass of a dozen locks on the Marne-Rhine Canal, ascending west of Strasbourg, consists of such a chamber riding sideways up its inclined railway. One can appreciate that on a steep incline the car construction would be simplified, but it must seem that one's progress is all leeway. And one can but wonder what new and mysterious engineering awaits us to carry our boats across the watershed from the Main to the Danube below Nürnberg, where the plans call for "Hebewerke" or lifts.

The real problem at any watershed is, quite clearly, water. If you are already up on top, where will you get the water to lock through a constant flow of traffic? Usually, sufficient water can be diverted from higher lakes or streams, or artificial reservoirs constructed, but where these resources are lacking, some form of water-saving lift is essential.

A canaling adventure is filled with admiration for the skill of man.

One might think that upon arrival in flat Holland we had come to an end of locking, but this was not quite so, as we still had fifteen locks between us and the sea as we descended the Dutch rivers to the Ijsselmeer, then crossed Friesland to emerge finally into salt water at Delfzijl on the estuary of the River Ems. Enough has been written about Dutch canals so that I will embellish the literature with only two remarks derived from 350 miles of inland waters in Holland.

First, the Blue Flag, and this applies to all the Great Rivers of northern Europe. I know I am repeating others, but since it clearly had not been hammered into my skull, I will add one more try for the reader's sake. A vessel bound upstream has the right to decide which side of the channel to follow. If the skipper elects his left side (the right bank, in normal nomenclature)— which he will usually do if the turn is to his left, because this

puts him into less current, shortens his distance, and saves fuel for his owners—he will display a blue flag (not to be confused with the blue tablecloth or apron or blue jeans his wife has just hung out to dry). In such a case the downbound vessel must give way and take the outside of the curve. This is no great hardship for the downbound vessel, as it puts him into deeper water and a more favorable current. Some more modern vessels use a louvered screen, an infinitely more accurate symbol than a flag, which may be whipping directly in line with your sight. And if you aim to travel the Great Rivers at night, which this writer does not particularly recommend, please learn the corresponding light signals. I had failed to realize, as I descended the Maas, that we were now on the Great Rivers instead of still in canals, and the first blue flag we met did not even impinge on my consciousness until it was too late and both boats were headed for the inside of the curve. Too late to turn across his bow and risk his turning simultaneously, I held my course and my breath and thanked God for a steep bank and a muddy bottom as I slipped between his foaming wash and the grass alongside.

On a pleasanter note, I would like to comment on the Hoendiep. At the mouth of the Ijssel River one can step one's mast again and carry on to the North Sea across the Ijsselmeer or across Friesland, the latter if, and only if, one's mast will clear the fixed bridges near Groningen. Ours would not, but there was one possible alternative, the Hoendiep, a narrow backwater leading into Groningen's back door, devoid of fixed bridges, but perhaps devoid of sufficient depth as well. We would try it, and on the appointed day we labored hard transferring weights forward and bringing our draft aft up an inch or two. The guidebook rated the Hoendiep as having a controlling depth of 1.6 meters; an American who had lain next to us at Hoorn had said he could hardly make it with his 1.5 meters, and his wife was saying, "Never again." As we swung out of the heavily trafficked main canal we were probably drawing 1.7 meters, and there was little left we could do to change our balance. But the last gauge had showed a surplus this day of 26 centimeters of depth, and this was reassuring. Cattails and lilypads grew out of the water beside us, and the kilometers and little drawbridges crept past; and at times we were moving down the middle of the main street of some little red-brick village, our bridge deck a few feet from families' front windows, and for our only time in Holland we were treated to that *National Geographic* picture, the old bridge tender, in Dutch breeches, holding out a wooden shoe on the end of a pole for his tip for opening the bridge. The whole trip was delightfully intimate, and not once did we touch bottom. If the water depth is up, I can recommend the Hoendiep.

We had left Delfzijl to commit ourselves to the mercies of the North Sea, although there is an alternate route from the Ems to the Weser, below Bremen, but this would mean lowering masts again, and anyway, we were ready for some open sea by now. We entered Germany at Borkum, the westernmost of the German Friesian Islands. Here we were trapped by fog and

wind and rain and the white seas breaking over the Borkum Riff
outside, and we began to study the inside passage over the
sands to Norderney, part of the route made famous by the
Dulcibella in Childer's *The Riddle of the Sands.* When the
young captain of the local lifeboat urged me to take his father
as a pilot and go over the sands without a care, I was on, and
concurring in the calculation that with an early start and full
speed we would be able to get over the hump just before high
water, a plan which allowed a few minutes and a few inches of
safety if we should happen to stray from the channel. On a day
which would thin to misty drizzle and thicken again to fog
and in which the sky and sea and shore looked all identical so
that one hung suspended in a dimensionless sphere of gray,
we moved off on the flooding tide, running 8 miles back up the
Ems in forty-five minutes to cut across the spur of sand known
as Emshorn and into the shallows behind the invisible islands.
Traveling at 2,000 rpm, almost full speed for us, over water
charted as having one meter of depth at low tide, with no reference points and no sun, and with currents eddying in unknown
directions, is not my idea of relaxation. At times like this, I
wish it were someone else's boat. Running from buoy to buoy
in the mist, we entered Bants Balje, where our pilot seemed
temporarily lost and, I felt positive, had just driven us across a
shoal area dry at low water; but with a quick council of war he
recovered, and soon we picked up the first of the brush stakes
which mark the winding channel over the sands. Since everyone
has read *The Riddle of the Sands,* you all know that this is a
channel only in the sense that at high water it is slightly
deeper than the surrounding sand, for at low water everything
is dry for miles. One is counseled to stay close to the brush
stakes, and they mean really close, but even at its beginning,
where the channel has a depth of six inches at low tide, our
pilot continued at full speed, throttling back only when he
reached the area shown as having three inches at low tide. We
were a comfortable half-hour before high water and cruised over
the watershed, running a fathometer trace as we did and finding
eighteen inches under our keel, and coming into the channel on
the far side with such perfect timing that we now caught the
first of the ebb to boost us out toward Norderney.

Our narrow waters ended here, for the moment, as the next day we crossed the bar into sparkling sunshine and a glorious reach in open sea to Helgoland; but this respite was short-lived, as we drove in the following day before a rising gale and riding the crest of the flood up the Elbe River to the Kiel Canal, where, to our surprise, we locked down, not up, into the inland water, it being high tide with an onshore wind.

This monster, the Kiel Canal, about 60 miles in length, is just a great boating experience. As I have said, the lock chambers are big, 1,082 feet by 147.5 feet, yet two of them are kept operating, side by side, at either end. The flow of traffic is constant, flags of all nations, vessels of every description, the whole waterway on so vast a scale that it seems more a long, broad lake. At Flensburg one may moor to a quay on the north side in a freeport area for the purpose of buying bonded stores.

Returning to the Mediterranean two years later, we spent more time in German waters, being flushed out the Elbe by an ebbing tide into a rainy and sloppy North Sea, then skirting the outer edge of the sands, the water a yellow-gray and the seas cresting as they crossed the shallower spots, until the lonely tower of Alte Weser loomed through the murk and we were able to alter course, make sail, and catch the flood up the sea channel of the Weser estuary while a dramatic rain squall washed the salt from our sails. As we lowered down off Bremerhaven another dramatic squall burst over us, the black loading cranes along the river reaching into the torn black cloud, the dirty river lashed white. It was as if the North Sea, angry at our escape, were making a last effort to strike back. But we were home free, the salt water finished for that season, and for the next 1,000 miles we would be a canal boat again.

The German waterways we traversed were all on a bigger and more commercial scale than were the French, and while the countryside was not unpleasant, it tended more to flat plains and lacked the intimate charm of France. I don't doubt that charming waterways exist; I have heard reports of the beauty of the Moselle and of the Neckar; but these did not lie on our chosen route.

From Bremen we moved up the Weser River 75 miles, and through seven locks to Minden, running aground only once, where a sign directed *Sportboots* to detour a commercial lock. In Germany we normally qualify as a *Sportboot*, but this channel, we learned as the *Cynthia R* climbed out of the water, was for canoes.

The reader likes to hear about the worst storm or the worst stranding, so let me tell you about our worst locking. Of over five hundred locks we traversed in Europe, Minden stands out as our worst experience. Here a short spur of canal leads from the Weser's channel to the lock entrance let into the face of a formidable turreted castle-like building. Coming up to it in the early afternoon, we found a crowd of barges awaiting entry. Being small, we cruised forward, saw a space big enough for us in the chamber, which was otherwise filled, and started to move in. No human was visible, except for the spectators lining a gallery built across the front of this castle, but we had already seen the TV monitors observing us as we approached, and now a stentorian voice from an invisible loudspeaker bellowed: "Shportboot hinaus!" It was eerie, this disembodied voice from a controller who saw us only on a TV screen somewhere in the interior of this building, but we backed off, played at being the good soldier, and were rewarded by being told we could go up with the next lift. So we tied to the right bank at a little landing and were rewarded instead by being thrown out a few minutes later by the arrival of the tour boat whose landing it was. With the next lift an enormous motorship moved in, and it was clear no other boat would go up with him. Then came the call, "Shportboot herein!" We crept in under the dripping overhead gate, doubtful that enough room existed, wondering if the TV cameras would note that our davits and the truck of our mast were still under the gate and that we would go no farther, when the barge beside us, presumably on orders to squeeze ahead, gave a little burst to his propeller. This was opposite our forward waterline and his rudder was set hard right, as is customary in a lock, and a six-foot wall of white water lifted our bow high and smashed it sickeningly into the lock wall, forward of any fenders. Obviously we weren't going to fit in here, and I backed out through the gate while the squawk box hurled imprecations at me. To hell with being a good soldier. You run your lock and I'll run my ship. Incredibly, there was no serious damage; the blow had been taken on the heavy rub-strake with its stainless-steel nose and transmitted throughout the arch of the plan forward and through the heavy deck timbers to the opposite side. Except for a bit of crazed paint at the edges of shelves we had not suffered; nor had the masts been hurtled from their strongbacks.

Now we tied alongside a small Dutchman, who volunteered that if we just stuck with him he would see that there was room when he went in and that he would be gentle with his engine; an hour later we made it again, this time with room enough, the squawk box commanding us not to take all evening about entering, to face the 40-foot lift with no floating bollards. Small bollards were inset into the lock wall every three feet of height, and with two spring lines we managed to leapfrog as the water rose and as we kept our engine turning over to keep a tension on the lines and the fenderboard against the lock wall. Even this required constant adjustment of engine speed and turning of the wheel in addition to handling one of the two springs, as the boils of incoming water snatched first at one part of the keel and then at another. We had approached this lock just after lunch, and it was dark by the time we emerged into strange waters at the upper end. Fortunately, a substantial mooring basin here offered refuge and the opportunity of becoming observers ourselves to the entire operation in the morning.

It may have been a rough ride, but the Minden complex is an impressive bit of engineering. Here the canal crosses the Weser River on a long bridge, 40 feet above the river surface, and around the next bend of the river to the south lies the old town of Hamelin, of Pied Piper fame. Remember how

> The river Weser, deep and wide,
> Washes its wall on the southern side;
> A pleasanter spot you never spied.

But now it was not rats that were drowning in the Weser, it was fish. All day the surface had been dotted with the bloated bodies of a carp-like fish about a foot in length, and even numberless dead eels. It takes a lot to kill an eel. Some chemical spill must have occurred upstream, yet people were swimming and skiing and fishing on the Weser. At Minden a pumping station is constantly at work lifting water from the Weser into the canal, and no doubt most of it drops right back into the river again as the lock is operated.

The canal itself offered a bit of relaxation, since for the next 105 miles on this and on the Dortmund-Ems Canal there would be but one lock, followed by the short descent of the Wesel-Datteln Canal, whose six locks drop one 140 feet to the Rhine.

The Rhine is a big river and a busy one. We were to spend the next three weeks upon it and our memory of this time, while it includes castles and vineyards, is far more of barges. There are little barges, and big barges, and bigger barges, the maximum now being about 360 feet in length; there are barges in tandem pulled by other barges or by tugs, barges in rafts being pushed by modern river towboats; often the river both upstream and downstream ends in what appears to be a solid wall of shipping, twisting and turning, crossing and recrossing the channel, passing or overtaking on either side, running at many different speeds, some asserting the right to blue-flag the opposing traffic, others not; and a little Sportboot having no idea whether a big vessel will respond to the rule that he should give way to our blue flag, as we were bound upstream, or whether he would follow the rule that commercial traffic has the right of way over the Sportboot, and would ignore us. As we were being constantly overtaken by giant vessels, we never knew when one of these would flip his blue flag on or off and start across the channel, leaving us alone with everything hanging out. All this takes place in close quarters, at full speed and all day long, in a current that swirls and boils around you; and if you try to get out of the traffic you will very likely run aground.

I did just this myself on our first day on the Rhine. Cynthia and I were still alone, heading for Düsseldorf, where we would pick up two couples for the trip to Switzerland, and still unused to the Rhine, I assumed buoys marked the outer edge of the channel. They don't. They mark the channel ends of groins, long diagonals of rock which serve to deflect the current into mid-channel and thus keep it scoured to a navigable depth. But

in low-water stages there may be considerable shallow water between the end of the groin and the usable channel itself, where
gravel bars stream down-current from the end of each groin. Although we knew that the level of the Rhine was low that
autumn of 1973, we didn't yet know that we were shortly to
enter stretches where the buoys were all high and dry on the
gravel banks. Here below Düsseldorf they were still afloat, but
perhaps in 3 feet of water, and as I cut corners, running from
buoy to buoy on the inside of a curve, I soon drove the
Cynthia R hard up on the shoreward side of a horn of gravel.
The current at once swerved us sideways to the stream, locking
our keel into the bottom, and no amount of reverse would
budge the boat. And we knew that the Rhine was continuing to
fall by a centimeter or two every day.

We sat there, I feeling very stupid, watching the barges proceeding up and down in the proper channel a hundred yards

away, and by and by a powerful patrol launch spotted us and pulled over. He would take a tow line, and he did, but despite his twin screws we failed to budge again. Now he tried it from astern, which I allowed rather against my better judgment, but ready to try anything now, with the only result that he was caught by the current and swerved his towline, with full power, across our stern pulpit and davits, wiping out considerable hardware. Now we temporarily abandoned ship, while the patrol boat took us ashore to the office of a coal company, from which telephone calls were made to the home base of a nearby towboat. Almost before we were back on board a massive pusher was coming around the bend. Three decks high, twin screws, but shallow draft, she looked a brute, but her skipper placed her within heaving distance of our bow, holding her there with such precision that one would think he too were aground, while I made fast the hawser around the mast tabernacle. He then began to apply power so gently that the hawser never snapped or vibrated, just lifted from the water and slowly grew taut. Then the *Cynthia R* rose grandly over the gravel and slipped smoothly into the channel beyond. Here our towboat lashed us alongside and proceeded at 10 knots back upstream, while I assumed we would be taken to his haven while salvage awards were agreed upon. But this was not so; a few miles upstream we came to some moored barges. It was these he had actually come to pick up, and by luck had been diverted on his errand of mercy. Here he slowed down in the stream and told us we could proceed on our own.

"But can I not pay for your help?" I asked.

"Well, if you would like to give a bit of *Trinkgeld* to the men who handled the lines, it would be a nice thing," the captain said.

Thinking that a *Trink* might be as welcome as *Trinkgeld*, I rewarded the crew with a bottle of Johnny Walker, and left them with grinning faces. And we stayed in the channel with the barges from then on.

Having now done the Rhine I cannot think it the most rewarding boat trip in Europe. The romantic Rhine of cliffs and castles and terraced vineyards is a rather short 35-mile stretch out of the 400 miles we covered climbing up to Switzerland. It is also the most exciting piloting, as we ran the narrow channels, passed signal lights, took on and discharged pilots, and approached the Bingerloch, where the stream has cut a deep, narrow channel through a ledge of rock. A large motorship ahead of us seemed suddenly to slide obliquely over to this slot, waggle her tail, and stop like a cork in a bottle. As we came up on her she worked her way through, and it was our turn to come nearly to a halt with the engine pounding out its 2,000 rpm and white water cascading over the shoals on either side.

Above here the land flattens out again, but above Mannheim the slope of the river increases to 23 inches to the mile, creating a powerful current, while the channel meanders under the murkey water. Our view was for the most part of gravel banks and barges. With the water level still low, these barges were picking up baseball-sized stones with their propellers, which could be heard drumming against the steel hulls, and sometimes could be seen being tossed into the air with the prop wash. We ourselves managed to scrape bottom even with a pilot holding us in the channel. With the completion of the Grand Canal d'Alsace on the French side of the Rhine this run will be easier, and for us, beginning the canal at Strasbourg, it was now an easy run on to Switzerland, with a delightful overnight stop at Alt Breisach thrown in for good measure.

In the harbor of Basel, Switzerland, we were 817 feet above sea level. We had climbed less than half of that amount in locks, and thus had pushed our boat uphill against the current for well over 400 feet of vertical ascent. We also learned here that references to the Swiss navy are not all in jest, as the Swiss merchant navy is responsible for 33 percent of all imports arriving in the country, all coming up the Rhine. Traffic passing outside our little port was constant, while in it there was a steady movement of ships to and from the warehouses, elevators, tanks, and pipelines that lined its various branches. All this time *Cynthia R* lay under a spreading tree along a grassy bank in one corner and enjoyed the scene.

The Rhine itself is navigable for a few more kilometers above Basel, but only to an industrial and tank-farm basin, not appealing to a yacht unless one must say one has been to the bitter end. There has been talk for decades of canalizing the Rhine the final 150 kilometers to Lake Constance, a thrilling challenge for the engineers, but hardly cost effective, as I learned from a visit to the Rhine Traffic Control Office. The young man who gave me information here was so intrigued at the presence in Basel of a sailboat which had crossed the Atlantic that he later came down for his own interview and we found ourselves written up and photographed for the Swiss magazine *Strom und See* (*River and Lake*).

The greatest test of our ability to traverse these narrow seas still lay ahead of us as we left Basel to cross the watershed back into the Mediterranean Basin via the little-used Doubs River route. Leaving the Rhine near Mulhouse, we were soon back in the small French locks with their hand-cranked lock gates, covered with fern and moss and grass. A quick ascent of 385 feet from the Rhine by means of about 40 locks in 30 kilometers of canal, a day and a half of work, saw us at our summit at an elevation of 1,160 feet above sea level, although what with our ups and downs we had actually ascended 1,344 feet since leaving Bremen, having descended the difference in various places along the way. It was mid-October, the days were cool, the mornings misty, and although the first rains of autumn had begun, the water level of the Doubs was still extremely low.

At first it merely crossed the path of the canal, building a bar of sand in the channel, over which we scraped our way. Later we joined the stream itself, creeping along at idling speed 15 meters from the conspicuous towpath and feeling for the bottom with our keel. From time to time an ascending *péniche* would complicate our problem, and we might lie hard aground on the channel's edge as it slowly scraped along our fenderboard, dragging bottom itself. But scenically and culturally this was a most rewarding run, in contrast with the dull canal we had left behind, the river dropping into a deepening watergap between the limestone foothills of the Jura Mountains, already sporting the first fall colors. Ancient Besançon lies here, embraced by a great horseshoe of the river, its high cliffs crowned by a gigantic citadel, under which the canal passes by tunnel—a city well

worth a lay day or two. And the town of Dôle, too, is worth a stopover to prowl its medieval streets and enjoy its food.

And then we were back in the placid Saône. We had made it, 132 miles from Basel, with 116 locks, on a route much of which was "déclassée," declassified as commercial canal. Suddenly the Saône no longer looked like the narrow seas, but like a broad sound after the waters of the Doubs.

If one goes on and on talking about these inland waters, it is simply because there is more variety in a thousand miles of canal than in a thousand miles of open ocean. This doesn't mean it has to be better. Everyone to his own taste. And I find I have still not mentioned our trip on the Canal du Midi nor the narrow waters of Scandinavia, which are endless.

To take you briefly to the Midi, then, let me say that here even our encouraging friend Irving Johnson told us we would probably find it sticky going. "But you can't hurt the boat," he said. "It's all soft mud, no rock anywhere, and if you get in and find you're getting stuck, it's so soft you can always warp the boat around and come back out." I did want to get a picture of the boat under the walls of Carcassonne. The reason this canal was so questionable was that it was built three hundred years ago to a depth of 1.8 meters, just about our draft in fresh water, and had been silting up ever since.

To tackle this problem we off-loaded our masts and booms in the port of Grande Motte, sent our aft trimming ballast ashore, left our sails, unshipped our davits, and generally emptied the lazarette of all excess weight, and then ran with fuel tanks not over half filled. The water tanks, being forward of the center of gravity, probably helped lift our stern. And despite our nervousness at the start, we actually made it to Carcassonne and back in two of the most delightful weeks of canal cruising we have ever had. I won't go into details of the canal itself here, except to say that when anyone asks me about chartering a boat in the French canals I recommend the Midi first, and I go on to recommend to all who do it, and to all those who are interested enough in canals to have read this far, that they read L. T. C. Rolt's most excellent account of the canal, *From Sea to Sea.*

It would take more than a book to describe all the narrow passages of Scandinavia, and almost a book just to go into detail about those we visited in the course of two years there. There is no other place I have seen other than Georgian Bay which begins to compare with it, but in the Baltic it goes on and on. While Lake Ontario boasts its Thousand Islands and Lake Huron its Thirty Thousand, the Baltic lays claim to 150,000 islands. And a million rocks between.

It is mostly on a smaller scale than the coast of Maine, and as we carried full sail through these islands and passages day after day we found it required two on watch at all times, one with a finger on the chart and pointing out the next buoy to the helmsman. A black line on the chart marks the buoyed channel, and if you stray from this the shoals are unmarked, although accurately charted on the Swedish side. Large areas surrounded by double black lines may not even be charted.

Lake Mälaren was a deep indentation of the sea in Viking days, reaching 75 miles into the heartland of Sweden; around its shores the nucleus of the present nation developed. But today it is a fresh-water lake standing a couple of feet above sea level, because of the slow rise of the Baltic coasts. It is entered by lock either from the south or from the east at Stockholm. It is rich in history, and we spent five days there, reaching north to Sigtuna, one of the early capitals of Sweden, where a local resident told us ours was the first American flag yacht she had ever seen in the harbor. But it was Midsummer's Night, and if her dreams were sweeping her on, they are to be forgiven. On this evening we watched the dancing on the greensward around a decorated pole; old couples in traditional costume, teen-agers in jeans, little girls in white with wreaths of daisies and oak leaves in their fair hair, and finally, when the five old fiddlers shifted from the polka and the schottische to the waltz, the crew of the *Cynthia R.*

We now enjoyed the best of a warm summer as we spent five weeks in the Finnish archipelago. We were here farther north than the northern tip of Labrador, north of Cape Farewell, Greenland, but for days on end shorts and swimming were in order. This archipelago lies roughly east to west for a distance of 120 miles, with an extreme north-south width of 60 miles, and has absolutely countless islands, channels, and rocks, which continue east to the Soviet border and north into the Gulf of Bothnia. It is a temptation to write about one's favorite harbors, but the truth is that in five weeks we saw but a small selection of the hundreds available, and we have no reason to believe that the next cove around the point may not be even better. The real joy lies in discovering your own, and repeatedly we learned that we were the first American yacht to have visited, when the owners of summer homes which dot these islands would come out to invite us ashore for a sauna or a drink. And you can choose solitude, if you will, simply by ducking around the next point or islet.

The narrowest of our narrow seas on the Swedish side was our passage of the Dragets Canal, an extraordinarily narrow stretch which (we realized as we entered) had a "Restricted" sign beside it. But it was too late to back out and far too narrow to turn around; in fact we probably had less than six feet of clearance on either side, and we proceeded, branches scraping the rigging, and emerged to meet a Swedish patrol boat. Far from arresting us, however, he was merely waiting his turn to go the other way, and we now turned back in his wake and came out again into unrestricted waters without observing any military secrets.

On the west coast of Sweden and the south coast of Norway one can again navigate behind a barrier of islands through channels which are sometimes no wider than city streets. In the entire run from Gothenburg up to the Oslofiord and south again to the southern tip of Norway there need be only two open stretches of 8 miles each and a few more of 4 miles. And while the west coast of Norway provides a couple of open-water stretches, still the bulk of it can be sailed in inside waters at least as far north as we achieved, which was the town of Ålesund, about 100 miles north of Bergen.

Again it was Midsummer's Night when we visited Ålesund. Instead of dancing around a pole, the Norwegians celebrate, as I have mentioned earlier, by lighting huge bonfires of oil-soaked herring barrels on the rocky points, fires which burn far into

the night, while the revelers observe from erratically navigated fishing craft.

It was the morning after this that we tried another narrow passage. An ancient wooden church on a nearby island beckoned us, and the approach through a passage with no soundings appeared to be worth a try. With five people on watch for shoal water (Cynthia was doing up the breakfast dishes below, but we had guests on board), we entered this pass, noting that it was too tight to turn around in, but the hand signals from forward beckoned me on until, when we were almost through, and with no sense of shock, the bow suddenly lifted and we came to a sudden stop. Our eyes went up and there was a wire around our mast, stretched between two waving poles on either shore. May

I say in self-defense that it was not shown on our Norwegian chart? Always worrying about the wrong thing, you see. I slammed her into reverse so hard that the normally floating dinghy painter was sucked under the stern and wrapped snugly around the wheel. The engine stalled, the beginning of the flood current set our mast ever tighter against the wire, and our powerless stern now swung across the channel until the rudder wedged against the rocky shore.

And this is a good place to drop the subject of the narrow seas, saying only that the Norwegians are a forbearing lot, ready to forgive much on the morning after Midsummer's Night.

VII

Spare Parts

"You see," he went on after a pause, "it's as well to be provided for *everything*."

The White Knight,
in Lewis Carroll,
Through the Looking Glass

Our friends who are contemplating ocean sailing are full of questions about how to handle storms and star sights and sharks and waterspouts when what they should be asking about is spare parts. There is only one way to keep a proper supply of spare parts on hand and that is to tow a fully found duplicate of your own boat wherever you go, preferably equipped with an acrobatic midget who can crawl into the cabin locker and shaft alley and under the engine bed to do the work. Month by month your spare boat can be cannibalized, a winch handle here, a stove burner there, perhaps a mast by and by, and sooner or later the spare diesel engine, until, shortly before starting your last ocean leg to return home, you can sell the now-empty hulk to some do-it-yourselfer. There will be little left but the ballast keel. Because unless you can carry a spare part for everything on the boat, which so fills the storage spaces that there is no room for food and drink, you are going to find that the part which goes is the very part for which you have no spare.

Far away in one of the remote Exuma Cays the vice president

of a large bank approached me with a sheepish look. No, he
was not about to call an overdue loan; when they do that bank-
ers have learned to look serious, businesslike, and very firm. This
banker was one of a party of four guests on board, and he had
just broken our only toilet.

"Don't worry about it," I told him. "We have a complete set
of spare parts. What broke?"

"The waste line from the bottom of the toilet bowl to the
pump," he said. "It seems to be made of plastic."

"The waste line!" I shouted. "Plastic?! They're supposed to
be solid bronze, and I've never carried any spare waste line!"
But hard plastic it was, and it had developed a spiral fracture
down its length through which our waste water poured over the
floor of the head and down the shower drain into the sump.
Unsavory! The injured part was removed and cleaned, the skipper's job, and placed on deck for study. What we needed was a
plumber or an organic chemist, not a banker. None of our glues
or adhesives would bond to this plastic, and I had no paraffin
wax on board or I would have treated it as we used to treat the
old oaken water cask on our first little boat, melting a block of
it and pouring it in to line all the cracks. We would then roll
the cask around the yard while it hardened and coated the
wood, assuring us of sweet water for the next year. At length
we had to content ourselves with taping it as tightly as possible,
which reduced flooding to seeping, and putting a diaper under
the affected part, which I changed twice daily. A diaper? Yes, a
diaper. We supplement our normal ragbag with ten-pound packages of used diapers from the diaper service, cleaned and ster-
ilized, of course, but rotated out of service. After all, what is
more absorbent than a diaper? And for the next month we were
the diaper service's best customer as we changed our soggy baby,
awaited spare parts, and sat down very gently. Cables to Miami
went unanswered; our vice president cabled the assistant vice
president in New York, an action which brought no results of
benefit to the toilet, but, by happenstance, was the cause of our
meeting Bob Manry, who had crossed the Atlantic in *Tinker-
belle*. He was now sailing with his delightful family of four, and
with a large German police dog, a cat, and a parrot, on a 26-

footer, reveling in the spaciousness, and had been pressed by the cable company's local office to deliver the reply to us, because he "was sailing in the same direction" as we had gone in earlier. Such is communication in the Bahamas. In due course I did what I should have done at once: I cabled the factory in Baltimore, and the part came immediately.

When we began outfitting the boat, stepping up from a 29-footer used for two-week vacations to a 44-footer on which we would live for months in remote places, a supply of spare parts was a priority item. I tried to analyze each system in the boat in turn to make up its requisite of spares. I talked with the Perkins diesel dealer, with the yard mechanic, and with owners of the same model engine, to learn what component parts of the diesel each felt might be a critical replacement to carry, and I built up a large carton of these. I wrote to the Hiller Stove factory and ordered spare burners and carburetors. For the toilet I had not only the standard repair kits, but an entire spare pump unit, everything except the bowl and waste line. In New Bedford we had a visit with the president of Edson to discuss spare parts for the steering system. So it went, item by item, from stem to stern, from truck to keel. Thorough and complete, all in order, and every item alphabetically indexed and cross indexed in a little telephone tickler book, indicating exactly where, in the complexity of a 44-footer, each item was stowed.

"Cynthia," I said, "I may not be a mechanic, but no matter what breaks down, at least I can take one look at the book and produce a spare."

A week later I lost the book. For two years, each time I needed a spare engine part, I would say: "Cynthia, what the hell did you do with my spare parts list?"

And any time Cynthia needed a new needle or a spool of thread she would say: "Bob, just try to remember where you put my list of supplies."

After two years it was time to dust behind the Bowditch and the H. O. 214s and there it was, fallen flat behind them. By then we knew it was out of date.

That broken toilet occurred when the boat had less than a year's use, but already we had been forced to replace an engine part for which no one had ever suggested a spare. When an engine is equipped with a hydraulic clutch, it is considered prudent to lock the shaft while under sail. There is an ongoing argument whether a boat sails more efficiently with her propeller locked or spinning, and I suspect the answer is "That depends." It is probable that a two-bladed prop, locked vertically behind the deadwood of the old-style conventional keel, offers very little additional drag, less than if it were spinning free, while the large-diameter three-bladed one may possibly drag less when spinning. But that isn't the point; the point is that when the engine is not running the hydraulic fluid may not cool properly and may tend to build up excessive heat, not to mention an inevitable wear on packing and bearings, from thousands of miles of free wheeling. The analogy of the maple seed falling more slowly when it spins is perhaps a better argument for buying a folding or feathering or variable-pitch propeller than for locking a solid prop. But we were a bit mistrustful of the reliability of the folding prop, and didn't want to put the money into a feathering prop; and we allowed ourselves to be talked out of the variable-pitch prop, probably wisely, and decided in favor of the standard two-blade prop and shaft lock. For canal and river work, where free wheeling is of no consequence, but where thrust is desired, we would make use of a three-bladed solid prop, which would otherwise be carried as a spare. The shaft lock must be of such a nature that the prop is always locked vertically, with positive control and release from the cockpit, and the one we chose operates rather like the "Park" control on an automobile, inserting a steel pin into a slot on a plate attached to the shaft coupling, operated by a Morse control.

This system also contained an interlock with a clutch control, so that when the shaft was locked the engine could not be put in gear, and when the engine was in gear the shaft lock could not be actuated. This all sounded pretty foolproof, so I violated my desire to avoid mechanical complications and installed it. After five months use, the aft plate of the gear box, to which the shaft lock housing is bolted, fractured from repeated shock of locking the shaft under way, and we found ourselves looking for a spare cover plate in Palm Beach, the installation of which requires uncoupling and backing out the shaft.

From then on we tried to come head to wind and slow down the rotational velocity of the shaft to lock it, and this reduction in impact allowed the next plate to last several years. Of course this slowing down, head to wind, would find us from time to time caught aback and forced over onto the other tack on top of a lee shore with the shaft just locked, particularly if we had guests on board who wanted to talk to Cynthia at the helm during this maneuver, engendering a few muted words from me and a quick debate on the virtues of sailing her out of this spot versus unlocking the shaft and starting all over again.

By then the fail-safe interlock was wearing, and one of our guests, in a moment of panic, forced the engine into gear while locked, thus stalling the engine and fracturing the plate, which was replaced in Gothenburg, Sweden. It was only when, despite the extremes of gentleness, I fractured the third plate, which was replaced in Malta, in the process of doing which the shaft was recoupled 90 degress off center so that the propeller now locked horizontally instead of vertically, that I abandoned the use of the lock altogether, and now, when Cynthia brings the boat head to wind and the shaft's rotation slows down, I clap a flat slab of leather to the outer rim of the shaft coupling, which luckily is readily accessible and smooth, brake it to a stop, and stick a bit of broken batten under the coupling set screw head, of a length to hold the blades vertically. The forward way on the boat clamps it in place; the tiniest nudge in reverse when we start the engine knocks it clear; and if any of us forgets it and throws the engine ahead to begin with, the bit of batten breaks. And believe me, we have an inexhaustible supply of broken battens to draw upon.

At last we have the foolproof shaft lock. Ah, simplicity! Remember how Davies, in *The Riddle of the Sands*, kept emerging from the cabin with some other part of the *Dulcibella*'s gear and heaving it overboard?

Our greatest triumph of simplicity arose from another missing spare part. I say "our" because the credit for this goes to my late friend Arthur Fairley, then Dean of the Maine Maritime

Academy. The Fairleys were with us on the first leg of a trip from Malta to Denmark in 1971, and we had come into the western cove of Vulcano in the Aeolian Islands north of Sicily, the home of the God of the Winds. This cove, lying between two small and barren volcanic cones, is open to the northwest, and we had northwest gale warnings on the air. It didn't really look like weather, but if it should come in, we would gun the engine and zip over into the lee of Lipari a mile away. I had let go the anchor on the black sand bottom and called to Cynthia to back her down, but all we did was idle astern, and not to interrupt the lively conversation in the cockpit, I stepped aft and opened the throttle. Nothing happened. Wiggle, waggle, and still nothing. Hm! Neutral's OK. How about ahead? Yes, she goes into gear, but advance the throttle and nothing happens. Idling speed, either ahead or astern, is all we have. And so to work.

In the locker behind the engine-control bulkhead I found the throttle control cable responding in its sheath, but down in the engine room, having removed about twenty one-gallon tins of stove fuel, I found no motion of the throttle. Somewhere in the 14 feet of Morse control cable, there was a break. No one had suggested I might want a spare cable, and certainly I had never thought of it. Previous boats had either had solid rod connections or engines so primitive that they apparently predated the invention of the clutch or throttle. Naples, 175 miles away, would be the closest place we could even hope to find a replacement.

I lay against the oily engine bed and wiggled the throttle control at the engine. No problem, and clearly if I spent the rest of my summer lying in the engine room and operating on command from above, like an engine man on a steamship, we could proceed. Then I discovered that closure was positive. The broken control cable could clearly push the throttle closed; it just wouldn't pull it open.

"Hey, Arthur," I said, "This isn't too bad. All we have to do is tie a string to the bell crank on the throttle, and I can sit by the sailbin and pull it open, while the man at the controls can close it."

"Have you got a spring of some sort?" Arthur asked. "Maybe you could let a spring do the pulling for you."

"Well, we've got a couple of screen-door springs to hold pots on the stove. We could try one."

So with a piece of copper wire salvaged from a derelict lobster pot driven onto a beach in Maine, a length of marlin, and a screen-door spring, we pieced together a throttle opener. It worked—it worked with precision.

"You know," I said, "that might get us to Naples, or even to France. Surely we'll find a cable along the Riviera."

And it did. It got us to France and then it got us up the Rhône and across Europe to Denmark, maneuvering through 242 locks and an infinity of landings and close quarter maneuvers and passings of barges in the narrow seas. It worked so well that only once in the whole summer did I make an adjustment of tension, and it was not until winter layup that we finally bothered to install a replacement Morse cable.

I do, by the way, now carry a spare clutch control cable. It would really be embarrassing to have that break down at some point. But it hasn't—yet. What did break down (and I am losing the chronological sequence now, because this only happened in 1975) was the Morse control lever which operated it. This is the single-lever control which is equipped with a pull button to release the clutch connection in case one wants to pour on the fuel without going into gear, as is necessary in a cold-weather start, to start up after bleeding the fuel line or changing filters, or to charge batteries at anchor. For several seasons the pull button, increasingly corroded with salt, became more and more difficult to operate, despite massive doses of penetrating oil and WD40, until now, on the south coast of Turkey, it gave up altogether. Mistrustful of all the little things that come flying out of such a gadget upon disassembly, and the impossibility of replacing the guilty parts in Turkey, we lived with it until layup, purchasing an entire replacement unit that winter.

I will confess to not having a duplicate fuel shut-off control cable. This is because I once learned what to do if that fails to operate. We had just come on board the *Cynthia R* in Malta after winter layup and had started up the diesel for the first time. After warming up and charging batteries, I gave a pull on the shut-off control, which of course cuts the fuel supply, and found it wouldn't budge. At that moment a man stopped on the quay astern of us with the look of a person about to ask, "Who designed your boat?" Not wanting to get involved in conversation in the middle of my problems, I ducked below to try from the engine room. But the system was solidly frozen, and when I emerged again our man was waiting patiently. "Who designed your boat?" he asked in a pleasant way.

"Well, that was John Alden's office," I answered, probably less pleasantly. "But I can't talk now; I've got a diesel that doesn't want to stop running."

"I've had a bit of experience with diesels; maybe I can help," he said. "I'm from that ketch *Yankee* across the creek."

I did a double take and my first good look.

"You're Irving Johnson," I said, as if he would be glad to know who he was, with which he came on board, removed the air filter, slipped a piece of stiff clean cardboard over the air intake pipe, and stopped the engine.

"If you can't cut off the fuel," Irving said, "you cut off the air. Now let's take the penetrating oil and free things up."

Five minutes later it was all as good as new; we climbed out of the engine room and introduced ourselves and have had many a pleasant gam in various parts of the world in the years that followed.

By talking about simplicity, I have already gotten things out of order, but no matter. The fracturing gear-box cover plate was at least understandable, which is more than I can say for the case of the disappearing exhaust-manifold water-jacket cover plate (what a mouthful). This manifold is aluminum, and the plate in question carries the sea-water outlet, connected in our case by rubber hose to the water-jacketed portion of the exhaust line, which is stainless steel, with bronze connections for the rubber hose, a veritable orgy of dissimilar metals linked by warm salt water. Now I don't know anything about electrolysis, and those who do admit they can't figure it out, but I do know that a few days before starting across the Atlantic we found a salt-water leak at this connection, and upon tightening the hose clamp the entire piece crumbled into powder. It had been in service just one year. This was the same day we discovered the main boom had delaminated, so that we could neither sail nor motor, a discouraging way to start across an ocean. (Nobody had suggested a spare main boom, either, but this was repaired with a better glue and a massive array of giant hose clamps. I still carry the hose clamps and half a dozen 8-foot oak battens which would serve as splints in case of a broken boom at sea.) A new part was found for the manifold, and we thanked our stars that it had not occurred in mid-ocean; but two years later, in a small cove in the Ionian, I found the same connection weeping again. This time I touched nothing, and we headed for Corfu nearby, where a repeat performance of the crumbling part occurred and a new one was fabricated by a machine shop. That winter I bought two spare plates and a zinc insert for the bronze elbow to serve as a waster, and to date we have had no recurrence, although whether it is the presence of the zinc or the fact that I am prepared for the emergency that has caused this to relent, I cannot say.

It took less than two years of use for the key-operated starting switch to corrode, exposed as it was to the elements on the bridge deck. This is a nuisance, but not absolutely fatal, as one can always short over the terminals inside; it carries only the light load to the solenoid; and the replacement seems to have been more weatherproof than the original. Nevertheless a spare "ignition" switch would be a comfort to have on board.

More useful are spare keys. We now carry quite a collection of companionway padlocks, because we have so often lost one of the two original keys and been unable to duplicate American keys abroad, or vice versa. It's smarter to take your keys to the local hardware store at the start and run off a handful of duplicates, of course attaching floats to some.

For some years we have carried lengths of flexible exhaust hosing together with short sections of wide copper pipe, so that a ruptured section of the wet line could be pieced out from spares, but no one had cautioned me to carry a spare standpipe muffler. This is a vertical unit of stainless steel into which the exhaust gases enter from the dry line, there to be mixed with the sea-water coolant and discharged down a flexible hose. I suppose I had thought of stainless steel as indestructible. Not so, although it did last eight years. We were again in the Ionian in 1974, with 600 miles to go to Malta for winter layup and repairs, when we became aware of exhaust fumes in the cabin. By backing out panel after panel I came finally to the muffler and there found pinholes in the outer sheeting and gasses and salt spray escaping through the asbestos lagging where the hot line joined it. Should I take it apart and try to repair it in Greece? Prudence whispered, "No." I found that by running the engine-room blower while the engine was in operation we could keep the living spaces below reasonably clear of these fumes, although worrying still that each day might be the muffler's last. On arrival in Malta the repair shop refused to touch it until we were safe in our permanent winter mooring, and then, on lifting it out, the entire concealed side of the muffler collapsed in the mechanic's hands like so much burned tinfoil. It was a satisfaction at least to know that Prudence had given me a good steer and that if I had attempted any investigation of the trouble in Greece we would inevitably have been forced to face the problem of no muffler at all.

While we had made it to winter quarters, satisfaction stopped there. I really can't describe the mess of oily soot that covered every surface touched by those fumes, the hours of soogying out cramped corners, or the shock of learning that the list price of the replacement part was, even then, $550.

Early in 1975 I began to notice a spray of water coming from the drive shaft of the Jabsco sea-water cooling pump. For many weeks I looked the other way, hoping it would go away if ignored, like an annoying child, but by August it clearly was not responding to neglect, and on returning to the civilization of Rhodes from a month in Turkey I got hold of a mechanic and we removed the pump. The entire inside was shot, all the bearings, seals, rings, and little pieces with meaningless names. The impeller, the only part I was prepared to replace from my spare-parts kits, was missing several blades. Of course I had had enough trouble understanding my mechanic, who spoke no word of English, when he wanted a socket wrench with a ratchet handle, to expect to discuss how to locate and replace all these pieces whose names in English were abstruse, so ordered a new pump from Athens. It took about a week to get this, and at a price just about double its price at home. The moral is that, had I carried a spare pump on board, I would have saved a week of worry and lost time, and about a $150 markup on the pump.

In 1976 it was the lube-oil cooler on the diesel that let go, an item which even the engine manual says should cause little problem. I had become aware of an excessive throw of oil from our exhaust, more of a slick than we are used to, and on checking the dipstick found it covered with a horrid gray emulsion. One ought to check the dipstick daily, but we had been using the engine only in anchoring or getting under way, and it could have been several days since I had last looked. Anyway, I changed the oil at once, the same mess throughout, and changed the filter, finding the filter cup quite full of water. Being within a day's sail of Rhodes we headed there before a Force 5 to 6 *meltemi*, like a horse headed for the barn, pondering where our leak might be. Fresh water would mean a cracked head or ruptured gasket, but the fresh-water level in the header tank remained constant and did not taste of salt. Salt water could back up the exhaust and enter through the cylinders, but then we would have difficulty in starting. We had not been in that kind of sea, and the dry line, when a drain plug was opened, was dry and free of salt. The only other source of contact between lube oil and water seemed to be the cooler, and it made sense that oil would be forced into the cooling water when the engine was in operation and the oil under pressure, while water could work its way back in at rest, the cooler being 18 inches below the waterline.

Removal and testing at Rhodes confirmed this; we flushed the crankcase with multiple changes of light oil and then sat back to await the arrival of a replacement part from America, it not being a unit carried in Athens by the Perkins dealer. Had I carried a spare, a week's delay and concern would have been avoided, plus substantial air freight and handling charges.

But one could shout out one's pride in American efficiency

and logic, after years in the Med. I had telexed to a friend at 1000 one morning, Greek time, and by 1600 that afternoon, American time, the part was in the hands of the air-freight forwarder together with adapters just in case my pressure hoses had different end fittings from those the new piece called for (they did, and the adapters worked), and the freight forwarder had the good sense to route it direct to London and thence direct to Rhodes, so it was not sidetracked in customs in Athens. The part was actually at the Rhodes airport within three days of my telex, and within three more days we managed to get it cleared with Greek customs and brought in from the airport.

If pumps have been one of the major causes of problems in our space program, it is no wonder that they go to pieces on a boat. When some pumps fail to operate before the space craft is off the launching pad, just imagine what could be expected in an eight-year voyage in a salt-water environment, the pumps being operated by the likes of us and our guests and their children. No, the wonder is that they hold up at all. My first advice to anyone planning a world cruise would be to carry at least one complete spare for every pump on board. And there are more pumps than you think: even on our unsophisticated *Cynthia R* let me count the pumps. There is the navy-type bilge pump; an emergency diaphragm gusher pump; the galley-sink pump; the wash-basin pump, the toilet pump; a wobble pump for the shower; a Jabsco portable electric pump with hose for general use or for deck and anchor cleaning; a Par Super Sucker, whose straw-like proboscis gets into little corners and tubes; and an air-pressure pump for the alcohol stove, already replaced once or twice. There is also, one hopes an air-pressure pump in the rubber raft kit. The diesel has its sea-water pump, a fresh-water pump, a fuel-lift pump, the high-pressure injector pump, the lube oil circulating pump, and the hand-pump for draining the crankcase; and even the simple Seagull outboard has its water pump.

Most boats our size would have two heads with hot and cold water in each as well as in the galley, which might have a sea-water pump in the sink as well, or very likely double sinks. Most would have a separate sump for basin drainage with both electric and hand pumps for that and for the bilge. And most would have some form of refrigeration with one or more compressor pumps, and an auxiliary diesel generator with its complete set of water, fuel, and oil pumps. So with our "simple" boat we have at least seventeen pumps, and it is easy to see how we could have twice this number without being considered at all complex.

Perhaps in our effort to be simple we have really complicated matters. Would a pressure water system have less maintenance than all these pumps? I don't know, but if I were to start over again I would seriously study this alternative. It leads naturally into a hot-water supply in galley and head, so that hot and cold fresh water could be supplied to sink, basin, and shower, all driven by one pressure pump. The saving in stove fuel used to heat dishwater, and in cabin comfort in hot weather, would be worth weighing against the disadvantage of one more mechanical system to maintain, one more noise turning off and on in the night, and, biggest disadvantage of all, the lavish use of fresh water on the part of our guests induced by a pressure system. Back to our pumps.

Of our seventeen pumps only three have given me no problem to date: the gusher bilge pump, because it has never been used; the air pump on the life raft, because the instructions say not to open the factory packing; and the fuel-injection pump on the diesel, which, for reasons known only to itself, has operated faultlessly. I will ask it no questions. Every other pump has either failed or been a cause of worry. Don't let me throw the blame on the pumps alone. All of us really know that valves and cup leathers wear and springs corrode. Proper routine maintenance, by which I mean annual replacement of those parts and ample oil and grease in between, would go a long way to prevent emergencies, but it is no less work to remove a galley-sink pump and replace its leather and valves routinely than to do so only when it fails, failure usually being slow and progressive. One always hopes to get another season's use before having to do it. This is particularly true when one is a mechanical incompetent and faces the possibility—nay, the probability—that at each removal one will probably break a vital part by strong-arming it, drop a screw or nut into the bilge, forget the order in which all the little pieces fell out, and crossthread some component on reassembly. Unnecessary surgery whose risks outweigh the gains, that's what it is. Far better to carry a complete replacement unit to throw into service and then wait for some day when weather holds you in port to disassemble and repair the culprit while your wife reads to you, instead of asking you, "How soon would you predict I'll have water in the galley again?" And, even better, there's always the chance that your next guest really enjoys tinkering and will do the repairs for you.

You understand that this advice is the result of doing it the hard way over many years, so that when I finally caught on that spares were advisable, I learned that my originals were now out of production and replacement units were unavailable. That's why I suggest starting with them. This doesn't mean you don't need spare parts too; you should still have all the spare valves and springs and cup leathers and washers, and not just one of each, either. Buy them by the handful. If you don't use them yourself you can always be a hero to someone less foresighted than you.

Valves, like pumps, can suddenly malfunction or nonfunction, or the packing leak or the valve stem or handle fracture, and it is pretty nice to be able to throw in a spare valve in a hurry and repair the defective one at leisure. At the same time that we were about to start across the Atlantic and discovered we could neither motor nor sail, we also discovered that we couldn't cook a meal. The valve in the alcohol feed line, of the packless diaphragm type, was frozen shut. That is, the diaphragm failed to respond to the release of pressure of opening the handle, and no amount of fussing seemed to relieve it. Since we have eight similar valves in our diesel-fuel line system, which have never given trouble, we can assume that something about the alcohol fuel had gummed the diaphragm shut, but no replacement could be had in Charleston, and we were forced to substitute a simple gate valve, which weeps for attention at the start of every season but otherwise has served us well. But with nine identical valves, wouldn't it have made sense to have carried at least one spare from the start? And if you have a pressure feed line, be sure to carry spare lengths of tubing or hose with the proper end fittings for attachment. Also, carry a bit of tubing which could be wired in place as a sleeve over a break in a diesel-fuel line.

While your mind is on tubing and hose, remember that no two fresh-water outlets will be alike once you are off home base. In addition to 100 feet or more of light plastic tubing, carry shorter lengths of various diameters fitting snugly inside and outside your main line and each other, so that you can step up or down in multiple stages and adapt to any type of hose bib, faucet, or tap, or that dirty hose on the town quay, together with a supply (not just one each) of the necessary hose clamps. These adapters and hose clamps are too often "borrowed" by those less foresighted than you.

We seem to be getting down to the little things, but even if small, they may be of equal importance. So to start at the top, let us go to the masthead. That is where I went the day the American astronauts landed on the moon, and the crowd of Yugoslavs on the quay of Cavtat seemed every bit as interested in my ascent. The bulb in the masthead light had burned out, and I had gone up in the bosun's chair with a replacement (yes, I knew enough to carry spare light bulbs), pliers, and screwdriver to disassemble its housing. It ought to be simple, but you know what it's like at the masthead. Even two blocked, the bosun's chair sits uncomfortably far below the masthead assembly; one must lean back over space and crane one's neck, trying to focus through the distance portion of bifocal glasses on a tiny nut a few inches above one's nose and grip it with the pliers with one hand, while fishing for the invisible slot in the invisible machine-screw head with a screwdriver in the other hand. Two blocked and wedged into the converging shrouds and stays, the bosun's chair can in no way be rotated around the mast, and no matter how you twist and squirm, one machine screw remains elusively hidden, to be removed by touch alone. Of course a motor boat goes by at this point, or someone on deck crosses over, little realizing that an almost imperceptible motion at deck level is magnified ten times at the truck. Anyway, I was just congratulating myself on the cheerful "plink" of the last nut being deposited in my little bucket when the release of pressure on the gasket popped the last machine screw clear of its seat, to be followed by a dismal "plonk" as it disappeared into the harbor. Would I have ever thought of carrying spare machine screws for the masthead light assembly? Now, yes; then, no!

So my advice is, Start at the top and work your way down. Buy a replacement for every machine screw, nut, washer, pin, or cotter pin that might ever be removed, damaged, or corroded. Buy enough to replace a replacement when you drop it or cross-thread it. Put them in little sealed envelopes, labeled for what they are. Buy taps to clean out the threads of places these may have to screw into. In our case, for example, the lifeline stanchions and pulpits disassemble, like pieces of an Erector set, and machine screws vibrate loose. Since the pieces always seem to be under torque or tension, it is most difficult not to cross-thread on reassembly, and a tap for these machine screws, and ample spares, are a necessity. In the case of the Edson pedestal steerer, always out in salt spray, corrosion has been a problem and I early found all the fastenings of dissimilar metals frozen. When a repair was necessary, some of the fastenings had to be drilled out and the holes retapped. Have you spares for all these screws? Neither did I. Have you spare clevis pins for the jaws of your turnbuckles? This is a favorite item to roll out through a freeing port when you are working on your rigging. In fact, have you a few spare turnbuckles against the day one of these turns up flawed or perhaps snags a protruding bolt or re-bar of some unhappy pier? Yes, you probably do, although in truth we could get along without in extremis. For centuries rigging was set up with deadeyes and lanyards, and we could all fashion a jury rig to replace a missing turnbuckle. A schooner we sailed on in the Virgin Islands resorted to this twice when trade wind squalls snapped turnbuckles.

But let me ask, now that we are at deck level, if you have spare brush springs for the motor of your electric windlass. Really, you may think, that is going too far. But it isn't. In the Bahamas our windlass motor filled with salt water, which slowed its operation. I may be an electrical nitwit, but even I know a motor shouldn't be full of water. On taking it apart I found that the brush springs crumbled into fragments. A helpful tomato cannery assigned their electrician to me for half a day, gratis, and he brought the motor back to life. Since then I have carried a spare motor, never used, and a handful of brush springs, also never used, and have kept the windlass covered when not in use, which is probably what I should have done in the first place.

Now let us slip below decks. When I disassembled the stove burners for routine cleaning the second or third time, the heads of the machine screws began to go. Repeated overheating plus corrosion had taken its toll, and after cannibalizing our spare burners for parts, I learned to carry an envelope of spare stove-burner machine screws. When the rudder stops on the steering quadrant fell off, it was because they had been set up without lock nuts, and the original nuts rolled off to some hidden corner. When the rudder stock cap vibrated loose, luck was with us; it fell onto a little shelf, its bolts still with it. On the Danish island of Bornholm I had to close the seacock to the engine sea-water intake, and as I slacked off on its locknut, the nut disintegrated into half a dozen bits. Again luck was with us; a machine shop in Bornholm had bronze nuts to match this diameter and thread. Usually in Europe one finds everything in metric thread and quite incompatible with U.S. fittings, although if one can find English thread it can be made to do. It is at least the same number of threads per inch, only the cross-section of the thread being different.

So we have come from the masthead to the bottom of the bilge, not pretending to cover everything, but just giving random examples of places where our experience has called for spares. Next year it will be a new part that I've failed to anticipate.

Thus it was, when we hauled out for spring painting in 1970 in Malta and found the Cutless shaft bearing worn smooth, allowing what seemed to be a quarter of an inch of play. Did I have a spare stern bearing? No!

I expect I'm making my point; if your boat is going to remote places, she must be wholly self-sufficient. You should count on finding nothing—*nothing*—in the way of spare or replacement parts.

We do carry a spare compass or two, not the good spherical compass which rests in the binnacle, but a satisfactory hand-bearing compass and a small mountaineer's compass, either of which would get us into port; but when an air bubble appeared in our binnacle compass (on the coast of Turkey, of all convenient places), we had no compass fluid. As it turned out the fluid alone would have done us no good, for the bubble, like Elijah's cloud, grew hour by hour from the size of a pinhead to that of a dime and to that of a fifty-cent piece. At this point we dismounted the compass and found its rubber or neoprene diaphragm cracked and dripping. Previous compasses in my life had been of the old-fashioned flat type in their own bowls, and no one had mentioned the frailty of the diaphragm, a known weak point of our model. Cables home brought the necessary materials via our next guests, who joined us in Antalya with quite a tale of difficulty of explaining to a land-bound Turkish customs official at the airport, who had never heard of a compass, but was always on the lookout for smuggled drugs, what compass fluid is all about.

We are appalled at the number of yachts in remote places which carry no spare propeller, but the most surprising was a single-screw motor boat which had climbed the Rhône in late May 1971, a short time ahead of us. This boat had thrown a blade at one of the hairy stretches of the Rhône, of which there were many then, and had been instantly washed up on a gravel bar with a falling river. The natives were most friendly and reassuring: "Don't worry about your boat," they said. "In November the Rhône will rise and he will be afloat again." But luck was with them, the river had risen briefly the next week and a tow boat had plucked them off and towed them to Lyon, where they were lying indefinitely while a replacement prop from England was frozen somewhere en route by one of those many transit strikes.

In 1974 when we climbed the Rhône again only as far as

Avignon, we found there, lifted out on the quay, a twin-screw American cruiser we had seen preparing for the trip two weeks earlier at La Grande Motte on the coast. She had made it just the first 10 percent of the distance with her unprotected props before striking a bar herself, which had left one prop and shaft utterly demolished. And again no spares. Perhaps the desirability of a spare prop was no more obvious to that owner than the dozens of things I have listed above had been to me. I am in no position to cast the first stone, but only to let others, including the manufacturers of marine hardware, profit from our combined stupidities.

Long ago Cynthia and I were sailing out of Knight Inlet in British Columbia, where, to quote the majestic words of the British Columbia *Pilot*, "the shores rise in almost sheer precipices to stupendous peaks, clad in perpetual snow," to which we can add that their sole inhabitants are the grizzly bears. A gray southeast wind was gaining strength, the typical forerunner of a storm pattern on the Northwest Coast, and here it blew directly out the westward leading canyon, the outer 35 miles of the inlet. Somewhat to Cynthia's dismay I had set the spinnaker, not quite the chore it would be on the *Cynthia R*, but a big sail for our 29-foot cutter, as we carried a substantial J distance, and it was a masthead chute.

"Bob," Cynthia called from the tiller, "there seems to be a lot of vibration in the rudder."

"Just proves we're well balanced," I called back from the cabin. "When there's no pressure on the rudder it always flutters a bit."

Cynthia subsided, mumbling something like: "Seems more than just a bit to me."

"Oh, stop your mumbling," I mumbled.

When I relieved the watch, the wind was piping up, the gray clouds lowering on the mountains, and we were beginning to oscillate in the puffs, as I leaned and hauled alternately on the tiller. Then suddenly it was limp in my hands, and the *Carib* rounded slowly up and grandly drove for the cliffs, the full weight of the increasing wind now apparent.

"All hands on deck!" I cried. "We've lost our rudder."

And Cynthia came up clutching a copy of *Edible Plants and Berries of British Columbia.*

We are not racing buffs at heart, but believe me, there is no better school for sailing than going around the buoys in close-order competition. Our drill paid off now as we brought the chute in under the boom, then dropped the main and took stock. Our rudder wasn't gone, it had just lost its grip and was wholly independent of the rudder stock. Our destination was dead down wind, distant 20 miles, and a small jib held our head off while I drilled holes in a bit of plank and laced it with wire to one end of the spinnaker pole. With this passed under the taffrail and with ample chafing gear in use, we were soon in business again, arriving in cold rain squalls at Minstrel Island in time to arrange for haulout the following morning. The missing part, for which, of course, I had no spare stock, was the key that connected the rudder stock to the bronze rudder strap. This sort of incident has never happened again, perhaps because I have learned to carry spare key stock for critical shaft connections.

On several other occasions Cynthia has been right in insisting on spares. When we left for the Bahamas in 1967 she wanted a spare swimming ladder, and we had broken and repaired both before we returned in May of 1968. On entering the canal system of Europe she demanded a spare boathook, and both of them had gone missing before we had returned to the Med.

Cynthia accuses me of not worrying enough about such matters, usually in self-defense when I have accused her of spoiling her fun by worrying about too many things at once.

"*Somebody* has to worry about them," she says.

"But we're always worrying about the wrong thing," I reply. "We worry about a storm, then run aground instead. We worry about having our ship's papers in order and then get slapped down for not having an operator's permit. We worry about having enough Sparklets for the soda-water siphon, when the siphon breaker in the toilet overboard line is about to break."

"We're always worrying about the wrong thing" has become a truism on our boat, and while it seems clear that if you worry about enough mischances you can't help but hit a few right, nevertheless the majority of our real problems have struck from the blue. A minor example was in the stowage of our regulation USCG approved life jackets, the clumsy kapok-filled kind that take up lots of space, but which you don't put on just to work the foredeck at night. So I looked for a dry place to stow them, not inacessibly, but neither on top of everything in daily use. A nice spot was found under the aft ends of the aft cabin bunks, where simply throwing back the mattress and lifting the plywood would expose them, and, better yet, the driest spot on the boat, as there was no deck directly over these spaces and no circulation of air from the bilge into them. In fact it turned out they were as watertight as tanks, and I don't know how long they had been half filled with water before I finally caught on. Long enough, anyway, for the life jackets to have become waterlogged messes, their metal spring clips and fastenings corroded away, their fabric smelling of rot. What had happened to our driest spot on the boat? It doesn't really matter because the point is we should clearly have been worrying about the condition of our life jackets long ago; no question that the water had been in there from the year before, if not longer. But we had been too busy worrying about some wrong thing which in turn never happened, content that this dry spot didn't even need airing.

To assuage curiosity, what happened was that the main backstay chainplates came through the deck over this space and down the side of the boat behind some ceiling. The cover plates, where these chain plates pass through the deck, had worked their screws loose, and both sea water and rain water had been seeping in all the previous year.

Little things like this, which could have spelled disaster, but somehow didn't, are constantly showing up. Tins of alcohol stove fuel, stowed in the shaft alley, rusted through and lost their contents into the bilge. A change to plastic bottles saw some of them slowly cut or crack open and lose their load of alcohol in turn. Alcohol vapors were probably released at a very slow rate and flushed by the engine-room air vents or consumed by the diesel's massive demand for air; but still, alcohol vapors *can* explode. The strange fate of the *Mary Celeste* has been attributed to a spontaneous explosion of vapors from her cargo of alcohol. We should have been worrying about this all those weeks that our bilge fumes were rich with alcohol.

My next-door neighbor took off for Tahiti in a well-broken-in boat, only to have his main boom gooseneck break in mid-Pacific, leaving him unable to reef. Who would think to carry a spare gooseneck?

In a squall off Cape Spartivento on the toe of Italy, one of the aluminum alloy blocks suspending our dinghy from the davits fractured, an example of something I actually had worried about, as the 10-foot dinghy will dip her nose or stern into the water when we are laid well over and pitching, and tremendous strains must be set up on the entire system. We lashed it back temporarily with line and substituted an old bronze and lignum vitae block for the plastic and aluminum when the squall had passed.

One more little thing of which you should have ample spares is the hypodermic needle. If dentistry, accident, or illness requires any form of injection in remote places, the chances are good that the needle will have been used on many people, and it is well to carry your own.

And now we must get serious for a few minutes. Among the spare parts which we cannot carry and cannot fabricate are bits and pieces of the human body, or the whole thing, for that matter. An injured crew member is a deeper concern to the skipper than rocks and storms, and try as we will, we all get injured from time to time. It doesn't have to be the glamorous maritime kind of injury, like being bitten by a shark. No, one of our guests was bitten by a horse. Now what kind of injury is that for a sailor? One doesn't have to be hit on the head by a jibing main boom, but the number of crew who have cracked their skulls against the main boom while it is resting in its slings is legion. And we had a guest who slipped while climbing on the rocks and gave his scalp a nasty cut right through a heavy canvas cap and his own head of hair. I am sure he would have traded for a spare head at the moment, if we had had one. Perhaps a doctor would have stitched him up, and while I was once a trained Purser–Pharmacist's Mate and do carry surgical needles, I felt his head was injured enough for one day and he might prefer scar tissue to a broken needle.

But let's not start off by sounding like heroes at our guests' expense. We have our own problems to confess. On our first overnight passage after breaking in our boat on the coast of Maine we headed south from Portland for the Cape Cod Canal, the next intended stop being Marion, Mass. Forecasts mentioned east winds going northeast and strengthening, with high seas, but our attitude was that a following wind and sea should make for a quick passage, and as far as Cape Ann we had delightful sailing. Besides Cynthia and me on board we had my daughter, Delight, and her husband and Cynthia's Uncle Waldo, then 67, but an enthusiastic sailor. I remember the euphoric feeling as we sailed slowly south on a beam reach, eating supper and watching the coast of Maine slip by, with just that touch of excitement to spice our meal with the challenge of the forecast furnished.

Massachusetts Bay at midnight brought something else, a heavy swell from the east, and running across it a steep and cresting sea from the northeast. We were still carrying full sail and swinging off the pyramidal crests in pitch darkness when a particularly steep combination threw us widely to starboard, rolling our rail under. There was a crash from the black cabin below, and since only Cynthia was not on deck I asked Delight to slip down and make sure she was all right. In a moment she was back in the companionway.

"No, she's not all right," she said. "I think you'd better come."

I gave over the wheel and got below to find her on the cabin floor.

"Why are we out here?" she asked.

"We're on our way to the Cape Cod Canal," I said.

"Why are we going there?" she wanted to know.

"Don't you remember, we just started off for Florida."

"But why are we sailing at night?"

She was knocked silly in the true sense of the word. By the light of a flashlight I saw she was bleeding from the mouth and I had the horrified specter of a fractured skull, although in the morning we learned she had bitten her lip. It turned out she had climbed into the upper bunk in the main cabin, not designed for use at sea, as it had no bunkboard, where she could keep an eye on us in the cockpit, worrying about our going overboard in the slop. And I was worried about identifying the aids to navigation in Massachusetts Bay when I should have had my mind on what might be going on below. Always worrying about the wrong things.

There was little to do but wedge her where she wouldn't be thrown again and continue for the Cape Cod Canal and Marion, where X-rays the next morning confirmed what we were already suspecting, a broken arm, the type known as a comminuted fracture, which, like the crushed shell of a hard-boiled egg, still had all the pieces in place. Treatment consisted simply of immobilizing it briefly and then starting on curative exercises to keep the immobility from becoming permanent. Her head had cleared up at once, but the evidence of damaged capillaries in the shoulder lasted many weeks, and she was probably the only girl on the waterway that fall with one white breast and one black.

Cynthia redeemed herself ten days later at the start of the next passage south, from Mamaroneck to Cape May. This time we had a forecast of a northwest wind and clear weather, ideal for coasting down the Jersey beaches, but Cynthia thought she had heard some mention of a hurricane from a Coast Guard forecast. A hurricane had moved slowly north up the coast the week before, and then recurved out to sea, and since all forecasts later in the morning had confirmed the fair northwester, we dismissed the idle threat of hurricane. But a film moved across the sky as we romped down the East River with the tide, and it hardened into an ominous gray, a great circle around the sun, as we emerged from The Narrows into the Lower Bay. Here the wind was northeast and rising.

"Let's just put in behind Sandy Hook for lunch," Cynthia suggested, and I thought that a good idea myself, although Cynthia's Uncle Waldo, whom I have said was an enthusiastic sailor, tended to pooh-pooh our caution. But Sandy Hook was flying the small craft warning, and surf was heavy on the beaches, so we lay an anchor behind the Hook and did odd jobs while we awaited developments. At 1500 the small craft warning came down, and I was about to say: "Well, that's that," when in its place were hoisted the two red pennants of a gale warning. Now the radio was full of the rogue hurricane, which had reversed its course and was heading due west for the American shore, due to strike somewhere south of Cape May that night. That was all we needed, and we hurriedly searched the charts and *Pilot* to find a suitable haven up the Shrewsbury River, which runs south behind the Jersey beaches from Sandy Hook. By the time we had made it to Sea Bright, the wind was already giving us difficulty making a landing and securing, and when we walked over to the ocean front it was a wild sight, salt water flooding the streets as it cascaded over the sea wall. So we were glad indeed that Cynthia had worried, and this time about the right thing. It would have been a foul night at sea.

We had family with us far as Annapolis, but would be alone from there to Florida, Cynthia's arm still in a sling, and we decided just to take it easy, sail only when the weather was fair, and avoid getting into any situations where Cynthia could get thrown off balance again. On leaving Annapolis, after waiting for a fair forecast, I mistook a buoy for a turning mark of the channel and within five minutes of starting off alone we were hard aground under the windows of the Naval Academy. Worrying about the wrong thing again.

The next day we had selected Fishing Creek, a narrow dredged channel on the east shore, as our evening harbor, but a south wind was rising as we beat past the Little Choptank. A council was held on whether to put in right there, but Cynthia was for carrying on. By late afternoon, reefed down, and plunging into the steep chop of the Chesapeake, I lowered down to make a cautious approach under power and opened the *Pilot* for last-minute advice, to learn that the channel, shown on the chart as amply deep, was reported as now silted up to one foot. On a calm day it is amusing to poke into places like this, but with an 18-knot beam wind and cresting seas, a crew with a broken arm, and sunset coming, it seemed a mistake to run aground again. A look at the chart revealed that Solomons Island, a close reach of six miles back to the west shore, was our nearest shelter. So it was up with the reefed sails again, grand and wet, driving hard into the short seas, the sun burning gold and pink through the sheets of spray to leeward, Cynthia wedged to leeward and grinning, until the wind went down with the sun and she got up to put a chicken in the oven, while we drifted in with the last red glow in the west. So much for our promise to be out in gentle airs only. By the time we were in Florida she could lift her arm straight over her head, something she had been unable to do for years, and I was offering to break her other shoulder to cure its arthritis, too.

Toward the end of our winter in the Bahamas I had a more expensive accident myself. The genoa sheet hung up on a shroud as we tacked, a common enough occurrence, and I ran forward to clear it, rather than coming head to wind again. But when it did snap free we were hard over on the other tack with perhaps fifteen knots of wind in the sail, and it spun me across the deck with a whiplash motion which proved to have ruptured a spinal disk, although it was two days later that all the classic symptoms set in, and another two before we were back from the Exuma Cays to Rock Sound and medical advice. The nub of the advice was to live on pain pills until we worked the boat back to Florida or Charleston, and then go home for surgery, which we did, including a twenty-four-hour passage from the Abacos to Cape Canaveral, during which I learned where the expression "feeling no pain" in association with liquid pain killers came from. But it was only while lying in bed after surgery that I thought through the fact that the guilty shackle, supposedly of the non-fouling design, had been put on backwards (not by me, I would add). Always worrying about the wrong things, you see.

On our Atlantic crossing, as mentioned, we had enjoyed in Bermuda the company and the parties of the Bermuda Race veterans, and my crew of young men were becoming increasingly exhausted. On the morning we were set to sail for the Azores, Skip reported in with headache, stiff neck, dizziness, and mild fever, all symptoms which could be associated with flu, polio, meningitis, and other dread diseases. How could I be so heartless as to put to sea, to sail away from medical care, with death looking in his hatch? But the symptoms could also come from too little sleep and too much motorbike riding across Bermuda at 3 A.M., and if we were to stay in port with heat and humidity both in the nineties, rafted up with the racing crews pounding over our decks to get to shore, and joining their parties at night, recovery seemed doubly doubtful. The day was fine; a light northwester would allow us to reach slowly northeast in air fresher and cooler by 10 degrees, but to reverse our course and motor back at flank speed if anything more ominous developed. I gave Skip a couple of aspirin, recorded his TPR (temperature, pulse, respiration), confined him to his bunk, and we sailed. The noon TPR was encouraging. By evening it was normal, and by the next morning he was fit in every way and we were 100 miles on our way to the Azores.

Many of our guests have been doctors, and we have built up a formidable pharmacy from their traveling kits, as each one leaves behind his favorite cures, mostly free samples from the drug houses, whose instructions are in microscopic type which tends to blur in an emergency. The problem we face seems to be one of decision—when to start actually administering our patent medicines to guests or crew, who are generally reluctant to admit or to describe their problems, and wind up deciding that a stiff drink is what they need. So I find myself slow at resorting to heroic measures, which is probably a good thing for our companions.

However, an episode occurred as we were leaving the Azores in which I found great satisfaction in being as brutal as I could. John, in horsing around on the beach, had cut the arch of his foot on a broken bottle and then, for a day or two, being a doctor's son, had walked barefoot around the quays, which, of course, are paved in dead fish, horse manure, dog droppings, garbage, and spit. I am not opposed to nature children and the barefoot act, especially in natural surroundings, but in the filth of the big-city streets or of the seaport it seems an affront to both esthetics and intelligence, so, with the gray Azores lying behind us and the Portuguese Trades filling our sails, when John came to me with his diffident "Say, Skipper, I seem to have a sore foot," and I heard the story and saw the supurating, swollen wound and the red lines leading up the leg, I was so mad that it was a pleasure to bring out a stiff scrub brush and hot water and the surgical soap and "go in there," while John chewed on a rag and pretended he was Ahab having his leg amputated. With a jeweler's loupe and a needle I picked out the last bits of foreign matter, put a bit of ointment on the cut, and sent him to his bunk with a full dose of antibiotic and his rather sobered promise to report ingesting each pill of the three-day schedule. To everyone's relief and my own surprise, and either because of or in spite of the treatment, he was as good as cured in twenty-four hours. The resilience of youth, able to withstand simultaneously the onslaughts of infection and of my treatment, is a joy to behold.

We really have a pretty good record of health on board. Most guests are worried about the water, taken on from dirty hoses dragged through sewage-filled harbors, but in general water supplies are reliable, and one does ask first. Far more guests arrive with disorders, which subside afloat, than those who pick up a bug while sailing. Our own tummy troubles, when they do occur, seem to come from meals ashore, and just as likely from the good hotels and restaurants, another example of worrying about the wrong things.

But Cynthia was hit with a fever while we were lying in Corfu, a fever so sudden that between her admitting to its existence while shopping in the city and my getting her back to the boat it had risen to 104 degrees. Being in a city, I dug up a recommended doctor, who put her on a very halfway dose of whatever antibiotic samples he had in his cabinet, some in shots and some in pills. He spoke only Greek and German, but I was able to ask him if he recommended that Cynthia stay in the hospital while I returned the boat to Malta.

"No," he said. "It is my hospital, you see, and I think she will be better off on your boat."

Perhaps she would have been better off if we had never been in Corfu in the first place, if we had been in some isolated spot instead, as I might have treated her myself; although we will never know if the results might have been as dramatic as with youth.

In long-range cruising, illness and accidents are going to occur, but so do they at home. In balance there is probably less exposure to illness at sea than at a cocktail party and less exposure to accident than on the highway. But when it does occur it seems somehow more dire, and this has to be a product of our civilization. Our lives are so protected, our accidents so often beyond our control, and our responsibility for diagnosis and treatment so willingly referred to others, that it strikes us as hazardous to assume a position in which the accident will be a consequence of our own decision, where we must assume responsibility for the treatment of illness and injury, and where we must live with the results of our mistakes, even if the result be death.

I said we must be serious for a few minutes.

VIII

Red Tape

Mana siz muşkalat.
Turkish expression meaning
"Difficulties without logic."

"I bag the titl, to isued CUSTOMS APPROVAL that I can with Jacht *Cynthia R* under my comand to sitt at coast sea SFhJ. in the time of July 18 1969 year, to Sept. 30 1969 year. With demand I enclos Crew List and Pasenger too, like the things wich Jacht has, as the details of the goods."

I signed the document, the Customs officer placed a seal over my signature and initialed it, and apparently in response to my "bagging the titl" he now issued another document. This one read: "On the basis of the article Nel. 7 Regulation of calling sailing sejourn of forin yachts and sports sailing boats in the teritorial waters of the FPR of Yugoslavia, has been issued CUSTOMS APPROVAL. It is approved entry and temporary sejour in FPRY of a sailing object/yacht *CYNTHIA R* capacity 24 under mastership Robert S. Carter Without paying customs duty and customs fees respectively without depositing caution money. In accordance with approval sailing object may sail respectively stay in teritorial waters of the FPRY 90 days at the longest counting from the day the approval has been suce. The approval may be prolonged on sumbitting request to the Caustons House."

Now we turned to the Port Captain, dressed in the customary uniform of underwear top and khaki pants. Customs and Quarantine had been overdressed in open sport shirts. The noonday heat shimmered over the harbor of Herzegnovi, our own brains shimmered from having been up all night for the 120-mile run from Brindisi, Italy, and I asked Cynthia to pass up beers all around. At last the forms were filled, the officials stepped to the quay, and the Quarantine officer indicated we could lower the yellow flag, then turned back to ask, "By the way, is everyone healthy on board?"

In a few minutes the Port Captain was back; he had used the wrong forms; would I step to his office and work out new forms with him? Now it was his turn to send out for beers and we clinked bottles, saying *"Druzhba,"* or "Brotherhood," which I had heard was the magic greeting in the communist world, and went to work on forms again. Eventually they were merged into a seven-page document, the sheets affixed to each other with paper seals, the seals stamped with a rubber stamp and a flourish. I may have been in the communist world now, but the paper work was in part a holdover from the Ottoman Empire of the Turks, and perhaps inherited by them from the Byzantine world.

We were free to cruise the waters of Yugoslavia at will; we could go to the islands of Rab, Pag, Krk, Cres, Iz, Ist, Sit, Zhut, Mljet, Vir, Vis, Brač and Hvar. In Yugoslavia big islands have little names, but as the islands grow shorter the names become longer. We could also go to Tetovisnjak, Lukmarinjak, Hrobshnjak, Shkrda, Mrchara, and Krknjas. But three islands we could *not* visit were President Tito's Brioni and two detention islands appropriately named O Goli and Grgur. Well, that's all right; we didn't want to go to those two islands anyway.

We were by no means new at red tape by then. In fact, I have always hovered on the borderline between exasperation and fascination as I deal with officialdom. One of our friends in the Mediterranean has his hobby listed as combating officialdom in all its forms, and makes a virtue of fighting it out with each one of these petty tyrants in turn. He insists that his boat is English soil, that officials must request permission to board it, that he and his wife are seamen and therefore do not have their passports stamped in and out, as we tourists do. It may take him as long or longer to carry his point than it takes me to accomplish the paper work, but his satisfaction in maintaining his independence is his reward.

My own attitude is that these poor, underpaid government employees, no doubt crushed by some more powerful tyrant in a tyrannical bureaucracy, in whose absolute power they must live out their lives, respond to any deference to their own egos which we can create, and that a courteous and helpful approach eases the day for everyone. Sometimes it takes a bit of money or a bottle of whiskey to ease their day, too, and at first I used to get very up tight about it, but more of that later. My point is that while I would far prefer to live my life free of all officialdom too, it is not my hobby to fight it. There are other things more rewarding to do in my brief time in any area, and the officials, like the weather, are a part of life to be tolerated.

"But you're just encouraging them in their robbery; if you give in you'll find they try to get more out of you next time," says my friend.

"The little bit I give them is the least of my expenses in a year's time," I reply, "and, anyway, I'll get it all back by writing up the accounts of how they do it. 'How do I pay thee? Let me count the ways.' "

But the countries of shakedown are few in our experience, as we have avoided the banana republics and the emerging world and the Middle East, and officials to us mean more the capricious application of varied and sometimes nonsensical rules, administered by men who run the gamut from the extreme of pleasant helpfulness to the straight business approach to downright nastiness, although the latter is rare.

Our first experience with going foreign, other than innumerable trips into and out of Canada, was our crossing to West End on Grand Bahama Island. In Palm Beach we had been told not to fly the quarantine flag on entering, because the local officials would think we had plague on board. Actually the single flag hoist "Q" in the International Code means, "My ship is healthy and I request free pratique," and ought to be displayed on the first entry to any country. I looked up "pratique" in Webster's and found that it means "Permission to hold intercourse," and thought, "No wonder he suggests I don't fly it," but I read on to learn that it is "Permission to hold intercourse with a port, given to a ship that has satisfied health regulations." It is the signal "QQ" which means plague. But following the local advice I entered without the hoist, reported in, and immediately had my knuckles rapped for failing to show the proper signal. I apologized humbly, but since my only excuse was that I had been led to believe this official was too stupid to know the difference, which I sensed would not smooth our way, I let it go at that, and we were pleasantly received and given our papers.

So much for advice. Since then we try to play the game according to the rules, and it is only the odd situation when one's blood pressure builds up.

Now let me say that Americans are in no position to point a finger. Many lands place cumbersome or punitive rules in the arriving yachtsman's path, but reports from both Americans and foreigners of their treatment upon entering a United States port put us high on the list of undesirable places to enter. Our personal experience here is limited to our return from the Bahamas at Port Canaveral and repeated entries from British Columbia. Most of these have been met with prompt, pleasant, and efficient processing of the entry. Once, when Cynthia and I were cruising alone in a 29-footer, we both went together to the officer in Friday Harbor on entering from British Columbia, and I was reprimanded for not have come alone with a crew list and waited permission for her to land. In Europe they never worry about that kind of detail.

But I have heard and read of many a boat which, on entering the United States, was literally turned inside out by our customs officials, who perhaps thought this world cruiser's sole purpose in sailing an ocean was to smuggle a bit of grass into America. And there was that sad case during the Great Depression of the Australian who, having bought an open 18-footer, decking it with canvas, making himself a sextant of a bent hacksaw blade and hand copying the navigation tables from the public library, then sailed eastward across the Pacific, weathering two typhoons, and finally arrived in Los Angles harbor. Anchoring for the night he was blown ashore and wrecked, whereupon the local authorities put him in jail for landing without papers. No, we mustn't point.

All American travelers are experienced in the baggage search by customs, an experience we have never had on arrival in any other country in the last thirty years. True, we are trying to protect our land from the invasion of strange plant and animal diseases and I am reminded of returning by air from a non-sailing trip to Bolivia. Now in Bolivia, when a young man takes home a bride he buries a dried llama fetus under his threshold to guarantee fertility, and these objects, which closely resemble a skinned and desiccated rabbit, are sold out of barrels in the marketplace. So I had one tucked into the bottom of a suitcase when we passed through customs at the airport, with fifty people queued up behind me. The customs officer opened that suitcase and looking off into space, as customs officers will do, he plunged his hand into the laundry and trinkets and pulled out this one item, holding it aloft by one stiff leg. Wouldn't you know?

"What's this?" he asked, a bit startled.

"Why that's a desiccated llama fetus," I said, in a tone implying that any fool ought to know that.

"It's a what?"

"It's a desiccated llama fetus. You know, you put them under your bed for fertility."

There was an appreciative murmur from the waiting crowd. The customs officer eyed me thoughtfully.

"Maybe you do, bud," he said at last. "Now tell me, is it a split-hoofed animal?"

I knew about hoof-and-mouth disease.

"Well," I said, "according to von Hagen, although the foot of the llama is divided, it is not a member of the bovine family. It is a camel—sort of."

I think it was the "von" in von Hagen that did the trick, because the officer now said, "So it's a scientific specimen. Why didn't you say so in the first place?" And tossed it back in.

Anyway, that's the way customs people treat us here, and I have no doubt somebody with faulty English is doubly suspect and trebly confused. So if we Americans are ever given a hard time elsewhere, we might figure it an even swap.

Back to Yugoslavia, then, I will say that after we finally got our papers straight we had no problems. We sailed the coast for seventy days, visited 50 harbors, and only once had our fingers rapped. This was when we went up the Krka River to the head of navigation at Skradin without having stopped at Šibenik for clearance. At Skradin they didn't care, but at Šibenik on the way out the authorities were upset.

On another occasion, crossing the wide bay between Trogir and Split, the inside route, that is, we saw a square-rigged training vessel moored at an establishment on the eastern shore and dressed for Sunday, and altered course to stand over toward her. Before we knew it we were in a prohibited zone, which I ought to have seen, except that part of the chart with the cautionary note was folded under, and we were assailed with noises from a loud hail and frantic semaphore. We couldn't read either, but got the message anyway, and sheered off, wondering if we would be pursued and detained, but we must have appeared innocent. An English yachtsman had been less fortunate; having come upon this square rigger in another bay and photographed it, he was immediately arrested, his camera and film confiscated, and he and his yacht ordered out of the country.

"How come?" I asked the British consul, who had been telling us the story. "What's so secret about a square-rigged training vessel?"

"Oh, it wasn't the square rigger, you know," he explained. "What the yachtsman perhaps didn't even know was that a couple of Soviet warships were in the background in that bay, and Yugoslavia is not supposed to be granting harbor to the Soviet navy. It could have been embarrassing to have those photographs floating around."

We have missed a lot of good photographs in our day just

because some hunch told me that some suspicious underling would consider it his duty to guard his own military secret, like a twenty-year-old patrol boat armed with a 20-mm gun on its foredeck, and I refrain from bringing out my camera when anything more military than the guard at the royal palace are in view, or when riots are taking place. Rioters are always a suspicious group, no doubt not wanting their pictures around if they happen not to win. And certainly the police, when constabulary duty's to be done, are not happy with pictures of "police brutality." So I miss some pictures, but not as many as I would miss if my camera had been smashed or confiscated.

It is easy to be ordered out of an area even in your own country, as we learned while proceeding south on the Cape Fear River in North Carolina. I had crossed the main channel where the tide was flooding strongly against us and turned down the western channel past the quays where a couple of ships were working cargo. Soon a patrol car with flashing lights and wailing siren zoomed to the water's edge and by loud hail ordered us out immediately. It turned out that this was an explosives loading area, and while it had been noted as "Restricted" on the chart, it was described as "Prohibited" in the *Coast Pilot*, which I now read. So it is a universal problem.

The Swedes, who keep a very sharp eye on the foreign cruising yacht, seem somehow to exude a paternalistic attitude, as if it were as much for your own good as for theirs. Probably in no country have we been so frequently hovered over by patrol planes and helicopters or visited by patrol boats, the latter courteously checking one's papers and wishing one a pleasant trip. One feels their presence to be benevolent, and if I were in trouble I would be pleased to know they were around. When you run off limits there, you feel that they pick you up in a firm but kindly way, perhaps with a tolerant sigh, and put you back on the square where you belong.

At the same time they do not seem to enforce rules merely for the sake of enforcing them. On the Baltic coast, south of Stockholm, we stopped at Dalarö to inquire the true identity of Strindberg's island of Hemsö, and learned that it was really the nearby island of Kymmendö. The officer of the patrol boat giving us this information, having already checked our papers and found them in order, pointed out that Kymmendö was in a restricted zone, but then said, "We have to make a patrol through those channels this morning, and if you would like to see the island it will be quite all right to follow us. But landing would be prohibited." We declined with thanks; without landing the island itself would be scarcely distinguishable from many of the other 150,000 islands of the Baltic Sea among which we had spent the last two months. But that type of cooperation and consideration was the mark of the Swedish officials, always correct, dignified, courteous, but ready to apply the rules with common sense.

Not so the Russians. While in the Baltic I was determined to pay a visit to the Soviet Union, mostly, I suspect, because I didn't know anyone who had ever sailed there in his own boat. A West German had once gained permission to ship his very small sloop to Leningrad as deck cargo, where he was then allowed to lie at the sailing club for a week, at the end of which he was dispatched with his wife and six-year-old son to beat 100 miles down the Gulf of Finland into a night of rising storm, to be intercepted at daybreak by a Soviet patrol boat for having been blown out of the channel limits.

While at home during the winter I had written to the Soviet Embassy in Washington, which had not replied. I had then written to the Russian Bureau of our State Department, which replied promptly that they had referred my letter to the Soviet Embassy, where it clearly had the same treatment as before. In Stockholm I had visited the American Embassy, which had sent me to the American Consulate, which had disclaimed any interest in my project, and thence I had gone to Intourist, where a very pleasant girl with good English had explained that it was "not yet" permitted for a private boat to enter a Soviet port. When I mentioned that a West German had done so she said that it might be possible, but only if a Swedish or Finnish travel bureau would arrange it by writing to Moscow.

I had already got the message that there was little point in asking for Leningrad; that is a naval base and the nation's most important port, and given the paranoid quality of Soviet secrecy it was clear no American yachtsman was going to be welcomed. But another of the many roads to socialism seemed possible to a boat which had traversed so many inland waterways, and this was the Saimaa Canal. I hadn't heard about this before we sailed in the Baltic, but this canal joins Viborg on the Gulf of Finland with the interior lake system of that country. This vital link in transporting the forest products of interior Finland had been built across Karelia, which the Soviets annexed after World War II, and for some years the Finns had no water access to their own lakes, but lately the canal had been completely rebuilt and modernized by the Soviets who, with a good-neighbor policy, had now leased it to the Finnish Saimaa Canal Company and reopened it to shipping. Here, I thought, was the key to sailing my own boat to the Soviet Union; I would take the Finnish route via the leased canal and thus be able to say I had traversed Soviet territory, as well as having an interesting excursion to these seldom-visited lakes.

In Mariehamn in the Åland Islands I visited the Soviet consulate (and why do they need a consulate here?) situated in a magnificent old residence, and met the secretary, a most pleasant young man, who said that while it should be possible in principle for me to do so, he did not know how, and that I should inquire of the Saimaa Canal Company in Helsinki or of the Soviet Embassy there.

With the *Cynthia R* lying in Turku two weeks later, Cynthia and I took the train to Helsinki to make arrangements. The first call was to the office of Saimaa Lines, the steamship company which operates a service through the canal, where my reception was very pleasant, but where I was told I would first have to solve the Soviet part of it, which was all handled by Intourist, whose agent was officed in the Finland Travel Bureau in town. The American consulate offered little help, except to advise me to stay away from the Soviet Embassy, which had nothing to do with foreign visitors, and to confer with a Mr. Novitsky, the Intourist man. So we trolleyed down town and presented ourselves at Mr. Novitsky's office, but he sent out word that he was "busy" and suggested we telephone again in the morning.

"At what time should I telephone?" I asked.

"Just try any time," the girl replied.

"When does Mr. Novitsky come in?"

"Sometimes he comes late, sometimes he does not."

"When does he go out to lunch?"

"We do not know."

"I think I understand," I said. "Thank you very much for your help."

I could see my chances were dimming.

In the morning I went first to the office of the Waterway Authority of Finland, across the street from Mr. Novitsky's building, where a young engineer most helpfully found me an English-language copy of the canal regulations. It appears that the treaty, or terms of lease, between Finland and the Soviet Union classifies ships permitted to use the canal as:

1. All Soviet vessels.
2. All Finnish vessels except military.
3. All other commercial vessels.

So Finnish and Soviet pleasure vessels may use the canal, but no other yachts. And the Finns must follow a cumbersome procedure: they must give notice in advance, clear their passage, follow a prescribed route offshore to a checkpoint far out from the canal, arrive there at a fixed time regardless of weather, maintain radio contact at fixed intervals, proceed at prescribed speeds, and report for entry into the canal at a fixed time and place. Not the easiest set of rules for a small sailboat in strange, far northern, rock-strewn waters to adhere to. Anyway, we were American flag. The Finnish authorities would be delighted to have us visit their lakes and canal; all I must do is get Mr. Novitsky to authorize an exception to the rule.

"I'll go and see him now," I said. "Would you call his office for me and ask if he's in?"

The answer was that Mr. Novitsky would "perhaps" be in at 1000. At 1010 I walked into the office and told the receptionist that I had just called in and that I was here to see Mr. Novitsky. I was ushered into his inner office, a scruffy and extraordinarily littered cubby with just room for a chair for me between his unoccupied desk and that of a secretary, who was definitely not the type to excite the James Bond in me; surly and frowzy, she gave me a silent, sullen look and went back to her typing. Mr. Novitsky would be with me in a moment, the receptionist said and left. Time passed, the secretary ignored me, Mr. Novitsky remained absent. Then the receptionist was back, red faced and obviously flustered. Mr. Novitsky was "busy in a meeting"; could I leave word how long I would be in Helsinki and where he could telephone me? By now I had the message, but for fun I would play out the game.

"Yes, I'll be here all today and until noon tomorrow. Anytime he calls I can be available to come in to see him at once."

All day the phone was silent, our message box at the front desk empty. At dinner time that evening a report of a telephone message was delivered to our room. Mr. Novitsky would be "on a journey" tomorrow and would not return until after I had left Helsinki. I turned over the slip to note the hotel's time stamp on its back, 1635. He had called still during business hours and had, I assume, instructed the hotel not to deliver until after hours. Maybe I'd been reading too many spy stories. But I don't think so. I like to picture Mr. Novitsky cowering in some back room until the receptionist had carried out his orders to "get that man out of here." I sincerely hoped that Mr. Novitsky didn't know what I knew: that all he had to say was, "I am so sorry, but foreign yachts are not permitted. It is impossible." ("It is impossible" is a favorite explanation of Soviet authorities.) I hoped he was haunted by the problem of avoiding responsibility for turning loose a lone capitalist, worse, a capitalist with a yacht, into his socialist society, that he didn't know how he could plausibly refuse, that if he didn't he would soon be promoted to the Intourist office in Outer Mongolia instead of sophisticated Helsinki. So much for you, Mr. Novitsky.

But he could have had the last laugh. It was after I had left the Baltic altogether and had other plans afoot that I learned we could probably have sailed from Helsinki across to Tallinn in former Estonia, a short hop and the goal of various races and cruises from Finland. I never checked out what barriers might have arisen to that, but many Scandinavians felt sure that Tallinn was an open port to foreign yachts and that I had missed my chance to add the Soviet Union to the list of countries we have visited.

By then I was turning my attention to visiting East Germany. Just as there are many roads to socialism, there are many waterways leading to the Rhine, and it was our intention to go up the Rhine to Switzerland. Since we were in the Baltic we could go across to the Elbe River by one of two routes, the Kiel Canal, which comes in downstream from Hamburg, or the canal from Lübeck, which enters the Elbe upstream from Hamburg. Having arrived on the Elbe by either route, one can proceed downstream to the North Sea and reenter European waterways at any one of half a dozen North Sea ports, or one can go upstream and join the Mittelland Kanal near Magdeburg. This canal links via other waterways to the Rhine. Since we don't like the storms and fogs and shallows and dirty water of the German Bight, that North Sea coast of Germany, we preferred to go via Lübeck and Magdeburg. But one hindrance stood in our way. A day or two of this route would lie in East Germany, as the border had been drawn closely west of the junction between the Elbe and the Mittelland Kanal, and the new bypass canal being built by the West Germans would not be completed until the following year.

So I sought permission. I tried the East German tourist agency in Stockholm, where a very pleasant woman, speaking only German and Swedish, advised me that she had no written instructions about their waterways and was unable to discuss it in the absence of such instructions, and that I would have to write to the proper ministry in Berlin, which I did. Swedish nationals, she said, could sail to Rostock and Warnemünde, but could not proceed inland, and she had no instructions about other foreign flags. (It is my impression that it is quite all right, that the East Germans follow the normal conventions with respect to calling vessels, but one wants to watch one's step.)

Germans feel more compelled to answer their mail than do the Russians: Alles in Ordnung! The weeks went by, and in due course I received a reply from the Democratic Republic. It read: "It is impossible."

So we have never been picked up by Soviet or East German patrols ourselves. In fact the next place we *were* picked up by a patrol boat was, of all places, Switzerland. Having spent two weeks climbing the Rhine, we had arrived at Basel with little idea where to lie; you know how confusing it is to arrive in a strange port with heavy traffic and a swift current. For a short distance the Rhine forms the border between Germany and Switzerland, but then one reaches the spot where Switzerland straddles the river, and it is there, on the right bank, our port side, that the customs and immigration office lie at the entrance to an extensive basin out of the current. But as we brought this abeam we happened to have a large barge paralleling our course and effectively blocking our view of the scene, thus missing it entirely, and we finally edged alongside a Rhine steamer at a small quay in the center of town. We were still debating where to go when the patrol boat came. Why had we not stopped at customs? "Cast off and follow me."

I didn't know whether we were being assisted or arrested, but we got ourselves out into the river again and drifted downstream while the patrol checked some vessel in midstream, then followed him back to what proved to be an unquestionably better berth in a quiet corner of the basin, under a spreading tree, with a fresh water tap nearby. A wire mesh fence fifteen feet away proved to be the German border. We were in Switzerland, but not by very much. "Wait here," the patrol ordered, and motored off. We must have seemed innocent enough, because soon the customs came over, the formalities were easily concluded, and our explanation for slipping by them the first time accepted. They even changed some money for us so we could use the telephone on shore.

Our most dramatic arrest by a patrol boat occurred in Greece. We had come into the harbor of Kalymnos in the Dodecanese to get out of the wind for lunch, and anchored amongst a group of small fishing craft, ignoring the striped yacht berth onto which the *meltemi* was blasting with full force. At once one of the boys in the white middy, the uniform of the harbor patrol under the colonels, came off in a rowboat, and a conversation rather as follows took place in Greek (I never know whether a Greek on the other end of a conversation with me would report the same input):

"What are you doing here?"

"We have come from Kos and we are having lunch."

"If you come here you must tie up to the quay."

"But we do not stay here. After lunch we go to Vathi."

"No, you must come to the quay."

"No, there is much wind, too much wind."

"It is forbidden to anchor in the harbor."

"But all these boats around me, they are anchored."

"It is forbidden for them also."

"There is a big yacht anchored outside the harbor. I will go and anchor there."

"No, he is going to leave now."

"OK," I said, "so am I."

And with that we raised the offending anchor and all went below to eat while the *meltemi* blew us out of the harbor and we drifted slowly offshore. The first mouthfuls of goat cheese and resinated wine were just slipping down our throats when a launch containing about six troops with rifles pulled along-side and motioned me back into the harbor. They had the guns, after all, and I complied. In the harbor I was motioned to the quay, so I rounded up, dropped the hook again, and paid out scope until our counter was grazing the quay, where our friend in the white middy was standing, all seventeen years of him, I suspect, commanding what may have been his very first military operation.

"Well, what do you want?" I asked, leaning on the stern pulpit.

"I want a line to tie you up," he said.

I hoped he meant to tie up the boat, and passed a stern line to him.

"Now," he said, "I must get my superior."

Shortly a spruce young officer appeared and conversation resumed:

"What are you doing here?"

"We came here to eat our lunch in peace. Then we go to Vathi."

Poor fellow, I think he really grasped the situation and was on my side, but he had to save face for himself and for his young assistant. Blushing deeply he said, "That will be all right. But you must pay harbor dues for entering Kalymnos."

"Of course," I said.

"I will prepare the papers," he said and climbed back to his office overlooking the quay.

During lunch the papers came, with copies for me and for Athens, all signed and rubber stamped. And the harbor dues? Thirteen cents! Zeal had been vindicated; justice had triumphed; employment had been furnished and would continue to be, as clerks somewhere posted my harbor dues in great ledgers and accounted for its allocation and filed copies of the documents in government offices across the land. And we could now finish our lunch.

I mentioned that I had responded to the guns, which I guess is my usual reaction, at least if they represent authority, but I guessed wrong once in Turkey. On the south side of the peninsula that lies only a mile from the Greek island of Samos is little St. Paul's Port, and we put in there one Sunday with a mainsail torn by the *meltemi.* A fellow sailor had reported two weeks earlier that it was a suitable and frequented spot, but we found ourselves quite alone.

While I was rowing around checking depths after anchoring, a fairly usual procedure in a new and narrow harbor, two men appeared on the deserted shore, one with a rifle and wearing what might have been a fatigue uniform, and the other in plain clothes. The Turkish shores are full of hunters, often wearing bits of cast-off uniform, and this man looked particularly disreputable, so when he motioned in a most peremptory way for me to come in I thought of the four women I had on the boat and the isolation of this cove and pretended to ignore him. But he persisted—the Turkish gesture is not a beckoning, but rather a motion akin to slapping one's thigh, but with the arm slightly to one side, a gesture as authoritative in its appearance as is the Turkish word "Yok" for "No" in its sound. When I finished checking depths I went back on board to consult about taking in our papers, still torn as to whether I should get close enough to let them get their hands on the dinghy. When I came back on deck they had solved the problem; they were toiling away up and over a trail across the hills and soon disappeared. What we did not know was that directly over the hill on the extremity of the point was a Turkish military lookout post. This is not a reinforced concrete bunker with a slit window, as you might expect in our civilized world, but is a little roof of woven rushes supported on four frail posts, shading a table and two chairs. Very practical: cool, airy, and unlimited visibility. No doubt our man was on patrol from this post, and no doubt he had communication with Kuşadasi, the nearest Turkish control point twenty miles up the coast. Because in the late afternoon, as we finished our sail work, we noticed a power boat heading our way, throwing sheets of spray in the whitecapped sea outside the harbor. "Company at last," we said. And then, "Hand me those binoculars.—You know what that is? That's a patrol boat. Get fenders and lines to starboard; stand by to repel boarders, because he won't have any reason for coming in here except us."

Arriving at a mutual understanding in Greek is tough, but in Turkish it is tougher. I have always suspected that on Sundays these boats are doing double duty, as yacht and patrol, as we so often found girls and friends on a patrol boat making its Sunday rounds. Fortunately one of the friends this time, dressed in sports clothes, spoke a bit of English.

"What is your trouble?" was his question.

This sort of threw me, as I had been expecting the usual type of paperwork question: Where from? Where to? What hour will you leave? and had been trying to think of the right expressions in Turkish. I started to stumble into saying nothing was wrong and then realized I had to cover up for everybody. I had to produce an acceptable story for entering what might be a restricted harbor, our friend's advice notwithstanding, and for why we would stay there for the night, and one which would justify this patrol boat's joyride on a Sunday. Best, of course, if they could either arrest a spy or perform a rescue at sea, but I didn't really need either treatment. We showed them the new stitching, the palm and needle and sail twine, made blowing faces and ripping motions.

"You have motor?"

"Yes, we have motor."

"Motor is good?"

"Yes, motor is very good."

They must be considering ordering us on to Kuşadasi, but it was late and the wind was up to Force 6 and dead ahead.

"You have two motors?"

"No," sadly, "we have only one motor."

There was a conference; our papers were checked and found in order.

In my best Turkish I addressed the commander: "Tomorrow Kuşadasi to coming I am. Tomorrow that place at seeing you we will."

To my relief he accepted this, he took a last appreciative look at the girls on board, and with a roar of his twin engines and a cloud of black smoke they took off on their next errand of mercy.

Turkish patrols are funny; I really don't know what's going on in their minds. Sailing a straight course, miles from shore, at noon on a clear day, with all our colors showing, I have had a patrol come from the farthest horizon straight to me, fall in alongside to port, to ask where our Turkish flag is, which all boats show to starboard, and on my giving him a hard luff and pointing at the starboard spreader, get a friendly acknowledgement in return and see them zoom away. The only time that we should perhaps have been booked, we were ignored. We were beating up from Samos to Chios, Greek islands, and sailing on Greek papers and flying Greek colors to starboard. It's a long way to windward, and we decided to put into a completely uninhabited cove on the Turkish side as a harbor of refuge for the night. We did have the foresight to replace the cross of St. George with the star and crescent. The cove was good because a dogleg at its inner end afforded landlocked protection, and as we turned that corner, there was a Turkish patrol at anchor. Too late now to turn and flee, very suspicious action at that hour, we decided to give the appearance of being in the right, and steamed up to anchor nearby with a friendly wave, as if they were welcome to share our harbor. And we waited for the usual boarding party, but it never came. No one even much looked our way, and this was strange, as these coves are know as centers for smuggling activities. But we think we got our answer at dusk, when the commander of the patrol appeared from the woods near the shore, with a little box under his arm, and was rowed off to his ship, where they continued to ignore us. And at 0300, with a burst of engines, the boat took off and disappeared around the bend. All the time, we suspected, they were much more worried that we were going to visit them than we had been about their checking us.

Turkey is out in front the leader in officiousness of the countries we have visited, although I have heard tales of Arab and African and Latin American countries which sound worse. But I can give the would-be visitor to Turkey some helpful hints. The coast is dotted with ports of entry, which sounds convenient, but each of these serves as a semiautonomous control point for its local area, and each treats an incoming yacht as if it were an ocean vessel arriving from foreign lands, even though you may have sailed nonstop from the last control port between breakfast and the happy hour. Along the south coast between Cape Krio and Antalya, for example, there are Datça, Marmaris, Fethiye, Kaş, Finike, and Antalya itself. When you enter at any one of these it is wise to state your farthest out turnaround, not your next port, as your intended destination, as this may enable you to escape some of the routine at intermediate ports. Then again, it may not; there seems to be little pattern. And with documents to the outermost port you may find you can bypass the control ports. You can if you don't anchor conspicuously in sight of them, in which case they will probably send a small boat to order you in. On the other hand, any place which offers shopping and supplies will be a control port, so you can't escape them all. If we must go into a control port it is our experience that we will be handled more efficiently if we state that we are moving on the same day. Then we are handled on an in-and-

out basis, while if we spend the night we find we must clear in
the morning with all the same officials we entered with the
evening before.

On entering you may first have to fill out a form for quarantine at the office of the port doctor, the *sağlik*. The sad *sağlik*
will ask many sad questions, such as how many deaths occurred
in the thirty-mile voyage, the cases of smallpox, cholera, and
plague, and where you last took on fresh water. The immigration police will want to see all passports and to keep a copy of
your crew list, which gives dates of birth and passport numbers
of all on board. The harbormaster, the *liman başkanliği*, will
have his declaration to be filled out and long entries to make in
vast record books. I have counted thirty-three columns of entries
for one visit from our little boat. On the declaration I must
print such things as the owner's name and address and the captain's name and address (it will not do to say, "Same"); the
nature of my captain's license (which is always a problem when
the owner-captain comes from a country which has not yet
mastered the art of licensing everyone who sails his own boat);
the number of life rings and life jackets (any number in the
blank will do, as it is never verified); and the name, citizenship,
and passport number of all hands (even though a photocopied
crew list with all these facts has just been presented).

Somewhere along the line a form has been filled out and a
charge made for the lighthouse. If you can't produce a receipt
for the lighthouse fee from the previous port you will likely be
billed for both. It doesn't matter that you navigate only by
day; I'm not even sure it matters whether the port has a lighthouse.

Then one moves on to the customs, the *gümrük*, or in some
ports the Grasping *Gümrük*, where the same information is repeated on different forms, and I will say more about the *gümrük*
by and by. There is no precise routine in which these visits are
to be made; there seems to be a pecking order which varies
from port to port. Just when you think you have mastered the
fact that customs must come before the harbormaster you find
yourself in a port where he must be final. Nor are the forms or
questions the same from place to place. I just keep all the wad

of sheets, accumulated from prior ports, clipped together and present the pile to every office. Sometimes they extract a sheet and make up what appears to be a duplicate; sometimes they add a missing sheet; sometimes they are upset because the last port omitted some essential paper.

Nor are the officials we deal with all of a kind, and in due course of time one learns which doctor expects American cigarettes, to which customs officer one should slip a small bottle of duty-free whiskey, which harbormaster will appreciate the latest American porno magazine, all status symbols in the modern Turkey. And some shake you down for money and some are kind and generous.

In Bozburun, a tiny village and no port of entry, but still with a customs office, the officer asked our wants; when we said it was for fresh vegetables, he led us first to the only store and, their supply being exhausted, disappeared to come back with his arms filled with fresh vegetables from his own garden, for which he would accept nothing.

And there are the officious ones. I think of Ayvalik, a rather open waterfront down the length of which the wind off the Troad churns the anchorage into dancing whitecaps, the same wind that blew around the windy walls of Troy. We made to anchor in the slight lee of a small projection of buildings and were hailed by an officer on shore and ordered around to lie off the customs building, the windiest spot on the waterfront, where our stern was not too far off those same projecting buildings. The main sewer outfall is situated here, and the polluted water leaps in multicolored pinnacles of reflected waves. We were ordered to tie the dinghy, chafing along the stone bulkhead of the customs compound, which itself was filled with wrecked cars, no doubt of tourists who had come to grief and who had abandoned their wrecks rather than pay import duty on a car which could no longer be driven back out. Rusted sheet metal banged in the wind. Access to town was through a padlocked gate.

Having attended to preliminary paper work on shore and to save our guests this dismal landing, I now rowed them around to the landing in the lee, where we were met again by customs.

He allowed the ladies to get ashore, but ordered me back with the dinghy to the windy customs side, stepping in for the trip to make sure I did, and forbidding me to land elsewhere.

"But how do we get back past the gate at night?" I asked.

"That is all right," he said. "The padlock is never locked. Just pull on it and it will open."

Mana siz muşkalat!

We lay there overnight, restless and smelling the sewage, and the wind picked up so that I had to carry out a second anchor and then a line to shore. Although I had said we would leave at 1000, I was back in at 0900, all of us ready to go. But nothing could be done until 1000, because that is when they had told the police I would clear. The harbormaster filled out a large document in duplicate, stamped and signed by all parties. Then he hand copied my crew list, of which I had a photocopy for him. Then he opened his desk drawer, took out a key and a bottle of hair oil, put some oil on my head, unlocked a safe, and took out a pad of small documents and filled out a set, which were stamped and signed and sealed. So back to customs, where a long sheet of particulars was typed out, which I had to stamp and sign in two places, and with which he then disappeared, to return with a small form signed and stamped by them. He then took from his briefcase a pad of a third form, some of which had been filled out on our arrival eighteen hours earlier, and now made out a set of these for our departure. He then completed the last of the thirty-three columns in his record book, stamped and signed the document from the harbormaster's office, took his third copy of my crew list, which both of us now stamped and signed, and pinned all the papers together. Then six armed men stood on the quay and watched as we rowed back over the dancing sewage, warmed up the engine, and brought in our shore and anchor lines, heavily coated with foul mud.

No hard feelings, Ayvalik. It was all done in a friendly way, with innumerable glasses of tea at your expense. It's just that you'll never see me there again.

Venality is not new in the human race and while Americans seem to go through cycles of tolerating it or laughing at it from time to time when practiced by local politicians at home, we are invariably indignant when we are looked upon as a source of a bit of petty bribery by foreign officials. In our own case I do not recall encountering this anywhere other than in Turkey, where our reaction was a mixture of indignant shock and amusement. On our first cruise down the south coast of Turkey, Cynthia and I were alone on board and we came in due course into the little port of Kaş on a sizzling afternoon. This was before the present breakwater and quay were built on top of the submerged ledge at the harbor mouth, so we dropped an anchor in the center of the little round bay about two hundred feet from shore, and even before we were properly coiled down a shoreboat was bumping alongside, from which five leather-booted men, four with pistols on their hips, stamped on board and down into the cabin. I asked if they would like a beer. "No. Whiskey!" their spokesman said, bringing his fist down on the cabin table. We had been told not to give Turks whiskey, that they are unused to it and unable to handle it, a charge I very much doubt, but we were outnumbered and outgunned, and anyway I was grateful to get all the officials over with at one time and the red tape finished. So I gave each a shot glass of good whiskey (they refused water with it) and the ship's papers and asked the spokesman, who had a fair command of English, which office he represented.

"Customs," he said.

"And the man beside you?"

"He is my assistant."

"And these other two men?"

"All customs. All my men. When we finish you go on land. You see doctor, police, and harbormaster."

"But who is the fifth man with no gun?"

"He has boat to bring us out."

And there he was, smugly drinking my whiskey.

With sinking heart I realized they might spend the entire afternoon inspecting my whiskey, glass by glass, the Turks seldom being beset by haste, except when behind the wheel of a car, but their own unusual haste in boarding us proved to be their undoing. They had not given us time to rig the

awning or curtain the windows or open the hatches. The afternoon sun poured through the plate glass of the main cabin and
the four customs men in hot uniforms, huddled together in the
sun on our dinette seat, and having bolted their whiskey neat,
soon had more sweat running down their faces than we did.
The cabin air, with seven of us in it, was becoming rank, and I
am sure the open shade of the *taverna* ashore seemed more
appealing by the minute. Soon they left us, the boatman now
adding injury to insult by producing a bill for his services in
rowing two hundred feet to drink our whiskey.

This sort of thing would be infuriating were the amounts involved not so small as to be meaningless in the overall cost of
running a boat, and the methods employed so amusingly con-
spiratorial. But under any circumstances I found it a great
effort to go along graciously with what seemed to us to be an
affront to our moral principles.

Then, a couple of years later, we found ourselves on a tour
of Iranian archeological sites, culminating with Persepolis, the
site of the ritual capital of the Persian Empire under the Great
Kings like Xerxes and Darius. Here in the most magnificent
palace of the empire the Great King held court once a year to
receive the ambassadors of each of the twenty-three tributary
kingdoms, who came with their servants bearing ritual gifts to
the Great King. In splendid reliefs around the walls of the
palace foundation, marching on in endless procession, come the
tribute bearers, each carrying or leading some gift representative
of his own kingdom: bolts of fine cloth, necklaces of gold, hives
of honey, flocks of sheep, shaggy ponies from Scythia, horse-
drawn chariots. And, moving slowly along this drama of the
past, I was overwhelmed by the feeling that this is how the
Near East has been for the 3,000 years of recorded history.
When a stranger or a foreigner comes to the authorities, he
comes with a gift; it is a time-honored custom, simple courtesy
by their standards. Is it my place to come sailing in from an
upstart country in my fine boat and demand that they jump to
take care of me? They are public servants, yes, but do we expect
them to be imbued with the same feeling for service that we
hope to get at home (if we do)? The Turks are by culture a

most gracious and courteous people. The American who wants to "get it done" is in constant conflict with their custom that the process of doing it is of more pleasure than the completion of it. It should be done with relaxation, with graciousness and politeness, over countless little glasses of tea or cups of thick coffee, at their expense. They are generous with that on shore as they expect me to be with our liquids on board, for to complete our first episode at Kaş, when we once came ashore, we were at once invited to the customs office for coffee. When the last rubber stamp has been pressed onto the document and dated and initialled over, and the last column in the massive ledger filled in, the official seems a little sad. His day's work may be finished, his contact with the big world broken again.

In tourist centers, like Greek Mykonos, where the crowds are handled with cold efficiency and the townspeople regard any tourist as a thing from which to extract a bit of money and cast aside, we complain of the impersonality of the contact, but in the small Turkish port, where an hour or two may be spent on papers, we become at least very real, individual people. Years later when we return to Kaş, we are greeted with friendly smiles. "We remember you," says the present chief of customs. "You are the boat that gave us whiskey when I was assistant." And they are gracious and friendly and from time to time we drink their coffee and from time to time a quarter-pint bottle of whiskey is with my papers, and I tell myself this is not smuggling, not *bakşiş*, but simple courtesy, honoring the custom of the ages.

This paper work could probably all be done in an hour if the offices were staffed throughout the working day, but all too often the busy official is away, the office standing open and empty, communication with the children loitering in the door difficult.

In Kaş I once walked to the harbormaster's office to find it thus empty, then across the village to the customs office to ask if he knew where the harbormaster might be, only to find it empty, too. But I found the customs chief under an awning on the sidewalk engaged with the policeman in a violent bout of tric trac, the Turkish national sport, while four soldiers sat around to kibitz. A chair was pulled up for me and I was told that the harbormaster was in the mosque for the hour of prayer. It is true that we had heard the call of the muezzin. So I joined the kibitzers, passing around to them a Chamber of Commerce pictorial folder of Seattle: Puget Sound white with sails; Mt. Rainier white with snow; the Space Needle with its restaurant that goes around and around 400 feet up in the air; and it all seemed rather implausible to this group and less interesting than the game in front of them.

The customs chief finally slammed down his last counters on the tric trac board and began to tell us about the yachts.

"There are many French yachts this year. And those French girls, they are very sexuelle. Do you not find them sexuelle? But I am married now. I cannot look." And he covered his eyes and the soldiers laughed.

"But surely you can look. Maybe you can't touch, but it is all right to look."

"No, I am married. I cannot even look." And with mock sadness he covered his eyes again.

Then the doors of the mosque opened and the faithful came out, and I walked off in the sun toward the harbor office.

"When you finish, you come see me," called the customs man. "If Allah wills it, you may be able to sail today."

On the west coast of Turkey, which we visited first in 1976, although it is cruised more than the south coast, we found the shakedown a bit more systematized. On our first of three visits to Bodrum the customs took me for 50 lira (about three dollars), after sending everyone else out of the room.

On our second visit I cursed my lack of foresight when the same moment arrived and I found I had only a 100-lira note in my wallet. "That's all right," the customs man implied. "I'll take 100 now and when you come back tomorrow for permission to sail, I won't take any more." Then on our third visit to Bodrum the harbormaster, who spoke English, said most purposefully, "Customs, police, doctor, no money. Only lighthouse money. No money customs."

"Aha!" I thought, "a new day has dawned. They're clamping down."

And so to customs where a new man behind the desk, looking clean and crisp and blond and with a clipped reddish mus-
tache, more British than Turk, filled out our forms with expedition. But as he was finishing a very relaxed official came in
and slumped in an armchair. By and by he began asking questions. He tried to find out if our passports were in order (which
they were, but it was no business of his). Then about com-
pressors and air bottles. Then if it was true that only two of
us could be on such a big boat. Then about whiskey.

"How much whiskey do you have?"

"Four bottles."

"That's a lot of whiskey."

"I know."

"For two people you are allowed only two bottles."

"Yes, but usually we have friends with us."

"Where is the boat now?"

"It's across the harbor at anchor. Our small boat is over
there."

"I must inspect your boat."

This was the moment of truth, because Turkish inspections
are said to be a horrid nuisance, with everything turned out of
every space, a method of harassment, not of search. I was supposed to blanch and offer some preventive medicine, but I
jumped up and said, "Let's go now."

It worked. He backed away and suggested I might just bring
him the excess whiskey. I said I would be honored to make him
a gift from America and that I would bring it at eight o'clock
when we came in for dinner.

At 2000 I was crossing the quay with a tote bag holding a
water filter carton containing the bottle. The customs man met
me half way, grasping my hand, being a Grasping *Gümrük*,
and we walked across the square holding hands, Turkish
fashion, while it occurred to me that he wasn't going to let go
until he had his bottle.

I am always torn by such an exchange. Am I really trying to
go along with tradition, or am I rationalizing a cop-out? Am I
a coward, or am I simply pragmatic, paying a modest price to
buy freedom from interference and get on with my main

objective, which is comfortable cruising for my family and my guests? Am I an ambassador of good will for America? Would I be an ugly American if I insisted that my ship was American soil and the contents thereof none of their business? Or that they could seal the excess, if they wished, as was done in Bermuda? Should I fight the system in order to make it easier for the next yachtsman? If I have any moral principles, should I let them down for some petty Turkish official? Of if I hung tough, would I merely be indulging in the American sport of playing missionary to no good purpose?

These poor devils are underpaid, and when we have come in our yachts to enjoy their harbors and sail their waters, should we deny them this modest sharing of the wealth? Long ago I learned that life often confronts us with the choice of being a sucker or a bastard, and that if I knowingly choose to be the former I can sleep better and live more happily with myself. Each must make his own choice.

So up a side street we walked, hand in hand, to stop by the wall of a mosque, our backs to the street, heads bowed over the tote bag, while he made sure he was getting the real thing. We might have been commending our fates to Allah, bowing there by the mosque, so I said, "*Allasmarladik*" ("I commend you to Allah"), and he replied, "*Güle, güle*," which means, "Laugh, laugh," but connotes, "Go smiling," or, in American, "Have a nice day, now."

At Çeşme, farther up the coast, it was 100 lira, because I was planning to call at the Golden Dolphin hotel marina around the point, "and we must take taxi to control you when you come in and again when you go out." What I knew, although they didn't know I knew it, was that the last American to call at Çeşme had also been shaken down for 100 lira, although he had moored right in front of their office. I demurred, they insisted (and technically they could have been correct), and I paid.

"Now do we have to wait for them to come to the Golden Dolphin?" Cynthia asked.

"Don't worry," I said. "I doubt if there's any chance of their coming."

And of course they didn't.

At Altinkum, the port for the temple of Didyma, we had heard there lived a particularly officious grasping *Gümrük*, and since we had no intention of missing this site we decided to try to smother him with kindness and see what results we could get. Sure enough, he was alongside almost before we were well anchored, but I greeted him as best I could in Turkish with a "Do me the honor of coming on board, sir," instead of a "What the hell do you want," and I had the little bottle and the cigarettes laid out with our papers and was able to say, "Gift you for America from." He was visibly thrown off balance by this treatment and had the grace to say, "Thankings making I am," and then, "Very thankings making I am." But I can't say we gained much more than that, because he still managed to double as commission man for the local taxi company, who no doubt charged us double for a trip to the temple of Didyma, while his boatman outside was extracting his little fee for service from our guest on deck.

While Turkey has easily been the front runner in the race of producing difficulties without logic, Italy has been far and away the loser. It is almost as if the Italians didn't know how to make things difficult for the tourist. At our first port of entry into Italy in 1968 on the island of Sardinia we had to go ashore and comb the town to locate a policeman, who seemed as confused as we were, made some notes on the back of an envelope, and told us we were in. We then cruised Italy for four weeks before finally at Riposto down the east coast of Sicily officialdom caught up with us, and we were told we must have a *costitutto*, the document good for "all coasts." The main question I can recall their asking us was the names of the fathers of everybody on the boat, suspecting, no doubt, the presence of a kidnapped Sicilian bride on board. A romantic lot, the Italians.

A *costitutto* is good for twelve months, too, and we surrendered ours at Syracuse a week after getting it, when we cleared for Malta. In the spring we were back, and on reporting to the harbor office in Syracuse I presented my document, saying they would find a valid *costitutto* for my boat in their files. My document is a temporary one as the ship has not yet been in the Coast Guard District of her home port, and the word *Temporary* is typed into the top margin.

"*Bene, bene,*" the official said. "You and your friends, you go ashore and enjoy Syracusa. We will have it ready when you return."

But on our return that afternoon I found long faces.

"We have searched," they said, "but we find no *costitutto* for the yacht *Temporary.*"

"Ah, no, no, no," I explained. "The yacht is not *Temporary.* The yacht is *Cynthia.*" (In Italian it comes out *Chintzy.*) "That is the name of my wife."

"Ah, si, si, si," their faces brightened, "I understand. Your boat is *Chintzy.* Your wife is Temporary."

"It's a tough life," I mumbled.

IX

Ice Is Priceless

And ice mast high
Came floating by . . .
Coleridge, *The Rime of
the Ancient Mariner*

Ice is not the only thing which is priceless, of course. Calm after storm, wind after a calm, and the love of a good woman; safe harbor after a passage, blue waters after days in port, and a companion to share all this are among the truly priceless experiences of cruising. But I am thinking now that of those things for which we normally may expect to pay, ice is one of the most variable in price.

Within a certain range we know what we are going to pay for a gallon of fuel or a fathom of chain or a year of insurance, but ice? What is a pound of ice worth? Well, according to the economists it ought to be worth whatever a willing buyer is prepared to pay to get it, and in the Exuma Cays in 1968 it was worth ten cents a pound. This was good solid, blue, subzero ice, but still the most expensive we have ever found in ten years of fighting an increasingly iceless society. It is getting so that the more industrialized communities just don't sell ice any more. Everyone has his electric refrigeration, and no market exists, which makes it quite difficult for the little boat with the old-fashioned ice box.

And why have an old-fashioned ice box? There are all sorts of marine refrigeration systems on the market, and this was true some years ago when we were working out the specifications for the *Cynthia R.* We had a number of reasons: an aversion to the odd mechanical noises which turn off and on in the night, a desire for simplicity, the generally low opinion of artificial refrigeration held by the long-distance cruisers I knew at the time, the stories of boats arriving in Tahiti whose first act was to throw their refrigerators overboard, our own experience on other boats, where the refrigerator was used for storage of canned goods and the ice, if any, carried in a styrofoam-lined deck box, and a bit of panic at the mounting cost of our involvement in this project. But most of all it was the thought of running down the ship's batteries, the real essential in bringing every modern mechanical system to life.

Since then I have had no regrets at avoiding electrical, gas, or kerosene-fired refrigerators, but I will confess to second thoughts about the holding plate run off a simple compressor, belt driven from the main engine. I assume that such a system can be designed to furnish a deep-freeze compartment, create its own ice cubes, and hold the storage part at cooler temperatures than anything we achieve with less than a full ice compartment, while simultaneously releasing a certain amount of additional cold-storage space now occupied with nonproductive ice or simply air, as the ice melts down. The disadvantages are apparent. It costs money, it requires maintenance, it can break down even with maintenance (things do, you know), it requires sophisticated engineering to design and install—engineering unavailable where we have been cruising—and it requires operation of the engine for maybe thirty minutes twice a day to run the compressor. In normal cruising we probably do run the engine that much getting under way and coming in, and we would just have to swallow our pride when in port and join the group we now sneer at who run their engines at their moorings. On ocean passages the charm of silent sail, day after day, would perforce give way to some routine engine noise. Were we to leave our boat untended in port for periods longer than twenty-four hours, which is rare, we would simply have to plan ahead so that no valuable foods were left for spoilage. On a couple of occasions in ten years our engine has been down for several days, and here, no doubt, some wastage would occur after one had taken advantage of the emergency to live high on the freezer while it lasted. But still, the stories of hundreds of dollars' worth of spoiled food due to refrigeration breakdown, while the crew subsists on short rations, give one pause.

So let's see how we have fared with simplicity and with ice. From the launching of the boat in 1967 until the spring of 1976 we could accurately say that we had never involuntarily run out of ice. Then in April of 1976, when we moved on board and provisioned the boat, the ice plant of Rhodes was closed for repairs. Not only we, but all of Rhodes was out of ice, and we sailed for Turkey a few days later with no ice for the first time. I should add that within twelve hours we had filled the ice compartment in Turkey, but the record was broken. Would any refrigeration system have held us that long? Or been repaired so quickly?

Our ice box has been a joy. It is one of those rare bits of design which has worked out even better than we might have hoped. The massive ice compartment can easily take over 200 pounds of ice if the blocks are not just the wrong shape. The bottom shelf can hold fifty tins or bottles of beer and soft drinks, and the middle and upper shelves ample quantities of those foods which like to be cool. It is a top-opening box, so the cold stays in, and so commodious that even with a thirsty crew on board there is almost always one more beer in some invisible corner, known only to the skipper, to be reached only with a batten. The insulation is a product called Zerocell, for which I have the utmost admiration. Even in the warmest weather a full charge of ice may last nearly two weeks, although this is largely dependent on the self-discipline of the crew. If, with lavish American taste, every warm bottle goes immediately onto the ice itself, one can melt it down pretty fast, but we try to keep our cool in little ways.

When the sun shines down the hatch we cover the exposed top with a pillow; where frozen foods exist we will buy a couple of days' supply of this and add its cooling to the ice; we buy our soft drinks and beer in tins instead of bottles wherever we can, and if they are warm we let them cool down on deck overnight before stowing them in the icebox; we do not insist ourselves that our drinking water be ice cold, tank temperature is quite all right, although American guests will run through several bottles of ice water a day; we do not serve the ice in drinks, because it is always from dirty sources anyway; the drain line to the sump has an elbow in it, so the cold air cannot drain out nor bilge smells be admitted to the box. With these precautions we have spent months in the Bahama Out Islands, crossed the Atlantic by the warm-water route, cruised the hot shores of Turkey and Greece and Yugoslavia in midsummer, and until that moment noted above never run out of ice.

It becomes somewhat of a game, and actually our search for ice has led us into many situations which are a part of the overall experience of cruising, pleasanter memories for the non-mechanical than crawling into the bilge to repair a piece of machinery.

Ice was easy enough to find along the East Coast, where the sophisticated marinas carry it and many towns have coin-op ice dispensers on convenient corners, and it was not until we hit the Bahamas that we came into that other world, that non-American world of short supplies, broken-down machinery, plans which never materialize, the world of "Haven't got" and "Come back tomorrow," which is actually most of the entire world except for those little islands of efficiency of the north-western European culture of which North America is a part.

We had chosen Rock Sound on Eleuthera Island as our winter base because it offered daily jet air service then from New York and Miami; a choice of open Rock Sound, where one could lie at anchor, or Davis Harbor, a small basin where one could tie up, with the amenities of a laundry, fuel, water, high quality provisions, and ice. But the ice machine at Davis Harbor had not arrived. It was due any time, "maybe in two weeks." That was in November, and when we left Rock Sound in May it was still due "maybe in two weeks." Meanwhile we had scrounged ice where we could, principally from the ice machines of the Rock Sound Club and the Cotton Bay Club, which turned out quantities of little, wet, lenticular pieces of ice, and we would treat ourselves to a dinner at the club and then sneak around to the machine behind the bar and fill a sail bag or two to hurry back to the boat. This ice itself cost nothing, the club undertaking indirectly to make up for the deficiencies of their marina, but substantial tips to the bar boys seemed in order, and there was transportation to be assimilated as part of our overall cost of living, and we felt we were contributing to the economy of Rock Sound.

Every cruise we took that winter included the Exuma Cays. That is the reason we had picked Eleuthera: from the south end where one comes off the shallow banks into deep Exuma Sound it is a crossing of from 20 to 40 miles of glorious tradewind sailing to make one of the cuts between the cays and come into this delightful chain of islands. A couple of sources of ice existed there, of which the best was at Staniel Cay; this is where we paid ten cents a pound for what the grinning manager referred to as "frozen silver," and were glad to get it.

Up the west coast of Eleuthera a day's sail from Rock Sound lies Hatchet Bay, one of the few all-weather harbors (barring hurricanes). This small community contained a frozen-food warehouse with a most amiable manager.

"Hi, Mr. Albury! How's chances of ice today?"

"No," he said, "I'm afraid we don't have ice, but I'll tell you what. It's about time I knocked the frost off the pipes and you're welcome to that."

So we went in with a couple of mallets, I rather dubious as to how much good "frost" was going to be in our ice box, and soon we were knocking off 4" thick collars of clear blue ice, so cold that it actually picked up its own frost, like a mint julep, on its way to our ice box. It was not in the most efficient shapes to stow, but it held us through another week.

On crossing the Atlantic we clearly faced a problem of fresh-food conservation and adopted a policy of no chilled drinks, which was really a hardship for us, as the weather during the first half of the trip was extremely warm and sticky. But it did mean that we had the full space of food storage for perishables, including fresh milk while it lasted, and by topping up with ice before sailing, after first chilling all the contents, we found the ice held even throughout the longest leg of the voyage, thirteen days, although the ice box was on the sunny side of the boat, heeled upwards by the south wind toward the midsummer sun. When we restocked a day after our arrival at Horta there was still a nubbin of ice in a far corner. After this the shorter passage to Gibraltar in cooler weather presented no problem.

Here we entered the Mediterranean side of that other world of ice procurement where each country had its own system and the search for ice became an adventure. In general we found that ice in Spain was sold at the fishhouse, which was situated nearby in the harbor, inasmuch as all the Mediterranean harbors of Spain were artificial breakwater-enclosed basins. Ice would come out from a cavernous dark chamber and be deposited on the curb among the dead fish and burro droppings. No matter that I had a clean canvas tote bag at the ready; it was always dropped in the gutter, rolled around a bit, and only then slid into the tote bags, which had already been taken from me and set in the gutter themselves. At first I fought the system, unsuccessfully, but after some years in the Mediterranean we accept it.

I think the dirtiest little place we ever found ice was on the island of Ischaia off the Bay of Naples. We had a rental car that day, to see the island, and we had been given directions to the ice house, but somehow it wasn't there. We drove back and forth on the road and finally zeroed in on a crummy warehouse building into whose basement a dirt-floored tunnel seemed to lead. On exploring this tunnel, which reeked of drains and urine, we came upon a heavy insulated door, padlocked, of the type we associate with ice. Across the tunnel was the door to an apartment, although it was difficult to imagine what sort of troglodyte could live here, but we knocked and an old woman in black appeared. The naked light bulb hanging by its wire overhead gave the impression that she was holding high a lantern in front of her.

"*Ghiaccio?*" one of us asked hopefully, and she disappeared into her cave to be replaced by a consumptive-looking old man, who coughed and coughed as he unlocked doors and dragged columns of half-melted and dirty ice onto the mud floor.

"Conspicuous consumption," Cynthia murmured.

We do not put ice in our drinks.

In Malta the procurement of ice was always a pleasure. It was sold here at the ice-cream factory, which is staffed largely by girls who appear to be age 14 and up, and if one could time one's pickup of ice to coincide with their tea break, or whatever break Maltese girls get, one was surrounded by the giggling best of Maltese girlhood, all eager to talk to the foreign millionaire who bought ice 200 pounds at a time. Of course, as this was Malta, one had other problems to contend with: Malta is said to be more Catholic than Vatican City, and the number of feast days (legal holidays to you and me) is enormous, on top of which are various other holidays imported from England and Italy, and if there is no holiday there is the likelihood that the Maltese are suffering from another bout of the English disease and are on strike. So all in all it was a bit of luck to time things properly.

Yugoslavia presents a new challenge to the ice buyer. Instead of coming from the fish house or the ice-cream factory it comes here from the Mesopromet, the meat combine. But go early; the blocks have been delivered to local butchers along with the day's meat and may be gone by mid-morning, as there appears to be no surplus in their system. Having missed it one day and having with us the type of American guest to whom there is no such word as *no*, we found ourselves in his rental car looking for the main freezer plant on the outskirts of Split. On the second or third pass through a suburb we located it, just at closing time, to be greeted by merry laughter from the quitting workmen, who indicated that the day was done and they were not about to start reopening the ice room for some foreign capitalist in a rented car. But around the loading zone for the meat trucks lay large fragments of ice from fallen blocks, melting in the parking area, and we were welcome to scoop these up if we chose. We did choose, collecting perhaps 100 pounds in this manner, which held our ice box for another week.

Perhaps I am maligning Yugoslavia when I mention this. It was a one-time occurrence, and in the yacht marina at Dubrovnik one could arrange for ice delivery in a most civilized manner.

As in most countries where fishing is a major local industry, the procurement of ice in Greece seems not too difficult. Most towns and most major islands have a small ice plant, and while you may not arrive at a time when there are any unsold columns on hand, you can at least usually program it for the following day. The Ionian island of Kefallinia presents a special problem, as a cruising boat is probably on its protected eastern side at the pleasant harbors of Sami or Agia Efemia or Fiskardo, while the ice is at Argostolion on the west side, a 40-mile sail in the open sea. It is best to rent a car and enjoy a tour of the island, but the rental cars are all at Argostolion, too, and one winds up with a bus trip across the island just to start things.

There is a certain routine in this ice game. If we are going after it ourselves, we try to learn first exactly where the ice is to be found, a good way to learn your way around a small town, and whether we expect to use a rental car or a taxi or what for transportation. Then out come the canvas tote bags and we are off to negotiate. Unlike *beer*, which is one of the more international words, *ice* comes out in many ways: *glace* in French, *ghiaccio* in Italian, *pagos* in Greek, *buz* in Turkish, each mutilated by varying dialects; but in any language it is delivered in columns, slightly tapering, of varying length, some square and some rectangular in cross-section. A typical column may weigh 20 kilos before it starts to melt (a rare find) and should be broken in half to handle conveniently in a tote bag. As I have said, the dealer will usually do this by breaking it on the curb so that one half falls into the gutter if no dirtier spot presents itself. He then seizes the bag, which you have carefully held up to keep it clean, and sets it down in the puddle the melting ice has made, rubs it around a bit, and moves on to the next. The soggy bags now go into the trunk of a taxi, over the driver's grumblings, and we pay off the ice house and hope the taxi driver takes us promptly home. Probably 200 pounds of melting ice in his trunk is the best guarantee that he will not subject us to a tour of the town, once we are captive, while his meter clicks away. If he is a nice taxi driver he will help carry the tote bags to ship's side and be rewarded with a good tip or a pack of cigarettes, though in a tourist town he will contemptuously deposit them in the gutter across the street from the quay and receive a very modest tip indeed. But I do tip even the least helpful, because hauling ice is not really the best way for a taxi to make money, he deserves something, and I may need him again.

Or it may be that we are at anchor and the bags are carried by hand or pushcart from icehouse to dinghy, rowed out, and then handed up in a choppy harbor while the dinghy tries to slide from under.

On deck, if Cynthia is ready for me, are several kettles of clean water. The ice is dumped on the bridge deck floor, and while I lift any unmelted shapes from the ice box into the galley sink, and retrieve any lost and rotting bits of food, Cynthia is rinsing the dirt from the new blocks into the cockpit drains. A half-column at a time, each weighing about 20 pounds now, is lowered into the ice compartment, and the puzzle faced of how to make as compact a mass as possible. We don't know until we try if they are going to go better vertically or lengthwise or across the ice compartment, and this stowage pattern can make a difference of 20 to 30 percent in the amount we can stow; increasing mass while cutting down surface area is all part of the game. The odd chunks of old ice are now broken up and used to fill the chinks. On a lucky ice day we will get ice fresh from the brine, full-sized columns at a few degrees above zero, laid on clean with no rinsing necessary, and of such shape that the pieces exactly fit our box. Another time it will be airy, rotten ice, the columns half melted away, dirt deep in all its pores, and of dimensions which, no matter how it is turned, are incommensurate with those of our box. And we may have paid more for this.

In Turkey we usually find some little man, eager to be our agent, who will procure ice for us. He may up the price 100 percent, but it is still cheaper than taking a taxi, and I feel he has served a useful purpose.

In the interior of Germany it was the brewery where I found

ice, apparently only they having the requisite machinery.

One would think that in the more modernized countries of the north no problem would exist, but in fact our greatest difficulty in finding ice occurred in the interiors of Holland and Sweden. These are all-electric countries now, and the need for old-fashioned ice has ceased to exist. But apparently they have not found the corner coin-op ice vending machine a profitable venture either, as it would be in America. Coin-op machines there are, all right, but dispensing *smörgåsar* or pornography, not ice. On the Göta Canal I believe we would have spoiled our record had not the kindly proprietor of the Kanalhotellet at Karlsborg produced, in addition to a memorably fine meal, a small brick of extremely cold and solid ice to reinforce our dwindling supply, along with those ice cubes the hotel could spare.

This sort of help, always gratis, was typical of the generosity I believe would be afforded any touring yachtsman in these places where a boat from America is scarcely a daily event. But we had hardly expected it when we looked for ice at Karlshamn, our port of entry into Sweden and, incidentally, a principal port of departure for the great wave of Swedish emigrants to America of a century or more ago. Unlike the electrified interiors of these countries, the small ports of the north are a rich source of ice, usually crushed ice, with which the hold of a fishing vessel is filled before it sets out on its run in the North Sea or the Baltic, and a towering ice house is usually easy to spot. At first I thought this crushed ice would not hold up like block ice, but the ability to fill the ice compartment solidly from top to bottom compensated for its lack of solidity.

At Karlshamn, then, we inquired when we could come alongside at a time not interfering with fishing-vessel traffic, and were able to catch ice in our tote bags from a chute at dockside. Having topped off the ice box, I went in to pay, knowing that our small 100 or 200 pounds was hardly worth billing, when they think in terms of shiploads, and found it was the owner of the ice-house chain himself who had come down, not only to see that we got our ice for nothing, but to invite these visitors from America to his home that evening for dessert, coffee, and liqueurs.

This is the sort of thing I mean when I say that ice is priceless.

Alcoholic beverages are another thing for which there is no real price structure. I have before me a sales slip for some of our purchases in Malta in 1970, when they were somewhat apologetic at the second jump in prices since we had first come in 1968, and I find that we were now paying $.99 a fifth for Beefeaters Gin, up from $.83 the year before. Johnny Walker Red Label went for the same price, and Black Label was up from $1.83 a fifth to $2.45. Old Forester Bonded 100 Proof was transported from America, stored, retailed and delivered to the boat, with the customs officer paid to see it placed on board, for $2.64 a fifth. Or, if you take to wine, I see that we placed on board a mixed case of Château Mouton Rothschild '63 and Gevrey Chambertin '64 at an average cost of $3.75 a bottle, delivered to the boat. Maybe these aren't the greatest years, but try to meet it today. Or try to have met it even then in America. The Bâtard Montrachet '64, at $2.70, was selling at home that year for $8.00.

Later that same year, and for the next two summers, we were in Scandinavia, where Black Label was $26.00 a fifth, and gin about half of that. Even today, on the island of Rhodes, Greece, Aalborg Akvavit costs less than it does in Aalborg, Canadian Club less than in does in Canada, Kentucky Tavern less than in Kentucky. Only Jack Daniels had been marked up to some astronomical figure bearing no relation to other prices.

So shopping for these things is rather fun, but marketing in general is a job I try to worm out of. A lot of gushy articles have appeared on the joy of buying provisions in those quaint market places, and when we have guests on board we hope they have read these and are looking forward to assisting in this bit of personal immersion into the local color.

Every two to three weeks it is inventory time. I suppose it would be possible to keep a running inventory, but we never do, and with the varying tastes of our guests and our ready stores always available for the odd snack or drink it would be futile. So lockers are opened, a rough count taken of supplies, and a rough estimate made of what we will need to see us through to the next spot where such luxuries as the Western palate requires can be found. For the most part this consists of examining the remaining contents of cartons in the permanent food storage behind the dinette, but it will also find me on my knees checking the voluminous ready stores in the galley. I am grumbling.

"Remember, there's always a flashlight right there in the ready stores," Cynthia calls.

"I did remember. It's just that it won't light."

"Well, you have to hold it upside down. Don't you know that?"

"I guess I didn't remember that."

"What is it you're trying to find? Maybe I know where it is."

"I was looking for the honey, the Greek honey. It's supposed to be in a blue-and-white can."

"No, I poured it into the Nescafé bottle with the brown top."

"That's salad oil in the Nescafé bottle."

"No, no, that's the wrong Nescafé bottle. Look for the one with the masking tape to hold the top together."

That's the way the typical marketing day starts, and if I can't think of something important to do like changing the oil in the diesel, I am likely to find myself in the market place. The typical market has nowhere to set down a tote bag except the pavement, covered with a litter of rotting fruit and vegetables or worse, unless it has just been hosed down and is all puddles. You have just been to the stalls selling tomatoes and eggs and grapes and are holding about ten pounds of these in a tote bag while picking out potatos and a melon from a huckster who speaks no known language and refuses to sell the desired quantity because the price is per kilo or per oka or some other occult measure, and since his knowledge of arithmetic is limited, he can only calculate in whole units, which may be several times what you need, and which is payable in an unfamiliar coinage from a currency whose value you have not yet grasped. While holding tote bags out of the filth, you must grub through your purse or pocket trying to figure which coins are of what denomination (and very frequently, due to repeated devaluations, a country may have several different sizes and types of coins in circulation for each denomination), meanwhile defending the eggs and grapes and tomatoes from having the melon and potatos jammed crushingly on top. Once is quaint. A lifetime of it is a bit long.

The meat stalls seem worse. A pervasive effluvium of death hangs over them; flies swarm over the newly dead carcasses, hung to display their various interior systems and their genitalia. Severed heads decorate the doorway, and in imagination one is carried back into the fifteenth century until they become enemies of the Crown, whose heads were displayed on pikes along the embankments. European beef is unlike American, although maybe healthier to live on, as it tends to be lean and fresh, not marbled with fat and hung for weeks, and is mostly stewing meat. Cynthia was trying to locate steaks at one market and she and our guest had used all the customary synonyms of the international cuisine to get through to the butcher: steak, *biftek, entrecot, filet, bonfilet,* to no avail, until suddenly he seemed to grasp it, held up his hand, dashed behind his storage locker, and came triumphantly out with a cow's head, the eyes still gentle, the teeth faintly smiling.

In Greece the method of cutting up meat is solely with the cleaver, the idea of separating a carcass into its components, such as chops or loin or leg, not having arrived. Cynthia had just had a kilo of some indescribable cut hacked off, a thin slice of which had fallen to the floor beneath the board, and as she went out of the store saw the slice scooped up and go into the meat grinder. Fresh hamburger is not a part of our diet in the Mediterranean world.

We all have our pet economies, though, and they become intensified in the close quarters of a boat. One of mine is the saving of empty bottles. I mean, not collectors' items, but returnables, the non-return economy not having arrived with force in Europe. And in the hot weather of a Mediterranean summer we and our guests do manage to run through a number of bottles every day, especially if we have been unable to get beer in tins. Cynthia doesn't really approve of saving bottles. She would like to knock the bottom out with a bottle tunker and sink them.

"Look," I say, "You're littering the sea bed with broken glass. Just think of some poor scuba diver down there in the dark, groping around on the bottom for an amphora and severing an artery in his wrist at 180 feet." (Cynthia is very conscious of her obligations to society.)

"He shouldn't be there in the first place. It's a silly and dangerous sport."

"And when the impoverished nations start mining the seabed for minerals, they're going to have to sort out all that broken glass."

"Well, if you want to get a bucket of water and fill the bottles and sink them whole, go right ahead."

"I don't want to sink them at all. I want to turn them in and get enough money back to take you out to dinner." (Cynthia loves to eat out.)

"You're going to take me to dinner when we get back to civilization anyway. You promised."

I know I've won the round if, later on, just as I've turned on the evening news from BBC, Cynthia says, "Where do you want me to put this empty bottle?"

She knows perfectly well where they go. If it is a Rhodian wine bottle it goes in an old liquor carton under her dresses in the starboard hanging locker, the one we had to sprinkle with roach powder; if it is a Turkish fruit juice bottle it goes in a carton in the oilskin locker; if it is a Schweppes Tonic bottle it goes in a container under the spare fenders in the lazarette; and if it is a Turkish carbonated beverage bottle it goes in a tote bag in the sail bin. Oversize wine bottles go on the outboard end of the shelf under the galley sink to be used for bulk wine later on. It's all perfectly organized, and she knows all this, but I explain it patiently once again, and she says: "This is a maple syrup bottle. Where do you want it?" I haven't won the round after all.

One of Cynthia's pet economies, on the other hand, has been paper napkins. For the most part the only ones available to us are the kind a few inches square which collapse into pulp with a drop of water or which, on wiping the lips, convert instantly into a thin tapering roll, leaving a generous frosting of loose fibers on the male lip and chin. So when good quality paper napkins can be found, I say, "Grab a season's supply."

"Do you know what they *cost?*" Cynthia asks. "They cost a drachma apiece."

"Well, OK, so they cost a drachma. Let's give our guests back a drachma in the form of a decent napkin. Every day they're giving us about a thousand drachmas to share the expense."

"The plural is *drachmes.* Well, how many should I buy?"

"Let's see, if we average three meals a day for four people for a hundred days, that's 1200. Get 1200."

"We *can't* get 1200. That's sixty packages. We can't even stow that many. Where would you put them?"

"Let's get them and we'll find a place. They don't weigh anything. I'll stuff them into the forepeak."

"They'll get wet up there."

"They're wrapped in cellophane. They'll be OK."

"Well, all right, I can't win. But sixty packages is too many. I'll get six."

So I say, "Cynthia, I'll be returning enough empty bottles to buy decent paper napkins for everybody."

"No, you're going to use that money to take me out to dinner. Remember? You promised."

And perhaps this is a good time to discuss Sex and Violence.

X

Sex and Violence

And all men kill the thing they love,
By all let this be heard,
Some do it with a bitter look,
Some with a flattering word,
The coward does it with a kiss,
The brave man with a sword!
Oscar Wilde,
The Ballad of Reading Gaol

" ' "I'm gonna kill her! I'm gonna kill her! I'm gonna kill that woman!" And he kept walking around the waterfront, brooding, repeating to everyone he met, "I'm gonna kill her!" But of course none of us believed him and we didn't do anything, and one day he got together a crew of young hippies who wanted to sail to the Greek Isles (I don't know why they're always isles in Greece, they're islands everywhere else), but instead he took them straight to Malta.' And I asked him, 'Do you mean he made it non-stop direct from here to Malta?' And Bill said, 'That's right, those hippies never saw a single isle.' And I said, 'Bill, if I had a crew of hippies I'd go non-stop, too, because if I stopped anywhere they might desert.' 'Anyway,' Bill went on, 'they made Malta in four days and he anchored off Ta'Xbiex and rowed ashore with his shotgun and he found his wife on the boat with that professional diver. And I guess she knew he meant it, even if the rest of us didn't, because she and her man jumped over, one to each side, but he shot them both, killed the man, maimed his wife, and then he turned the gun around and killed himself.' But you know, Annie, I remember that fellow in Malta, very pleasant chap and there was a very pretty girl on the boat with him then. I wonder if it was the same girl. Anyway, he was helpful in telling me how to get away with breaking the law against scuba diving in Turkey."

"Thank God you didn't," Cynthia said. "But you're telling the story with too many quotation marks. You pretending to be Joseph Conrad or something?"

"No, I'm just telling it the way Bill told me."

"Well, what else did Bill have to say?" You see, she's really curious about gossip, too, after she's finished needling me. It's just a case of first things first. We do this instead of shooting each other. It's more intellectually stimulating.

Not everyone feels this way. Cynthia asked the wife of one couple who have sailed with us often, after her husband had made some husbandly remark, "Don't you feel like divorcing him?"

And she said, "Divorce? No. Murder."

So some of the people in the sailing world are not always pleasant, in fact it draws an even larger share of the world's rebels and misfits than the average for most population groups, and when the end of the season approaches and one finds oneself in port with old friends once again, comparing notes on the season, sitting round the cabin fireplace, relaxing with a glass, the conversation will go something like this.

"We're short on whiskey just now, but plenty of gin and tonic, plenty of local wine, plenty of *ouzo*."

"I'll have the wine, thanks."

"And you?"

"*Ouzo* for me, you know that. And a little water."

"Well, keep it simple; make mine *ouzo* too."

"Right. Have you met this fellow, Bull, who's lying near you?"

"Bull Dog?" Oh, we've known him for years."

"Marvellous name; a boat full of dogs and always on the hunt himself."

"Seems to have a hard-luck story. His engine's broken down half way through a charter, his charterers have left him and are threatening suit to recover their advance, and he's already spent it, and his girl friend left him to go off with the charterers. He's suing his employer to reinstate a terminated contract and his employer's suing him to recover equipment on the boat and his daughter's just left him to go back to his divorced wife in Sussex."

"Typical, typical, but that's all old. The latest is that he went down to the nudist beach and brought back two gorgeous French girls who went right to work cleaning up his boat."

"Didn't think that was possible."

"Yes. Worked like dogs themselves. Upset the whole marina. Throwing out all that junk, disturbing the cockroaches. All the workmen knocked off to watch."

"How does he get the girls to do all that?"

"Yes, it's hard to believe. You'd have to see him in the nude yourself. But I think he promises them a glamorous cruise, drifting off into the sunset down the Adriatic to the Isles of Greece."

"But he can't go anywhere. His engine's completely shot."

"Of course. But he tells them that later on. Anyway, there were a couple of American boys working nearby. We could hear them arguing all night over which one should tackle the girls, and the next thing we knew they had all sailed off to Cyprus together and Bull is alone with his dogs."

"I thought you said the girls wanted to go to the Greek Isles."

"Well, they did, until they found out that the American boys were going to Cyprus. Then they voted for Cyprus."

"You've been in Cyprus this year. Are things pretty tense there?"

"No, no, not a bit of it. The Cypriots were so busy smuggling cigarettes and liquor into Beirut and carrying refugees out at $100 apiece that they didn't even know we were there. But did you hear about the murder?"

"Is this the one Bill was telling me about? The chap who was wandering around saying, 'I'm gonna kill her'?"

"Has to be. Did you know the man?"

"No, only the fellow who sold him the boat, that professor."

And this is where Cynthia may have asked, "What's this? What about a murder?" And I found myself repeating my third-hand gossip.

"But you know, it's sadder than that. They had these two little children with them, very precocious the way children get on a boat when they're showered with adult attention in every harbor, and one day one of the children came over to us and said, very casually, 'Mummy ran away today.' And I said, 'Oh? How soon will she be back?' And this child said, 'Oh, Mummy shan't be coming back. She's run away.' And so she had. She'd gone to Malta and was living with a charter captain on his boat there."

"You know, the single-handers are the ones who've found the solution to this."

"Oh, hush up," Cynthia said.

"More *ouzo?* Help yourself. But the young people have another solution; they don't marry in the first place and they're free to come and go."

"Trouble with the young people is, you never know. They only have first names these days."

"But their point is, it shouldn't matter."

"No, it doesn't matter, but it would be nice to know how to address a Christmas card."

"I've got the solution to that," Cynthia said. "If they sign our guest book 'John and Jane Smith' I figure they're married, and if they sign it 'John Smith and Jane' I know damn well they aren't."

"But you know there was another case here that some people think was murder and some think it was an accident, but we have our own ideas."

"Well, let's hear about it. No, go ahead, take it, John, there's another bottle right under where you're sitting, Mary. I'll get some more water out of the ice box."

"I think he was a Frenchman. Anyway they had this high motor boat, and one day when it was blowing hard they took off across the open channel—you know, nobody in his right mind would have gone out there in a motor boat that day—and a few hours later he was back acting very distraught and reporting that his wife had been lost overboard. She'd been up on top of the pilot house doing something and had been rolled right over. Likely story. So there was a search, but of course nothing was ever found, and it turned out he had a lot of insurance on her, which is why some people thought it was murder, but he waited around until he'd collected from the company and then he disappeared."

"So you don't think it was murder?"

"No! I'll bet he just put her ashore on the other side—you know it's completely deserted there—and now he's joined her and they're living happily somewhere over there with different names."

"Well, there one's couple who were faithful to each other, anyway."

"You know, what surprises me is when one of the two thinks the other one is all his and then is shocked into reality. I remember once being with Jack on that big schooner he had in the West Indies. 'Jack,' I asked, 'Did you get this big bucket down to the West Indies all by yourself?' 'Oh, no,' he said, 'I had a little girl with me.' 'A little girl,' I mused, picturing a ten-year-old. 'Was she any help on the boat? Could she steer?' 'Oh, she was a great sailor,' Jack said. 'She'd handle this boat alone as well as I could. In fact I'd of married her, except the little bitch went home and married Hank.' "

"Is *that* where Mrs. Hank came from? It's always a shock to learn people's backgrounds."

"Not as much of a shock as it was to have my mental picture of sweet innocence suddenly become 'the little bitch.' "

"Then you know that Madge left Andrew and Andrew's got a new girl on board. He's a lucky fellow, Andrew; he always has such lovely girls."

"Andrew's too old for that. Isn't he 84 this year? It's about time he settled down and got married."

"That's just what I said to him last year." Cynthia chimed in. " 'Andrew,' I said 'you really ought to have a wife.' And Andrew said, 'Oh, but I *do* have a wife. Lives in Cornwall. She's really rather a dear and I go home and visit her every year. We have a lovely time. But she simply loathes yachting, says it's so dirty, says, "Yachtsmen are such dirty people." ' "

"OK, Mrs. Conrad," I said, "now who's doing it?"

"Tell them about Will," Cynthia said.

"Oh, yes, Will. Did you know he finally made it back to the West Indies? We hadn't seen him for two years, and then he and Christine dropped into our house at home one day, and he'd done it. We'd thought he never would because we'd seen him preparing for so long and so meticulously that we concluded time would run out on him before starting, especially when he said he couldn't go until his dinghy had a new layer of gelcoat applied. What difference would that make out in the middle of the Atlantic? But here he was and he'd done it and I tried to pump his adventures out of him and all he wanted to talk about was his crew. 'Well, I found this group of young people in Spain,' he began, 'and I interviewed them all and checked them out and they didn't seem too bad and there was nobody else available and it was the time of year to sail, so I signed them on. But, you know, they were an odd lot. They were all right, but they just didn't seem to want to work, just to lie around and sail the boat.' I couldn't help needling William. 'Well, Will after four years of preparation was there any work left to be done?' But he was serious. 'They didn't seem to care if the decks were dirty or the varnish needed attention. Odd bunch. Lazy,' he said. And I asked him, 'But wasn't it fun just to be with young people again and watch their lives?' But Will said, 'There just didn't seem to be any communication. I couldn't figure out what went on in their minds. Maybe nothing. They were an odd bunch, sort of nature worshippers. There was one girl who went back to the stern deck every morning at sunrise, stark naked, and would kneel and bow down to the rising sun. First thing I'd see every morning was this view of her salaaming to the sun. Odd bunch.' And I told Will it sounded rather charming to me, but he said, 'No, it wasn't. All you'd see was a view of her bottom. Couldn't tell the rising sun from her backsides.' And I said, 'Some people have all the luck, Will. Sounds to me like you never had it so good. Something to look at besides the ocean.' But Will was glum and only said, 'Not really. Glad to get rid of them when I got to Antigua.'"

"Do you suppose nudity at sea is on the increase?"

"Oh, sure, it's like a rising market. You just don't know how far it's going. But it's been around a long time. Did you know Wes in Malta? That retired Alka Seltzer man?"

"No, I don't expect we ran into him. We haven't spent that much time in Malta lately."

"Well, we were there at Manoel Island waiting for a new shaft to be turned out and we were tied up with a fairly substantial motor cruiser alongside to starboard and I had been admiring a girl on board who was stopping work in this part of the yard, as well as my own work, by sunning in a bikini almost too small to count. It isn't really fair to say she was stopping work, because this spring not much work was being done anyway, because labor was trying to topple the government by the simple expedient of not working, and we were all frustrated and it was very pleasant when the boat to port produced a steaming jug of Glühwein and we all gathered on the boat to starboard, which effectively ended our working day, and we met Lola. And when we were alone again I said to Cynthia, 'You know who that girl is? That's the Polish girl who was crew for Wes!' When Wes retired he and Olga elected to try life on a small sailboat in the Mediterranean and they'd bought this fine, little character ketch on the Riviera, and the way he told the story, he said, 'Here we were; we'd bought this boat and then Olga said, "What are we supposed to do with it? We don't know how to sail." And I said, "That's right. I never thought of that. We'll have to find someone to help us sail the boat." So we looked around and made inquiries and we found this Polish girl and she said she had sailed all over and would have no trouble sailing our boat to Malta, so we took her on. And the first thing she did when we got out of the harbor was to take off all her clothes. I mean, *all* her clothes. And Olga and I looked at each other and I said, "Well, I suppose that's something else we didn't know about sailing." But we're old and we didn't really feel comfortable about going around naked, so we didn't do it ourselves, but we never thought we should stop her. And pretty soon the novelty wore off. This is a small boat, you know, only one cabin, and you see everything that goes on, and I got so accustomed to seeing her backsides disappearing up the companionway steps, about twelve inches from my face when I'm eating a meal, that it seemed just as natural as if she were fully dressed. And she really didn't know anything about sailing either. As soon as we got out of sight of land she announced she was lost. And she got us into more scrapes going in and out of harbors. But it was fun and here we are and now we know what to do ourselves.' But it didn't last, you know. After a couple of years of it they sold the boat and took a flat in Andorra and finally, when America got out of Viet Nam, they went back to the States."

"Look, stick around," Cynthia said. "We don't want to break this gossip off half way. Bob will walk across the quay and get one of those grilled chickens from the *taverna* and we've plenty of bread and wine and olives. And while you're getting it you can be trying to remember your poem about Yugoslavia."

"That's right; you know, this nudity isn't only afloat. There's plenty on shore right now. When we were along the Riviera a year ago, coming back from Scandinavia, it was nothing to see these good-looking French girls right there in the marinas in their topless bikinis swabbing decks and polishing brass. And dinner dress ashore in a restaurant was often an almost totally transparent blouse over a braless top. Very fetching!"

"I can remember eating dinner and asking him, 'How do you like them?'" Cynthia said, "and Bob said 'Very fetching. Can't take my eyes off them.' And I said, 'Silly. I meant the snails.' And Bob said, 'Snails? Huh? Oh, snails! Is that what I'm chewing on? I—I was thinking—I mean . . .' And I said, 'You're blushing.'"

"Remember Susie," I said, to change the subject.

"Yes, I remember Susie, but run along and get that chicken. You can tell us about Susie later."

So I thought about Susie while I was negotiating the grilled chicken. On one of our early visits to Rhodes we backed in between two heavy, old motorboats whose decks were somewhat higher than ours, and I remembered how this created a charming illusion to starboard, how Susie lived to starboard and spent most every day wetting down the old wooden decks to keep them tight in the hot summer sun, as well as taking care of a new litter of kittens. How all day my view, working at the cabin table, was of Susie's shapely legs coming and going, truncated by the top frame of our window just below the hem of her scant shorts. How later, when we got to know Susie, she told us she had shipped as crew for a gentleman who had several children and no wife. When I got back over the gangplank with the hot chicken, stuffed with the usual handful of soggy french fries, the conversation had deteriorated into an analysis of the emotional state of the creative writer at work, and I could see it needed livening up.

"All right, I was going to tell you about Susie," I said.

"You were supposed to tell us your poem from Yugoslavia," Annie said.

"Did you remember to pick up some paper napkins?" Cynthia asked.

"No. No to both of you. Susie first. Are you all one ahead of me on *ouzo* now? Susie lived on the boat next door in Rhodes and it appears she had previously signed on as an *au père* girl on this gentleman's yacht."

"That's not *au père*," Cynthia said, "it's *au pair*."

"How do you know how I'm spelling it?" I asked. "You haven't seen how I'm going to write it yet."

"No, but I know what you're thinking."

"That's my problem; my wife understands me. But, yes, it's true. What a disillusionment it was to learn that an *au père* girl, I mean an *au pair* girl, wasn't meant for the paterfamilias. But you've got me off the track. What I meant to say was that Susie's first order of the day was to have everyone take off all their clothes. 'Saved no end of bother with the wash,' she said. So you see, it isn't so new after all."

"And now tell us your poem."

"I forget it."

"Poor old Jan," Cynthia said. "Remember Jan on the other side of us."

"I do indeed," I said, "but give us some clean glasses. We can't possibly drink wine out of glasses that had *ouzo* in them."

"Jan who?" Annie wanted to know.

"Jan Hooggracht. Sorry, I never can pronounce these Dutch names without hawking. Some old aristocrat; had a moated castle in the Low Countries. Caught our lines for us when we were backing in, trying to back in, across the wind, just Cynthia and me. Great chap. Never said a word when our davits hit him."

"Remember how he would say, 'My wife is coming tomorrow'?"

"And each day that went by he would say the same thing, 'My wife is coming tomorrow.' "

"Until finally we made up all sorts of stories about how his wife really had been killed in the Rotterdam blitz, or mashed on the highway, or had gone down at sea, and how he now sits alone on the deck of his boat, and the seasons come and go, and the grapes are harvested, and then the olives, and he says, 'My wife is coming tomorrow.' "

"You actually shed a tear over our own stories one evening, and then in the morning we came on deck and his rigging was hanging with bras and panties and we gave a shout, 'She's real! She's real!' "

"And then you asked him where they would cruise to now, and he said, 'Well, things aren't quite what I had expected; it seems she's leaving me.' "

"And after she'd gone we most hesitantly asked Jan if he'd join us for dinner, and he did, and then, again not knowing how bad form it might seem to butt in, but remembering the story of Parzifal, I asked him if he would rather talk about it or prefer not to."

"I'm sure he was glad of the chance," Cynthia said, "to have us almost strangers to tell it to. But wasn't it sad? His new young wife announcing she had decided to run off with the gardener?"

"Maybe she missed the tulips." Annie suggested.

"Tulips? No, this was the Spanish gardener at their villa in the Balearics. All he knew how to grow was corks."

"And what a blow to the ego. My God, you give a woman a villa in the Balearics and a yacht in Greece and what does she want? She wants the gardener."

"Well, look at you, wanting an *au père* girl."

"Yes, Susie was the *au père* girl for me. When we helped

Jan winch his mini car into its chocks on deck and he sailed away to put his yacht and villa up for sale, Susie had the grace to shed an honest tear. Loved her for it. Not too many like that any more."

"Why do you suppose it is that everyone who sails around the world seems to get divorced as soon as they're home?"

"Probably too complicated to get divorced abroad."

"That's OK, use your fingers. No, seriously, what is there about sailing that breaks them up?"

"OK, let's analyze them. How about Carl and Mary?"

"Well, Carl was insufferable. Imagine dragging your children out of school to go sailing. And such a grubby little boat. I don't blame Mary at all."

"And then there's Steve and Ruth. Luxury yacht. Paid crew. Went to all the big-name tourist places. Never went anywhere else, of course."

"But Steve was unbearable. Ruth would have been out of her mind to stay with him."

"Well, what do you say about Don and Sally?"

"Don was impossible. Sally should have left him long ago."

"I think we're getting somewhere," I said. "Analysis proves that men, at least skippers, are insufferable, unbearable, and impossible. Can you name one, just one, you'd want to be married to?"

"You," she said.

And when we got home that fall I bought her a mink stole with all the money she'd made cleaning toilets after our guests.

"We've come to a pretty dilemma," Bill said.

"If you can still make 'pretty dilemma' come out straight, you need some more wine. No, Cynthia, you'll have to take the cork out of the bottle before it will pour."

"They're obnoxious, too," Cynthia said.

"What I mean is," Bill went on, drinking from my glass, "a little while ago we were talking about all these women who had walked out on their men, and suddenly it seems to be all the men who are at fault. Don't you suppose it takes a certain type of man to sail around the world, independent, indomitable, impatient?"

"Insufferable and impossible," Cynthia added.

"And it isn't every woman who can handle this situation," he went on, ignoring her. "They feel threatened that a new mistress, the sea, has intervened."

"But don't you think they're better off than the many couples we meet between whom there is neither sex nor violence. They live in a world of armed neutrality, of silent hostility, he with his bottle and she with her dog, or vice versa. How about them?"

"I think they're cornered," Annie said. "They're cornered by habit and by finances and by warrants for their arrest in various ports where they have left unpaid bills, until they are shrunk into a little world from which there is no escape."

"Here they lie, under awnings, in sewage-filled harbors, and from time to time they make a run to some foreign port in order to avoid the import duty which comes up if they outstay their time, or to take on more duty-free booze, or to earn a bit of side money with a short charter. They're the sad cases."

"They aren't the only sad cases. There's another type we see quite a bit of in this work, and that's the middle-aged husband who finally has it made and dreams of sailing off around the world on his dreamship, but he wants to test it out on his wife first. So he sets up a cruise with us to show his wife how easy it is for a couple even older than they are to handle a boat or how 'Sailing is so relaxing.' "

"That's what they're always thinking about us at home," Cynthia said. "They think we're sitting out here under an awning, tied to a palm tree, with a tall glass in our hand, and they say 'Sailing is so relaxing.' "

"Anyway, these wives are a pretty savvy bunch and they're not about to be conned into giving up their big homes and their bridge lunches and their kaffeeklatsches in favor of all this nonsense of being cold and wet and seasick just to get somewhere where they'll be eaten by cannibals."

"So they arrive having made up their minds that they aren't going to have a good time, no matter how much they like it, because if they show they like it their husband's going to pick it up and run with it. So they dig in their heels and sit and stare at one corner of the cockpit all day, looking unhappy as they can, until he gets the message."

"So they compromise and he buys a big power cruiser, all electric, with central heat and a TV, and they keep it tied up at the nearest marina, and she lets him go sit on it on weekends."

"But you Americans think that's good for the economy, don't you?"

"We're much happier to be alongside young love, which may or may not represent marriage, but we suspect and hope represents a maximum of sex with a minimum of violence."

"Yes, young people, at least those who go to sea together, seem to be generally turned off by violence at this time."

"A lot of them are turned off by hard work, too, but they lead quiet lives. And they're always generous and helpful. They don't earn much money, and they spend less, but they're enjoying the sea and the people and nature and themselves. Don't you feel protective toward them?"

"Maybe I feel it; so many of them are learning about the sea and life the hard way, but they don't need our protection. They have their own armor of disinvolvement."

"Come on Annie, the conversation's getting too philosophical for this late at night. We'd better get back to the sack."

"Let's just do the washup first."

"No, no, it's too late to start that. Anyway, the water's cold. We'll do them with the breakfast things." That from Cynthia.

"Yes," I say, catching that word *we*, "Cynthia will take care of them tomorrow."

"Wait a minute," Annie said, turning back from the ladder. "We still haven't heard your poem from Yugoslavia."

"All right, and there's still a couple of inches of wine in the last bottle. But I've got to give you the background first. We'd never seen these nude beaches until we were in Yugoslavia. Well, they're not really beaches; all the shores are these beautiful flat slabs of clean white limestone, shelving down into the water like giant steps. The first time we came around a rocky point and found ourselves just off one we didn't know what we were supposed to do. I mean, do you stand up and strip off your own shorts? Or do you stare rigidly straight ahead? Or grab for the binoculars? We did the last and found we were being stared back at by people wearing *nothing but* binoculars. One girl, who was more bashful than the rest, or new to the game, knelt on her air mattress and pulled the end up under her chin. We waved one hand and she waved back. Then we waved both hands. Wasn't that a dirty trick? We're bastards, aren't we?"

"Who?"

"We. Us. People. You know, Cynthia gave me an anthology of ancient Greek poetry for my birthday this year and the first poem in the book, the oldest Greek poem * extant, maybe, goes:

> My ash spear is my barley bread,
> My ash spear is my Ismarian wine,
> I lean on my spear and drink.

but I had to rewrite it the way I thought it had to be to reflect how people really are, and it goes like this:

> My ash spear is my barley bread,
> My ash spear is my wine,
> When my spear is in my hand
> Whatever's yours is mine.

> The housewife working in the field,
> The virgin in her bed,
> When my spear is in my hand
> What's yours is mine instead.

"Is that his poem?" Annie asked.

"I said it was time to go home," John said.

"Never heard it before," Cynthia said. "Now hurry up and tell us the one from Yugoslavia. These nice people want to get to bed."

"Huh? Oh, yes, we were off the nudist beach, weren't we? Well, we saw these all over, and we learned later on that there had been a head-on collision between two motor boats, both skippers so busy with their binoculars that they never saw each other. They're a real hazard to navigation."

"Hurry it up," Cynthia said.

* Translated by Guy Davenport in Peter Jay (ed.), *The Greek Anthology* (London: Penguin, 1973).

"We came down past the big one—the big one is on the island of Lošinj, and it must be half a mile long, and the nudes
are as thick as barnacles—we were coming toward it with the
spinnaker up, and just as we brought it abeam we dropped the
chute so we could drift down the beach and give our guests a
good look. It's steep to, so we were close in. And one of the
wives was too embarrassed to stare at them through her binoculars and went down into the cabin, and then we found her
looking out the cabin window at them with her binoculars.
Never let her forget it."

"Just tell them the poem," Cynthia commanded.

"Yes, oh, yes, the poem. Well it goes like this:

> On the Island of Lošinj
> All sorts of things are seen.
>
> There on the rocks the nudists lie,
> Regarding each other with curious eye.
>
> Bare white busts from shucked bikinis.
> Roast red rumps that look like wienies.
>
> On sun-baked slabs and secluded notches
> They bake their bellies and warm their crotches.
>
> All this skin and hair en masse.
> We find less pleasing than one bare fact."

"I knew we should have gone home," John said.

"We'll try to cross tracks in the spring, Cynthia," Annie said.
"And don't let him beat you too much this winter."

The autumnal wind whistled in the rigging, a bit of motion
crept around the breakwaters into the harbor. It was the end of
another season. Spring was five months away.

Now Spring returning beckons the little boats
Once more to dance on the waters; the grey storms
Are gone that scourged the sea. Now swallows build
Their round nests in the rafters, and all the fields
Are bright with laughing green.
                              Come then, my sailors:
Loose your dripping hawsers, from their deep sunk graves
Haul up your anchors, raise your brave new sails.
                              Second Century B.C.
          It is Priapus warns you, God of this harbor.
                              Antipater of Sidon
                              Second Century B.C.*

   * Translated by Dudley Fitts in Peter Jay (ed.), *The Greek Anthology*
(London: Penguin, 1973).

XI

The Sunken City

Man marks the land with ruin . . .
Byron, "The Ocean"

The Turkish word *Asar* can be translated as "monument" or as "trace, remnant or remains," but it can also be translated as "legend," and this is the meaning I like to choose. There is on the coast of Lycia in southern Turkey a bay known as Asar Bay (although the bay remains nameless on the American chart) whose history must contain the stuff of which legends are made.

Everyone dreams of discovering a sunken city, and here one day Cynthia and I did. At first we didn't even know we had discovered it, and as the tale unfolds you can decide for yourself how much credit for discovery you want to accord us. Actually I regard the whole episode as a fine example that a life of sailing can lead into other paths of adventure than collecting trophies and getting seasick.

In 1970 we first sailed eastward from Rhodes along the south coast of Turkey, that part known from ancient times as Lycia, of which Strabo, writing at the time of Christ, said, "The coast of Lycia is rugged and dangerous, but filled with many harbors." George Bean, the late British archeologist, wrote of it, "Mountainous and inhospitable, this is ancient Lycia, the land of tombs." We were using the latest edition of the largest-scale chart available from the U.S. Hydrographic Office, a scale of

about three and a half miles to the inch, and a set of harbor plans whose title stated it was based on a British survey of 1811, and we had with us a tracing from a map of archeological sites.

We were into archeology at that time in a minor, amateur way, that is to say, when we were near a known site we went to see it, and we had worked our way a little beyond the Acropolis or the Roman Forum, but not much beyond the tourist beat of Delphi, Delos, Olympia, and Knossos. But our interest was up, we were alone and at leisure, and we began to observe less-known sites. Of Asar Bay, lying between the two southernmost points of this coast, the *British Admiralty Sailing Directions* state only: "The Shores of Asar veya hisar limani appear to be steep to, but have been only partially examined." That's all. The Turkish phrase we translate roughly into "Ruin and/or Castle Harbor," but it is generally known as just Asar Bay. Our chart showed nothing there, but our tracing showed a ruin at its head, and we turned in before a gentle breeze to see if anything might be visible. The steep and featureless ridge of the peninsula on our starboard, climbing to a height of 1,000 feet according to the chart, converged slowly on the more broken mainland shore to port, and the breeze began to funnel between the opposing hills. Ahead of us now, where our chart showed nothing, we could see substantial walls climbing the hill to port, and, busy looking at them through binoculars, we were almost too late in observing rocks awash across the bay ahead of us, the wavelets from the now-brisk wind breaking over them.

Abandoning archeology, we became sailors again, executed a 180-degree turn, and beat out, to test a narrow strait in the southern wall of mountain back into open sea. A trace at slow speed showed a least depth of 80 feet and there being no discoloration of shoal water visible, we logged it as a safe passage into Asar Bay and proceeded to the landlocked waters behind Kekova Island, about 4 miles to the east. We did not know then that in avoiding Asar Bay's inner reaches we had just repeated the actions of probably every pilot for the last thousand years. Nor did we know that we had just duplicated the work of Captain Beaufort in 1811, who wrote in his *Memoires*, published by Mr. Hurd, hydrographer to the Admiralty: "The Boghaz (or strait) of Kar may be safely used, if chace or other sufficient motive should render it necessary."

But our curiosity was aroused, and time, for once, was on our side, so we felt our way to the western end of what the Turks know as the Ölü Deniz, or Dead Sea, and which we generally call Kekova Roads; anchored; and walked back across the isthmus between here and Asar Bay. This is flat land, dancing in the heat of a Turkish summer, and here we came upon a family, a father in his torn pajama suit and his wife in baggy pants, driving a team of white horses around and around a circular threshing floor of stone. It was late June, the grain had ripened and been harvested, and threshing time was here. A little boy and girl stared at us shyly, the father stopped his work to fill Cynthia's straw hat with ripe tomatoes, and we walked on through a cluster of Lycian sarcophagi toward the ruins.

They were those of a fair-sized town, climbing the hillside over Asar Bay for perhaps a quarter of a mile, and almost the same distance along the water. We picked a high wall and climbed it to look down on Asar Bay, and there we saw, to our delight and surprise, a checkerboard of foundations beneath the clear water, the lines of a submerged breakwater or pier, and quays, deep water beside them. The rocks awash were more ruins, the safe anchorage conspicuous, and if weather permitted we would snorkel here on our return trip from Antalya with guests.

And we did; we swam and dove until exhausted. Under the water seemed to lie limitless pottery, marble tessera floors, fragments of columns, hundreds of feet of foundations. Best of all, there was no sign of digging or recent looting, no archeological trenches, no dynamiting of tombs to find the gold which Uncle Achmed had dreamed was within the solid rock. Except for a few goats, the ruins were deserted. From the apse of a Christian chapel, roofless and with its south end fallen into the harbor, grew a large fig tree.

"Hey, what a great place," was our reaction. "We'll have to find out what it is when we get back to Rhodes."

And we sailed away.

But at Rhodes no one we knew had any idea what we were asking about, and we looked forward to Malta, where the nucleus of Mediterranean sailors would surely produce the answer. In the course of the summer we visited Samothrace in the northern Aegean, where Cynthia's old friend and classmate, Phyllis Lehman, then Dean of Smith College, had been involved in digging since 1939. We thought she might tell us what it was we had seen, but instead we had our first insight into the vastness of the archeological world and the intensity with which the professional must concentrate on his own site. In this part of the world every island, every promontory, every bay, holds its traces of vanished civilizations: Minoan, Mycenean, Classical, Hellenistic, Roman, Byzantine, Seljuk Crusader, Venetian, Genoese, or Ottoman. It requires an encyclopedia of archeological sites to trace them, and we must not expect the professional to know them all, much less their histories. To know one area in depth or to know a broad application of one aspect of culture is more the pattern.

In Malta then that fall we renewed our questioning, and one by one our friends who had sailed the coast of Turkey disclaimed knowledge of the site. Then one evening John Marriner brought *September Tide* back from her summer's cruise and was assigned a berth near us. Marriner spent every summer then cruising some segment of the Mediterranean coast, writing a series of books on his adventures, and had recently done the south coast of Turkey. Yes, he could recall the spot I described; it was called Polemos. But of its history he knew nothing.

Of course, I bought a copy of his book when I got home and learned that he had not actually entered Asar Bay, but gone straight to Kekova Roads and returned on foot, as we had done at first, to glimpse the ruins in the evening light. But he did not trace its history or advise where to go to do this. *Polemos* was a peculiar name for a city; it is the Greek word for *war* (from which we get our word *polemic*), and we wondered where this name could come from.

In New York City, on our way home to the Northwest, I had dinner with Mel Grosvenor of the *National Geographic*, who had had his *White Mist* on the south coast of Turkey that year; and Irving Johnson, who had taken *Yankee* there recently. Neither of them could place either my description or the name Polemos. By now it was becoming clear that while we could hardly expect to "discover" a lost city, at least it was not a commonly known tourist attraction for other cruisers. I would have to consult the professionals and their literature to know what we had seen.

That winter, while visiting in Berkeley, a series of telephone calls brought me into contact with Crawford Greenewalt, Jr., who had worked for some years with the team digging at Sardis in Turkey. Most helpful, he brought out maps and reference books and guided me with a framework within which to approach the subject. I could start, he said, with Captain Francis Beaufort, who surveyed this coast for the Admiralty in 1811, the first survey to be made, and whose journal, *Karamania,* he had drawn from the library. Many other expeditions had gone through the area in the first half of the Nineteenth Century, culminating in the Petersen–Von Luschan expedition about 1880, which was possibly the last to be there. I would probably learn all about it from these accounts.

So we played in a small way at being scholars. We learned that Admiral Beaufort, who was one of that golden age of English navigators and seamen which produced Cook and Bligh and Vancouver and Nelson, was not only the practical seaman who introduced the Beaufort Scale of Wind Velocities and charted the coast of Lycia so well that we were still piloting from his chart, but a self-made classical scholar in his own right, who, after plotting the latitude and longitude of every landmark, proceeded to identify the ruins by reference to their classical names as derived from Strabo, Pliny, and Ptolemy. We learned that he, like Marriner after him, had sailed directly from Kastelorizo, the Greek island, to Kekova Roads, bypassing Asar Bay. But while anchored behind Kekova Island he had taken a shore party across the same isthmus where Cynthia had been given tomatoes, and recorded the following in his journal:

On a rocky hill, which rises from the isthmus, stand the ruins of a town, containing a profusion of half-destroyed dwelling houses, towers, walls and sarcophagi. Though beautifully situated, it is entirely deserted; during the entire day only one voice cheered us from the distant hills.

So we hadn't discovered the ruins after all, but perhaps we could lay claim to discovery of the underwater portions. No mention is made of them by Beaufort; either he considered them not worth recording or he never saw them. Nor does he identify the site.

I dipped into Col. William Martin Leake's *Journal of a Tour in Asia Minor,* published in 1824, but recording travels by land from a period even earlier than Beaufort's survey. He does not seem to have been at Asar Bay himself, but in notes to Chapter 5, having referred to the Stadiasmus of Ptolemy, he concludes:

To the westward of Andriace we have two ancient sites determined by inscribed sepulchres, which record the name of the city, and the inscriptions upon which have been copied by Mr. Cockerell:—that of Cyana . . . at the head of Port Tristomo, as the inner part of the bay behind the island of Kakava is now called—; and that of Aperlae . . . at the head of Assar Bay.

Beaufort had tentatively placed Aperlae some 30 miles east of here above the port of Finike.

And now I was comparing the Stadiasmus of Ptolemy with our log book, and although I believe Gibbon has referred to the remarkable geographical sagacity of Colonel Leake, something was wrong. The Stadiasmus was a form of *Sailing Directions* or *Coast Pilot* attributed to the geographer Ptolemy of the Third Century A.D., giving distances between all known ports around the perimeter of the known seas. There was an anomaly in Leake's interpretation of the Greek symbol δ representing four stade, and who was I to go questioning Leake or Gibbon or even old Ptolemy? I didn't even know how long a stade is, but clearly from other known measures in the table, four stade was meaningless here.

And who was this Mr. Cockerell who had copied inscriptions? Cockerell was a young English student of architecture and the classics who found himself on this same coast in the year 1812, sailing alone with a Greek skipper in a Greek caique, sketching ruins, copying inscriptions, and keeping a journal. Unfortunately he never got around to publishing this journal; this was done in a condensed version by his son, and no reference to inscriptions at Asar Bay is included, although we do learn that Cockerell, like Beaufort, sailed directly from Kastelorizo to Kekova. If he did in fact visit Asar Bay, it must have been on foot across the isthmus. Farther along the coast Cockerell was overtaken by Beaufort, who was shocked to find an English gentleman traveling alone on this pirate-infested coast and insisted he abandon his caique and join the comfort and safety of the wardroom of one of His Majesty's ships. One wonders if Captain Beaufort, a scholar himself, may have tired of his lieutenants' grumbling, "When you've seen one ruin, you've seen them all" and valued the company of another classicist in the wardroom.

The Frenchman, Charles Texier, came along the coast a few years later and was becalmed for the night nearby, recording: "We were to the south of the large bay Hassar: so our pilot named it, in which there is an anchorage sheltered from all winds, but which is completely deserted." He went on to place Aperlae at the site of the present village of Kekova Kale, and never saw the ruins at Asar Bay.

The English traveler Sir Charles Fellows came down the coast traveling in the opposite direction in 1838, but this gentleman was no sailor. "I never was at sea," he wrote, "without forming a resolution in future to travel by land." Thus it was that, when he arrived at Kekova, he could write, "I determined to change my mode of traveling for one less tedious and affording more amusement." And he headed inland by donkey and so missed knowing of our site.

Other travelers and scholars came and went, but when I came to the account of the Petersen–von Luschan expedition, published in 1889, a massive German tome, I learned that this party had sailed from Rhodes directly to Kekova, traveling in an Austrian paddle-wheel steamship designed for river service, thus also bypassing Asar Bay. In this case they did not even go across the isthmus, their attention being on other ruins inland and to the east. But a purpose of the trip was to establish the identity of the twenty-three cities of the Lycian League of classical times, and our author was able to terminate this discussion by saying, "But then Aperlae of Hirschfeld and Müller must properly be placed on Asar Bay where there are ruins which, since Beaufort and Cockerell, no one has seen, unfortunately also not I."

If it was really true that this was the last expedition here, and it confirmed that the ruins had not been seen since Beaufort's day, and Beaufort had not noted the sunken seaport, perhaps we really had discovered it.

We reread Freya Starck's *The Lycian Shore*, beautifully written, but somewhat lacking in a navigator's sense of geography. And there was a picture of *Elfin*, David Balfour's cruiser on which he was traveling, at anchor in Asar Bay, captioned "Polemos (?)." The question mark was hers. So somebody had been there—we could match a ruin in the foreground, stone for stone, with one of our own slides—even the dust jacket on the volume bore a drawing which could be no other view than that looking out Asar Bay through the doorway of a roofless building on the water's edge. But search the text as we would, there was no mention of putting in here. If you want to accept the definition of discovery as being the first to publish a site, clearly she had muffed it here. And she had placed Aperlae on Kekova Roads. Was our site Polemos as she and John Marriner indicated, or was it Aperlae, as Colonel Leake and Eugen Petersen claimed? We consulted the *Pauly-Wissowa*, an encyclopedic work on known sites, to find that Aperlae was shown as having been first on Asar Bay and later shifted to the more protected bay of Tristoma. More protected from what? The winter storms or the Arab raiders? And anyway, we had observed no ruins on the shores of Tristoma to compare in extent with those on Asar Bay.

But while our excitement was now aroused, we were committed by then to other plans; we were to spend the next four seasons crossing Europe by inland waterway and exploring Scandinavia. Asar Bay, while not forgotten, was filed away as an intriguing mystery to which I hoped some day to return.

And finally in 1975 we did. The *Cynthia R* was back in Malta that spring, our intended routing would take us around the Peloponnese, across the Aegean to Rhodes, and then allow us a leisurely period for exploration on our own. I bought a Nikonos underwater camera. Cynthia and I took scuba lessons and became card-carrying scuba divers, going 40 feet down in the cool waters of Puget Sound in midwinter. We read the accounts of George Bass and Peter Throckmorton and Nicholas Flemming, all of whom had done underwater research in Turkey. I photocopied Flemming's article on "The Eustatic and Tectonic Components of Relative Sea Level Change" (what a marvelously impressive title to drop in the right places), noting that he had examples from Kaş and from Kekova, thus closely bracketing Asar Bay, but apparently like everyone else had not been to Aperlae itself. He had measured the depth to which datable ruins from the past are now submerged along the coasts of

Greece and Turkey, corrected for worldwide changes in sea level, and thus the rate of subsidence or emergence of these coasts, which in the case of our area should be about one meter per millennium. (In fact our own experience indicated a more rapid rate, as you will see.) We thought how we might construct a grid with the primitive equipment at hand, prepared to buy air tanks, valves, a compressor—probably $2,000 worth of equipment.

Then we thought we ought to check on Turkish regulations. And behold! It is all illegal. Of course we had known right along that removing artifacts is illegal, call it what you will; what looks to you like souvenir collecting or safeguarding an antiquity looks mighty like looting to the authorities, and they are fed up with it. Not only are digging and probing and lifting archeological objects illegal, but scuba diving, measuring, and mapping are illegal. Making a site survey is illegal. These things can be done by permit only, and permits are sometimes arranged for eminent archeologists from Harvard or Berkeley or Bryn Mawr (actually many leading universities are working there), but the wheels grind slowly. Patience, often for months or years, is needed; contacts in the right places are needed. I don't mean to say that permission is dependent on friendship, but rather that one must know which are the proper officials whom one must convince that the intended work will be of some benefit to Turkey, and this requires a framework of identification and support; the expectation of employment of Turkish labor is a help; an agreement that all finds are Turkish property is self-evident. No, it was dreaming to think that an unknown charter boat skipper would get a permit to swim around mapping a harbor a few miles from Greece at just the time his own commitments left him conveniently free.

It is not even fair to ask that these regulations be explained. It is their country, after all, and they can make such regulations as they see fit. But the history of the past two centuries is explanation enough. We are dealing with an intricate coastline where smuggling and piracy have been major enterprises. In the name of science or greed the treasures of the past have been systematically collected or plundered, depending upon your point of view, by Europeans, English, and Americans. Repeated war and threats of war with their Greek neighbor breed a suspicion of foreign boats lingering in deserted coves. It is difficult for most of the population to comprehend the level of affluence and the level of freedom which allows yachtsmen to roam the world for pleasure. Man does not subject himself to the heat and discomfort of the Turkish coast in summer, or the danger of life on the sea, except for gain. A sensible man moves to the cool mounains for summer, coastal villages are half deserted, and the yacht which comes to anchor alone must be engaged in smuggling or looting or spying out the land. If treasures are to be found beneath the Turkish sea, Turkish divers can find them.

So what could we do? We could do what was legal, that's what. We could be tourists; we could look and observe and make notes and sketches and take photographs. We could snorkel over the site and we could look down through the clear water from the masthead and hillside.

It was almost a relief to know that we would not have to encumber our aft deck with a compressor and bottles, that we would not have to worry about valves and gauges and the medical problems of diving and above all that I would not have to spend that $2,000.

The best policy, we decided, was to be quite open about our presence, but to maintain a low profile in order not to overstep the bounds of tourism. Above all avoid putting any Turkish authorities on the spot. We would report to the authorities at Kaş, we would move by broad daylight. I had a letter to the Department of Antiquities in Ankara in my typewriter (which was not camouflage, it was sent in due course), but we would avoid planting floats in the bay as reference points, or laying out lines to grid the bottom. The length of an anchor line was the only measure we would use; a sailor's eye would serve to sketch in relative positions and sizes of identifiable objects below the water, while the rocky, thorny hillside of tumbled walls defied measurement without instruments, even had it been legal. Indeed, it seemed that our own abilities and equipment tied in completely with obeying the law, unless the very time we took to satisfy ourselves that we had described the site should arouse suspicion. As one of our professional acquaintances said, "You know what you're doing is legal and *I* know what you're doing is legal, but how do *they* know what you're doing is legal?" A good question.

So we sailed from Rhodes and entered Turkey at Fethiye, where the first of the Lycian cliff tombs frown down on the modern town; and we revisited Gemile Island, the name of which translates loosely as "The Isle of Ships," marveling again at the seawashed mosaic floors and the covered ambulatory climbing 1,000 feet of hillside to the ruins of a church, and the old wall paintings in Christian tombs, still bright with color, and the utter desolation of what had once been a thriving commercial seaport. And we sailed again around the Seven Capes, whose rugged mountains somewhere conceal ancient Cragus, and past the rolling sand dunes at the mouth of the Xanthus River, which hide the ruins of the silted in port of Patara, and thus we came again to Kaş.

The formalities were conducted this time with a feeling of ease over a table in the little harborfront cafe, and I reported to the patrol boat, based there, one of whose crew had been re-called from factory work in West Germany to serve his military tour, and with whom communication in German seemed possible. And then one day we sailed back into Asar Bay before a gentle wind, and rounded up to anchor underneath the walls, wondering if we would now find them overrun with German archeologists in lederhosen. But this was not so. Just as in Beaufort's day, 163 years earlier, the place was utterly deserted, and only one voice cheered us from the distant hill.

With an entire hillside and half a harbor full of ruins spread out before one, where does one start, logically, to explore or describe them? We sat on deck and examined the area with binoculars, and what stood out at first was that the city walls, where they approached the shore at right angles on either side of us, were built from the ground up of rubble and mortar, but beginning a few hundred feet up the hillside the walls were of large squared blocks of stone laid in rough courses to a height of ten or twelve feet, capped with an additional rise of rubble and mortar, clearly two very different periods of con-

struction, although we were not ready to date them. Was it not probable that the walls of squared stone, climbing the hillside about seven hundred feet apart, would have been connected by a lateral wall parallel to the shore, making of the city a rough rectangle, walled in on all sides, as were so many of the known sites we had seen in the Aegean world? The answer was, Yes; with the binoculars and later on foot one could trace the probable foundations of this old wall, more or less following a contour, which in many places was almost a natural cliff, fortified with a substantial tower, but most of the actual stone now missing. And see how sarcophagi are scattered outside the old walls, while those few within the walls are down toward the shore, where we can conclude that they can originally have been placed below and outside the old lateral wall. This positioning of sarcophagi helped support a conclusion about the original city plan, because it was customary to bury the dead outside the walls. Only when the walls were extended to the harbor did they come within the city.

Where the eastern of the newer walls came to the shore there stood a couple of very conspicuous white stones, and we chose to use this as a base point to work from. The submerged port ended at the west at that point on shore where the west wall, had it not been washed away there, would have reached the sea, and we would refer to the line between those two points as a base line, as it ran more or less along the rubble beach. While scarcely a grid, the geography now divided itself into five clearly defined areas: the upper hillside within the ancient walls, the lower hillside enclosed by later walls, the hillsides east of and west of the walls, and the submerged seaport.

It was at about this point that we began to get nervous about the rising west day breeze; rolled up our awning; beat out to the Kara Boğaz, the Black Strait, called Akar Boğaz, or Current Strait, on some maps; and ran down to the protection of Kekova Roads.

So began a pattern we were to follow for two weeks. In the morning calm we would motor back up to Kara Boğaz, plunging into the prevailing westerly swell, on auto pilot, and eating breakfast. By 0800 we would be at anchor in Asar Bay, the awning up, ready to start our first shore trip or our first swim over the port. By noon, either too cold from swimming or too hot from climbing, we would be ready for lunch and, Mediterranean style, a siesta, at which point a decision would have to be made. We would be missing the best light for seeing the bottom and sleeping into a rising wind which would cut short any afternoon work. Almost every day the wind did rise, and by mid- or late afternoon the *Cynthia R* would be tugging at her anchor chain, the awning at its guys. We would tell ourselves that if we only hung in there it would die at sunset, and we would save hours of daylight for writing up our notes instead of hauling up our anchor. And always the wind did die at night, often to come in as a faint, cool land breeze off the mountains before morning, but two afternoons out of three we would have been spooked by the rising chop in our narrow, dead-end bay, and when the boat began to plunge at anchor we would roll up the thrashing awning, bring up the anchor, raise shortened sail, and beat out to Kaza Boğaz. We would drift through this short passage in the baffling puffs which struck down from the cliffs, to drive spray off a glass-calm surface, and then run off four miles to the entrance to Kekova Roads, the flying fish scattering from our bow like the plumes from a rocket on the Fourth of July. We had found a deserted cove behind some flat islets opposite this entrance, where the breeze spilled off the mainland cliffs in gusts, but which afforded the closest anchorage and became our usual refuge for the night. Being uncharted and unnamed, we called it Flat Island Cove; we could have been Turkish and called it Yassi Ada Bükü, but that would have been confusing with the Yassi Ada off Bodrum, where the real scholars with proper permits were at work on sunken wrecks. We liked the breezy quality of the cove; it kept away the mosquitoes at night, always a curse on this coast, and after the hot day we could lie naked on deck in the dry wind, speculating about what we had seen. For two weeks we lay where not a single light was visible at night except a distant beacon to seaward, with the shooting stars of the Perseid shower duplicating in the cloudless night sky the flying fish of the day.

One evening we misjudged the wind and our courage and hung on in Asar Bay for the sunset calm, only to have the wind increase with evening. (I don't think it really increased, but as the light faded the waves looked more ominous, the singing in the rigging sounded louder.) At late dusk we caved in and made for shelter, to be rewarded by a rare sight out in open water. As we ran downwind for Kekova Roads, there passed a square rigger, silhouetted in the path of the rising moon, moving to windward with furled sails. She might have been a ghost ship on this deserted coast, but we knew that a square rigger had been engaged as a movie property in the eastern Med that year and settled for this prosaic explanation.

During our entire time at Asar Bay two other sails came in, a tiny Italian, which anchored for an hour's swimming and then moved out; and an English charter boat of our acquaintance, which lay there for a calm night. Other than these, in what

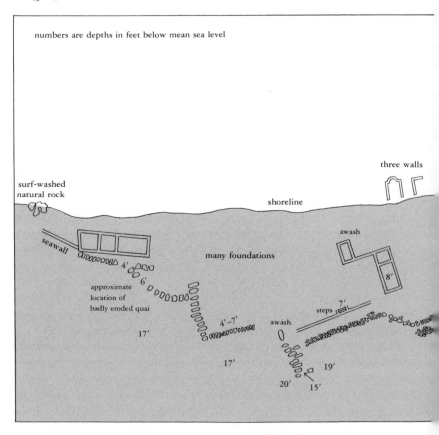

numbers are depths in feet below mean sea level

three walls

surf-washed
natural rock

shoreline

seawall

awash

many foundations

4'

6'

approximate
location of
badly eroded quai

8'

steps 7'

4'-7'

awash

17'

17'

19'

20' 15'

has now become many visits to Asar Bay, we have never seen
another boat at its head. From time to time the patrol boat
from Kaş would cross the mouth, heading for Kekova Roads,
where it would check the papers of boats lying there, but although we must have been plainly visible to their crew, as well
as to what we assumed was a military observation post high on
the nearby mountain, it never came to our site.

Day by day our acquaintance with the city grew, our sketch
plan filled in. We observed at once that our vertically standing
white stone at the water's edge was the frame of a handsome
gateway through the rubble walls, its carved stone lintel thrown

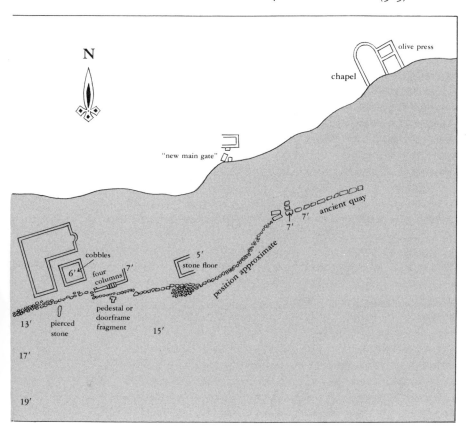

by earthquake onto the rubble beach, the foundations of square stone guard towers flanking either side. Along the trace of the older lateral wall a massive gateway of cruder stone gaped at the top of a steep and narrow approach, its lintel of a single block which was a good ten feet in length by three feet thick, still in place. Round sockets for massive hinge pins were cut into the stone, top and bottom, at each corner, and the recess for a powerful drawbar was built into the walls. Again a square tower guarded the path.

Since we had to begin calling things something, we used the terms "Old Main Gate" and "New Main Gate" which may well have been what they were, although we later came upon an even larger gate set into the east wall, well up the slope, and a rather small gate in the middle of the north wall, both indented between covering walls and towers.

In the northwest corner at the highest elevation in the city stood the ruins of a church, perhaps seventy feet in length, roofless, its windows partly blocked in with rubble, the capital of a column fallen amongst the rubble on the floor, and on the city walls outside this church rose a crudely constructed terrace in whose bottom course of stone, resting on the ground, was a similar capital. Does it represent a reject used for this mundane purpose? Or does it stand as mute testimony to the agonies of a dying city, the church destroyed by earthquake or invader, the survivors too reduced in number or too harassed by an enemy to rebuild, trying to create instead their last line of defense?

At the southeast corner of the older part of the city we came upon a slope of rubble, fragments of marble columns, scattered pieces of deeply carved and pierced stone in the acanthus pattern, which occurs in the capitals of columns in the church of St. Nicholas in nearby Myra, or in Hagia Sophia in Istanbul, colored tesserae as from a mosaic, fragments of plastered stone with a floral design painted on it, bits of irridescent glass. In the fallen walls above this slope were many handsome blocks carved with lettering, and no doubt these could be set straight again and an inscription read, but that was not for us; both a permit and a stronger back are needed. The professional might want first to observe them as they lie, but the slightly sad note is that the professional will probably never come here, this message will probably never be read.

Behind this complex, which we have assumed to be another church or chapel, built with an apse at its eastern end, we came upon a vaulted room, into one of the walls of which an older column had been laid on its side to serve as the lintel of an opening now stopped up with rubble, as the room had been used as a goat pen. Spraying ourselves with insect repellent, because a goat pen means ticks, we crawled through thorn to look more closely at the column and found eleven lines of inscription carved upon it. We copied what seemed to be the start of it, although part of it was covered by mortar and part eroded by seepage, assuming it would say something like "Demetrios loves Elena," and got as far as:

AYTOKPATOPCINI . . .

. . . AYPHΛIAI

before a tick got me. We didn't even know then that we might be looking at the Emperor Aurelian, or we would have been more excited and persevering. As it turned out, we weren't; we were looking at the Emperor Diocletian's middle name; but that comes later.

In fact we were in considerable doubt at this time as to the history of the entire area, as well as of our city (see how easily we have adopted it as "our city"), but there is no need that the reader should wait six months to piece together bits of information as we tramp or swim these ruins. From the Gennadion Library in Athens, from the American School of Classical Studies, from the New York Public Library, and from its warehouse, where some of our dusty references reposed, and from distinctly non-dusty professors of classics here and there, we later put together the bulk of what is known, or thought to be known, much of it disputed, much of it in medieval Latin, which I cannot read, or in stilted academic German, which I would prefer not to, with a good salting of French and Greek, and a little Turkish and Arabic for spice.

We had already conjectured that the older walls were built prior to the general use of mortar, that these had later fallen into disrepair, had been extensively quarried for building materials; later again a new period of wall building had taken place, this time embracing the seaport. And then had come a period of destruction, but whether man-made or natural was unclear, from which the city had never recovered. All this argued in favor of a warlike inception followed by a long period of peace when defenses became superfluous, then renewed threats of war amid a period of prosperity, followed by disaster.

All we must do was to fit this into the known history of Lycia, which begins more or less with the first Greek settle-

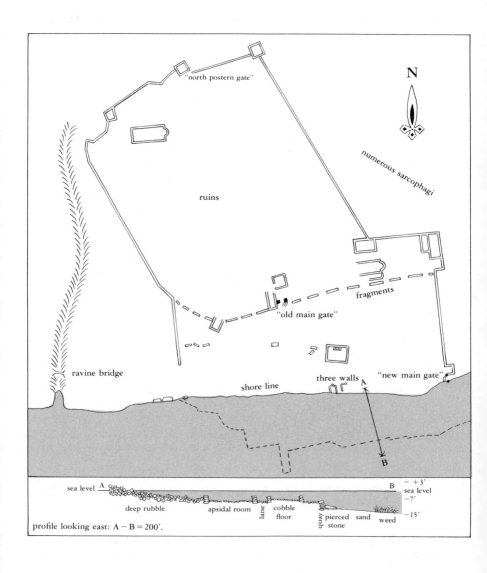

"north postern gate"

N

ruins

numerous sarcophagi

fragments

"old main gate"

ravine bridge

shore line

three walls

"new main gate"

A

B

sea level   A   B   − +3′
                                              sea level
                                              −7′

deep rubble   apsidal room   cobble   pierced   sand   weed   −15′
                            lane   floor   quay   stone

profile looking east: A − B = 200′.

ments along the coast, probably by Doric Greeks from Rhodes about 800 B.C. Prior to this and continuing, it was inhabited very properly by Lycians, possibly a remnant of the Hittite tribes. We have no reason to assume any settlement at our site this early, although the number of Lycian sarcophagi argue a mixing with this people. About 546 B.C. Cyrus, the founder of the Persian Empire, swept in, and for two centuries the cities of this coast were dominated by whichever side was in ascendency in the protracted wars between Persia and Greece, furnishing men and money and occasionally becoming battlegrounds themselves. Then in 333 B.C. Alexander the Great burst into Asia Minor like a storm, the Persian armies vanished like spray blown downwind, and the undefended cities of Lycia welcomed him with golden crowns. But in ten years he was dead and now there followed two centuries of bitter warfare as his generals and their heirs fought for control of Asia Minor. Lycia was early taken by Ptolemy of Egypt, its cities fortified and its shores patrolled by his navy, but it was held only by fighting off repeated attempts of the Seleucids, who at times prevailed, and when both sides were off guard the seafaring Rhodians took over the coastal cities.

But Rome was now on the scene. Greece had been subjugated, and the legions had incorporated western Asia Minor into a province of Rome. The Lycian League of cities enjoyed a period of independence until they, too, were embraced in the expanding power of imperial Rome, and it speaks for the ruggedness of the land or of its people that this was the last province of Asia Minor to be assimilated. With Roman rule and with the legions now forming a defense line as far east as Parthia and the Caucasus, there followed two centuries or more of peace.

So as we discussed our photographs with the professionals that winter it was no surprise to find general agreement that the early walls were Hellenistic, dating from those troubled times between Alexander and the Romans; that under Roman rule defense became unnecessary, or so the people thought, and the fine Hellenistic walls of squared and fitted stone served best as quarries.

But trouble was brewing; Roman power was losing its vigor; barbarians were on the march. In the fifth century A.D. Attila the Hun moved across Asia Minor. Walls were rebuilt, heightened, carried down to protect the seaport. It would seem that attack from the sea itself was not contemplated; the Mediterranean was still a Roman lake; and this may well have been a period of prosperity for the little city. Large buildings went up along the waterfront; the entrance through the new walls was of handsomely molded stone; the structures were embellished with marble and with columns, fragments of which are now strewn along the beach. Christianity had become the state religion, and churches and chapels were built in numbers, pagan monuments no doubt furnishing the building blocks.

And suddenly in the seventh century disaster struck from the undefended sea. The Arabs, spurred on more by greed than with the religious zeal of Mohammed, found the coastal cities of the Mediterranean easy picking, and within a few years of the death of the Prophet had laid waste the coasts of Asia Minor. Unlike the Greeks and Persians, the Macedonians and Romans, they did not come to colonize or govern or exploit; they came to rape and kill, to destroy the idols of the infidel and to carry off the survivors to slavery. Whether Arab or earthquake destroyed the church at the top of the city, the remaining population base was too depleted and too demoralized to attempt reconstruction. And then the curtain of history falls. The deserted city slowly crumbled with time and earthquake; the coastline gradually sank beneath the sea, and winter storms swept the buildings of the port into a rubble beach 200 yards in length and perhaps 10 feet deep in places. Probably no one knows what really happened. As Bury wrote in his *History of the Later Roman Empire*, "The history of the successors of Heraclius is veiled in the most profound obscurity." And Edward Ford in *The Byzantine Empire*: "The period 641–717 is in many ways the most obscure in late Roman history."

Byzantine armies, Seljuk Turks, Crusaders, the Mongols of Tamerlane, the Knights of St. John, Venetians, Genoese, and finally the Ottoman Turks moved back and forth across the land, but left no trace at Asar Bay. Another threat, too, was avoided, as no rivers flow into the bay, the threat of silting of the harbor, which in the case of so many harbors of Asia Minor turned the ports into malarial marshes. Perhaps malaria had been endemic before the Arabs, weakening the ability of the population to resist, but with depleted population the harbors could no longer be kept clear, and most of the quays, where ships from Rome and Byzantium had lain, became covered with swamp or sand dunes. Apparently a balance of some sort was struck, enough people remaining miserably alive to provide the protozoa with their human cycle, enough malaria to assure that the population would never flourish until determined Turkish efforts in this century succeeded in controlling it.

Medieval travelers visited Kekova nearby; in 1102 Saevulf, on a voyage to the Holy Land, described the island as *"omnino desolatam."* Dietrich von Schachten wrote in 1491 of the sunken city there, adding, "I didn't see it myself, because I wasn't there; but many of us had seen it before." And in 1521 Otto Heinrich Pfalzgraf bei Rhein wrote: "Forty miles behind Castel Rode lies the sunken city Cacuba, gone under like

Sodom and Gomurra; of which one sees from over the water houses and buildings." And then, like Dietrich, he adds, "We weren't able to see it, but it was said to be so." As I said, it is the stuff of which legends are made.

By 1812, when Beaufort was there, probably 1,100 years had passed by since the city had been deserted, and another 166 years had gone by before we were describing it. In all that time the only visitors we could trace had been Beaufort's party in 1812, and by inference Freya Stark and John Marriner shortly after World War II, neither of whom identified the site.

So there—that isn't very much history, but it is lots more than we knew as we snorkeled over the sunken port, and it comes pretty close to being all that is known of a city which probably had endured there for a thousand years. See what cruising gets you into that isn't in the how-to-do-it books!

But to come back to earth, we continued our scrambling and found above the Old Main Gate a small square building with stone benches built around the interior wall of its principal room, and with nicely cut stones of a massive arch lying both inside and outside its west wall. The benches would make one think of a bath, and we wished we could clear the rubble which completely obscured the floor to see if there was anything as exciting as a mosaic or the stacks of tile which would prove a hypocaust. But that would be illegal, and the most we could hope to do was to stimulate the curiosity of those who could legally go further than we.

Outside the western walls of the city, across a deep ravine spanned by a stone arch bridge, we came upon a bare slope covered by seashells and broken tile. Much of the shell was murex, and we tantalized ourselves with the romantic thought that there might be here one of the purple-dye factories of the past, of which few have been found, but it seemed more probable that we were looking at the raw materials which would be crushed to make the mortar we were everywhere finding, tinged pink with fragments of tile. But the thought lingers that, even if analysis of shell fragments in the mortar proved this, it could still be a convenient by-product of another industry. On the summit of this slope was a watchtower and beside it one building hidden in a cleft of the ridge, probably the bunkhouse for the off-watch.

On the 1,000-foot ridge across the bay we found nothing, only goat trails and thorn, and we wondered that no watchtower showed here, from which vantage the entire horizon could be viewed. Four towers, part of one still standing to a considerable height, do appear on the north shore of Asar Bay, set in positions to command a sweeping view of the approaches to the bay a few miles west of the city (as well as the ruins of a substantial building on Iç Ada, the island in the entrance to Asar Bay).

Immediately east of the city old foundations continued the few hundred yards to the head of Asar Bay, but on the isthmus itself we saw nothing convincingly ancient except the foundation of another tower and the occasional stone basin or drum of a column in the dooryard of one of the seasonal Turkish farmhouses, probably brought over for household use.

From the hillsides we took pictures of the sunken port and then, mooring over it, Cynthia cranked me up the mast in the bosun's chair and with a polarizing filter I photographed the most conspicuous foundations. With snorkel and mask we felt we were covering every inch of the submerged area, only to ask ourselves later, "What belongs in this blank on our sketch?" But the outlines of the port as it must have last existed were sharp. Beginning at the outer or western end, a sea wall capped with massive stones slanted out from the beach, rising from 15 feet of water to meet a stone pier which projected directly out into the bay for perhaps 75 feet. When above water, this would have doubled as a modest breakwater for the quay immediately behind it. This quay continued across the waterfront in a series of slight steps, the jogs coming perhaps at fifty- or sixty-foot intervals, and we thought this could well indicate the length of the trading ships which were accustomed to use the port: not the great galleys of imperial Rome, but small coasters, such as the Byzantine wrecks explored off Bodrum, which would have fitted quite nicely along the straight sections of quay. The top of this quay was now in most places about six to seven feet under water, and its side dropped vertically another six to seven feet. Beaufort reported that water levels along this coast were observed to rise and fall about two feet above or below mean water level, not tides, but wind and pressure fluctuations, and we must assume that the quays would have been built with this in mind, meaning that, in the absence of silting, normal depths alongside would not have been much more than four or five feet. Of course silting has occurred in a thousand years, but how much?

On the shelf from quayside to shore, which probably nowhere exceeded 150 feet in width, we photographed foundations of brick and of stone; floors of tile, of large, flat stones, and of baseball-sized cobbles, which seem to have been the undercourse for tile; apsidal walls; and in one place a wall built across four columns laid horizontally into its footing. What a passage of time is here, for a building with columns to have lived its life and for the columns to have been used as foundation stones for a second building which is now itself sunk a fathom deep beneath the sea!

From the east end of the whole submerged complex, and continuing the line of the quay, appears a row of large, flat stones almost completely silted up. That is, the depth of water on the harbor side was scarcely six inches deeper than on the landward side, and sea grass grew around and between them. Does this represent an earlier stage of the harbor, and are these the capstones of a quay from classical times? Would dredging of the silt uncover a complete wall here? Is the sunken seaport we have been describing only the latest in a series of ports, built progressively to the westward as slow silting occurred? What artifacts of bygone ages lie buried six feet beneath the waving seagrass? What traces of ancient wrecks may lie around the turbulent shores of the Kara Boğaz where the swift-running currents earned Iç Ada the name of Isla de Correntibus in the Middle Ages? We shall never know, and it is probable that the world will never know.

By now we had been in and out of Asar Bay for three weeks, and while it is true that we had been cheered by only one voice on our arrival, we had now been observed by any number of Turks, who have a unique ability to materialize in absolute silence from the most barren and desolate landscape. In fact, it was the hunting season and they were out to bag the *keklik*, the redlegged partridge, for which Kekova is named, and which haunt these ruins, so our constant swimming and snooping was probably common gossip along the shore. One calm Sunday morning we were resting late in our Flat Island Cove, in fact we were typing notes on the week's observations, when we saw the patrol boat from Kaş head our way. We set out fenders, helped ease them alongside with a "Hoş geldiniz" and opened the gate in the lifeline with a "Buyrun, efendim," my two expressions in Turkish, meaning, "Welcome," and "Come on board," hoping they would get the impression that we had nothing to hide, which was true enough unless they thought our sketch plan of the ruins was a master plan for a Greek invasion. But they did not want to come on board; they wanted to check our papers, which were in order. Then the young man who had worked in Germany and who had himself checked our papers in Kaş three times already—although you might think from his stern and impersonal manner that we and our boat were strangers to his coast—asked me in German if we had a compressor on board. No, we had no compressor. Did I know that diving with a mask was also forbidden? No, I had no idea at all that this was forbidden. Yes, it is prohibited. My surprise was genuine; everyone snorkels all the time in Turkey. Also, he said, taking pictures under water is prohibited. This also was a new one on me; the *National Geographic* is full of underwater pictures taken in Turkey, but this would be with benefit of permit.

But I thought I was getting a message; the time had come when we might be outstaying our welcome in isolated Asar Bay. Word had filtered back to the authorities at Kaş that those Americans were doing a lot of diving there, and it was simply unclear what this was all about. How embarrassing it would be if someone were looting their antiquities under their noses or charting their harbors for the Greeks. We had a good description of the city and our sketch maps of the sunken seaport, and many rolls of irreplaceable film; the authorities had treated us with tolerance and courtesy, and we thanked them for their information and decided to quit while we were ahead.

The next day we sailed back into Asar Bay for a final look and to confirm soundings with the fathometer, then beat up the coast to Kaş to come in to the quay alongside the patrol boat with a friendly wave each way. I guess I wanted our action to say, "Here we are, you see. Nothing to hide; inspect us, if you care to." I was most hopeful not to put ourselves in the position of being unwelcome in Turkey another year.

At home that winter we twisted the arms of some of the professionals to review our slides with us, a rewarding experience both for their own company and because they uniformly left more enthusiastic than they began, and with their help additional scraps of information filtered in. Otto Berndorf had been here in 1890 confirming inscriptions. There was little question that the site was ancient Aperlae, once a city of sufficient commercial importance to issue its own coinage. The large church at the summit was a basilica, and the city had been the seat of a bishopric. The inscription on the sideways column was worth a squeeze, that is, a paper impress. I wrote to George Bean in England, author of several volumes on the archeology of the Turkish coast, and learned that he had actually visited Aperlae for half a day eighteen years earlier. "Yours is almost the only account of the ancient remains of Aperlae," he replied. "And the underwater part in particular is quite new."

A copy of my report went to Hikmet Gürçay in Ankara. Hikmet Bey is director of antiquities for Turkey. While this did not necessarily call for a reply, I was pleased to get a request for a copy for the Antalya Museum as well.

I sent photographs of inscriptions to Louis Robert, in Paris, who holds the Chaire d'Épigraphie at the Collège de France, and learned that they were scarcely clear enough to serve a useful purpose.

The 1959 *Atlas of the Classical World* placed Aperlae at Tristoma; Asar Bay was a blank. So was it in the *Türkiye Atlasi* of 1961, the U.S. Army Military Map of 1968, the Turkish *Harita Umum Müdürlüğü* of 1956. Yet it had been clearly placed in a 1913 Gotha, in Richard Kiepert's Karte von Kleinasien of 1914, in the *Codex Kultur Atlas*, and in the U.S. Army Map Service Sheet J5 of 1943. The current Fodor Guide to Turkey places Aperlae at Kekova Castle. So the legendary quality continues; Aperlae remains elusive, now you see it, now you don't. And we must grant that the detailed sheets of the Turkish military maps bear the indication for ruins there.

We learned that the name *Polemos* is properly applied to the west end of Kekova Roads, where we would seek refuge at night, not to Asar Bay, and is used in the *British Admiralty Sailing Directions,* but its derivation remains unknown to us. Yet it is interesting to speculate that it may have derived from Ptolemy; Kekova Island has been referred to as the Dolochiste of Ptolemy, although it may be Ptolemy the geographer. This bay would have been a logical place for Ptolemy, the general and pharaoh, to have based the navy which guarded the Lycian coast for a century. And Homer is said to have used the names *Polemos* and *Ptolemos*, a minor war god, rather interchangeably.

Avassari, the name appearing in some maps on Asar Bay and on others as a shoreside location on the bay, crops up repeatedly in the literature. The German scholars spell it *Awschar*, which doesn't help at all, because the Avshahr were a nomadic race which moved into the Antitaurus and settled here and there around Lycia, giving their name to many villages, while *Avassari* as a Turkish word could imply the "Hunting Ruins," and clearly the ruins of Aperlae serve today chiefly as a hunting place of the *keklik*, the red-legged partridge. Could Tomaschek's obscure reference to this bay as *"Schoos, Bucht"* be some German's attempt to translate *Avassari*? Would that some scholar could tell us. Since most attempts at spelling Turkish place names came at a time when Turkish still employed the Arabic script, and since these names were pronounced in varying dialects and fell differently on the ears of early travelers, we have quite a choice.

The anomaly in the Stadiasmus, we learned, had been thoroughly discussed in the most pedantic German by Gustav Hirschfeld in 1885, although we did not uncover this until after we had drawn our own parallel conclusions that a line from the Stadiasmus was missing and that the word *akrotiri,* following *Aperlae,* did not refer to a city, as claimed by the Englishman Spratt, but to the promontory west of Asar Bay. As the southernmost cape of Lycia it was a logical landmark, and the distances conformed. I was tempted to think that the word was carried forward in the present name of the little cove inside this cape, Faktira, but the experts felt that that was reaching for it.

When Otto Benndorf had visited Asar Bay by boat in 1890, although he had previously equated Aperlae with Kekova, he now concurred that the inscriptions seen by Cockerell did in fact prove the identity of the site on Asar Bay. But of Cockerell's original journals we have found no trace.

In 1976 we were back in Turkey, not knowing if our efforts were well regarded or if word would be out to expel me, perhaps after a night in jail, but apparently our work was not that glamorous. To our great relief we were simply ignored; the authorities could not have been more courteous, and we sailed back to Asar Bay for a day to make the squeeze. This was dried and rolled and duly dispatched to the professionals, and it wasn't a discovery at all. It had appeared in print in 1853 and was included in the Le Bas–Waddington collection as No. 1293 and in the I.G. ad res Romanas pert., III, as No. 691. So we weren't first, but our squeeze did reveal a bottom line of text previously unrecorded, which proved that the column had been a milestone, set up by the city of Aperlae and dedicated to the Emperors Diocletian and Maximian about A.D. 300. And in

1977 we finally met the Turkish underwater archeologist Oğuz Alpözen, who we had suspected might have wound up with our report. This hunch was correct; he had, in turn, dived there, photographed it, and included it in a recent Turkish national television program and also in an article in a Turkish magazine, with credits to us for having brought it to their attention. And this probably concludes a most satisfying ego trip. The proper authorities now know of it and the decision to explore it further should be theirs. And so we nibble at the edges of intellect.

Already, though, we are on the track of other discoveries, in which the shores of Lycia abound. Looking up the narrow valley immediately west of Andriaki, the port from which Paul took ship to Rome after appealing unto Caesar, and now a waste of sand dunes, we saw the ruins of an early Christian church and of what appeared to be a small classical temple, standing solitary in a marshy pasture. By following a fish-filled stream in our dinghy we came to its head, where it emerged full born and bitter with salt from beneath a limestone cliff. Later research determined that these temples were associated with the city of Sura, whose ruins lie on the hill above and were unobserved by us in the valley, and that here we had indeed the temple of Surian Apollo, known for its Fish Oracle. Those seeking a sign from the oracle threw bits of meat from sacrificed animals to the fishes, the oracle announced the reception of this by the fishes, and the priest made his interpretation of the oracle. I am glad to share this information with the reader, who may at first think it one of the most useless bits of trivia in a lifetime collection. But reflect a moment: the priests and oracles and citizens of Sura are long gone; the salt stream and the fish are still there. And the written word survives.

To the south of the present small port of Kaş, the ancient Antiphellus, lies the little bay known as Port Sevedo in the guide. Sheer cliffs form its eastern shore, pierced with half a dozen Lycian cliff tombs, and these so focus one's attention that it was not until our fifth visit to this anchorage that my eye happened to discern rock walls high on the hilltop above.

Scrambling a rough goat track through thorn and brush, we arrived at these walls to find the ruins of another small city, appearing much older than the usual late Roman ruins along this coast, there being nothing standing other than the fortification walls of large unmortared blocks of stone. But in a central spot, directly before the walls of the upper citadel, stood a lone sarcophagus, built of three pieces instead of the usual two, its base cut into the bedrock, an entry way at one end of the type used in cliff tombs, and a short distance in front of it a high altar, also formed by cutting away the bedrock around it, leaving a single square shaft about 12 inches on a side, with a hollowed top, as if here also had burned an eternal flame.

This site had been visited in 1830 by Spratt, who decided it was the Akrotiri of the Stadiasmus, because it was a high tower, although geographically misplaced, and again by Benndorf in 1890, who wrote a long paper proving Spratt wrong and asserting that it was actually Phellus, and yet again by George Bean in 1957, who wrote another paper proving that both Spratt and Benndorf were wrong and that it was the more ancient site of Sebeda. We find no other reference to it, no further visitors except ourselves. All about is desolation except for a family of eagles who live at the cliff top.

On our last day of our most recent trip to this coast of tombs, as we were preparing to sail, we were approached by a launch with a man who presented himself as Mustafa of Uçağiz, identified himself in a mixture of French and Turkish as the Museum Department's man on this coast, and offered to show us a city beneath the sea in Kekova Roads. Perhaps this is the city which Diedtrich von Schachten and Otto Heinrich Pfalzgraf bei Rhein had also been told was there, but never saw. Maybe we will find Mustafa again, and maybe we shall see this city which has "gone under like Sodom and Gomorrah."

The mysteries lead one on. The adventures of the sea and of people and of the mind are synthesized. They must end one day, but the satisfactions and the memories will endure.

Log

For those who may like to trace the voyages of the *Cynthia R*, this abbreviated log contains the principal facts. In the count of harbors I have included not only overnight anchorages, but luncheon and swimming stops, that is, all those places where we lay at anchor or otherwise moored. But I do not count two different mooring places within the same harbor as being two harbors, nor do I count repeat visits to the same harbor during any one time span, although many of the harbors counted may have been visited repeatedly.

Miles shown are miles over the bottom on the route taken, rounded up or down to reasonably even numbers.

For each year I have also shown the principal passages, being those runs of about 100 miles or more, with the hours under way.

1967		HARBORS VISITED	MILES LOGGED
4/24	Launching		
5/24	Delivery		
5/24–8/31	On the Maine coast	42	1300
9/1–10/31	Portland, Me., to Palm Beach, Fla., via Intracoastal Waterway	50	1700
11/1–11/30	Palm Beach to Rock Sound, Eleuthera via the Abacos	23	600
12/1–12/31	Three round trips from Rock Sound to the Exuma Cays	18	500
			4100

PASSAGES: Portland, Me., to Marion, Mass.: 140 miles, 27 hours
Sea Bright, N.J., to Cape May, N.J.: 133 miles, 22 hours

1968		HARBORS VISITED	MILES LOGGED
1/1–4/12	Five round trips from Rock Sound to the Exumas, Cat Island, Little San Salvador	28	1000
4/13–5/1	Rock Sound to Charleston, S.C.	22	800
5/2–6/22	Laid up.		
6/23–8/1	Charleston to Gibraltar via Bermuda and the Azores	7	3800
9/1–11/1	Gibraltar to Malta via Ceuta (North Africa), Spain Balearics, Sardinia, Italy, Lipari, Sicily	45	1800
			7400

PASSAGES: Allans-Pensacola Cay, Abacos, to Cape Canaveral, Fla.: 190 miles, 29 hours
Charleston to Bermuda: 768 miles, 5 days, 7 hours
Bermuda to Horta: 1856 miles, 13 days, 7 hours
Ponta Delgada to Gibraltar: 1004 miles, 6 days, 17 hours
Minorca to Sardinia: 246 miles, 40 hours
Olbia to Ponza: 158 miles, 24 hours

1969		HARBORS VISITED	MILES LOGGED
4/19–4/26	Malta to Corfu, via Sicily	6	450
4/27–5/4	Corfu to Vouliagmeni via Corinth Canal	8	300
5/5–6/30	Aegean Sea	36	900
7/1–7/18	Corinth Canal to Herzegnovi, Yugoslavia	17	550
7/19–9/26	Dalmatian Coast	50	1600
9/27–10/10	Ionian Islands	6	300
10/11–10/14	Corfu to Malta	3	400
			4500

PASSAGES: Catania to Crotone: 145 miles, 25 hours
Brindisi to Herzegnovi: 119 miles, 21 hours
Herzegnovi to Othonoi: 190 miles, 26 hours
Corfu to Syracusa: 300 miles, 42 hours

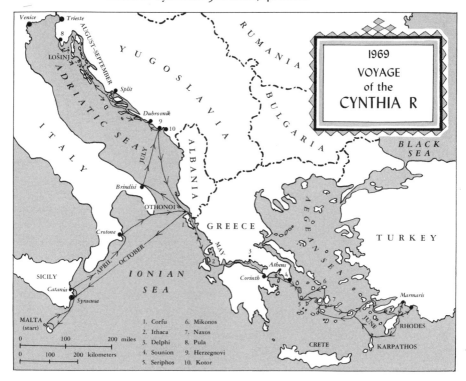

1970		HARBORS VISITED	MILES LOGGED
4/24–5/9	Malta to Cape Matapan	8	550
5/10–9/15	Aegean Sea and South Turkey	91	2250
9/16–10/19	Corinth Canal to Malta	26	800
			3600

PASSAGES: Syracusa to Argostolion: 261 miles, 43 hours
Othonoi to Crotone: 118 miles, 23 hours
Crotone to Syracusa: 152 miles, 24 hours

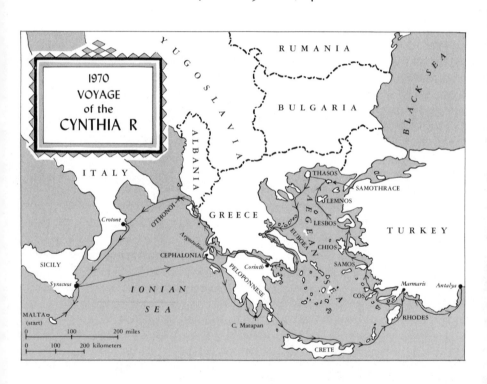

1971		HARBORS VISITED	MILES LOGGED
5/1–6/25	Malta to Port St. Louis, France, via Sicily, Lipari, Italy, Elba Corsica, Monaco, Riviera	39	1100
6/26–8/30	Port St. Louis to Delfzijl, 240 locks, via Rhône, Saône, Canal de l'Est, Meuse, Maas, Ijssel, Friesland		1050
8/31–9/23	Delfzijl to Faaborg, Denmark, 2 locks, via Frisian Islands, Helgoland, Kiel Canal, Danish Islands	16	450
			2600

PASSAGES: Calvi to Monaco: 97 miles, 15 hours
See maps following pages.

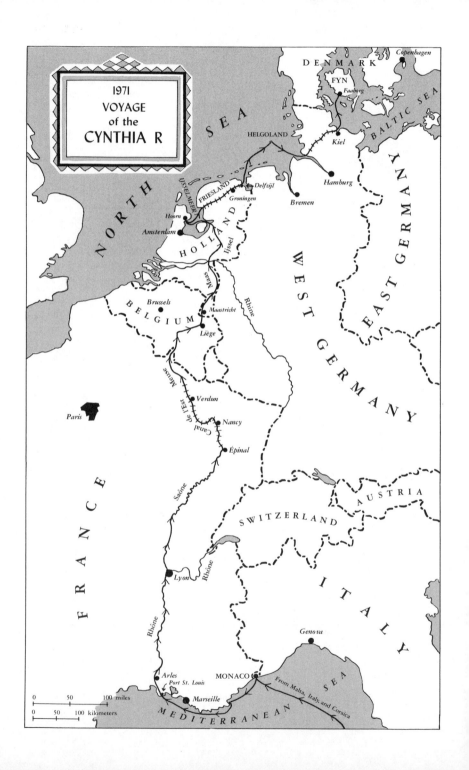

0 50 100 miles
0 50 100 kilometers

Venice

Genova

MONACO

LIGURIAN SEA

ITALY

ADRIATIC SEA

ELBA

Calvi *Bastia*

CORSICA

GIGLIO

Civitavecchia

ROME

Anzio

Naples

PONZA

ISCHIA

CAPRI

SARDINIA

TYRRHENIAN

SEA

STROMBOLI

LIPARI

Taormina

SICILY

Catania

Syracusa

1971
VOYAGE
of the
CYNTHIA R

TUNISIA

MALTA (start)

The Log

1972		HARBORS VISITED	MILES LOGGED
5/15–6/24	Faaborg to Stockholm, 2 locks, via Bornholm, Öland, Gotland	27	800
6/26–8/6	Finnish Archipelago	29	700
8/7–8/21	Stockholm to Gothenburg, 65 locks, via Göta Canal	18	400
8/22–9/25	West coast of Sweden	22	500
			2400

PASSAGES: None

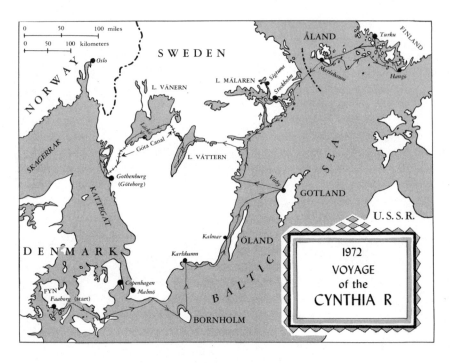

1973		HARBORS VISITED	MILES LOGGED
5/17–8/10	Gothenburg to Ålesund and return (West coast of Norway to 62° N)	82	1800
8/11–9/6	Gothenburg to Bremen, 2 locks, via Danish Island and Kiel Canal	25	600
9/7–10/26	Bremen to Arles, 157 locks, via Weser, Mittelland Canal, Dortmund-Ems Canal, Rhine to Basel, Rhone au Rhin Canal (Doubs River), Saône and Rhône		1000
			3400

PASSAGES: None

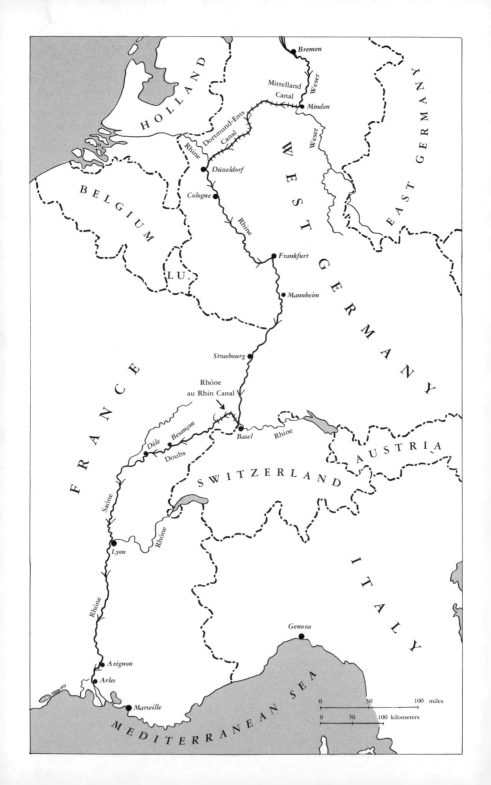

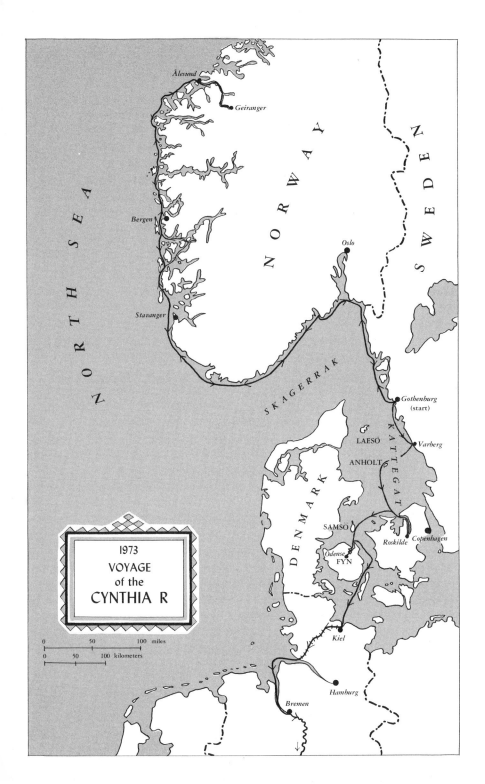

NORTH SEA

NORWAY

SWEDEN

Ålesund

Geiranger

Bergen

Oslo

Stavanger

SKAGERRAK

Gothenburg
(start)

KATTEGAT

LAESÖ

Varberg

ANHOLT

DENMARK

SAMSÖ

Copenhagen

Roskilde

Odense
FYN

1973
VOYAGE
of the
CYNTHIA R

0   50   100 miles

0   50   100 kilometers

Kiel

Hamburg

Bremen

1974		HARBORS VISITED	MILES LOGGED
5/9–6/19	Arles to Carcassonne and return, 78 locks, via Rhône, Rhône à Sête Canal, Canal du Midi		400
6/20–8/15	Grande Motte to Corfu via Corsica, Sardinia, Ponza, Capri, Lipari and Italy	45	1300
8/16–10/9	Ionian Islands	45	750
10/10–10/19	Corfu to Malta	7	450
			2900

PASSAGES: Port Cros to Calvi: 112 miles, 21 hours
Sardinia to Ponza: 160 miles, 30 hours
Milazzo to Crotone: 151 miles, 29 hours
Crotone to Otranto: 97 miles, 16 hours
Crotone to Syracusa: 158 miles, 29 hours

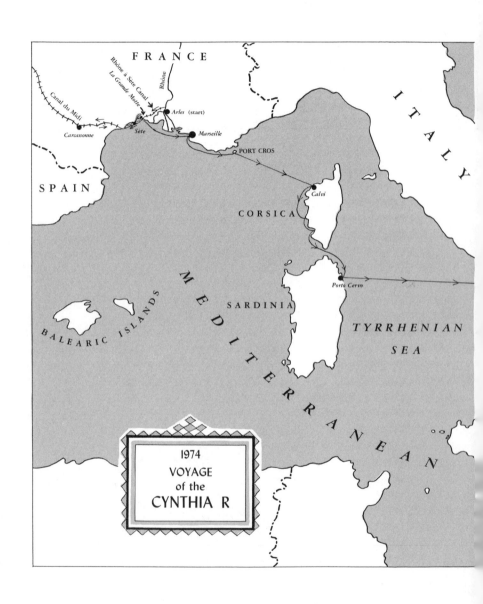

1975		HARBORS VISITED	MILES LOGGED
4/30–6/4	Malta to Cape Matapan via Ionian Islands	20	700
6/5–6/30	Cape Matapan to Rhodes via Aegean Islands	26	550
7/1–8/17	South coast of Turkey	26	800
8/18–9/30	Dodecanese Islands	23	500
			2550

PASSAGES: Malta to Argostolion: 320 miles, 55 hours

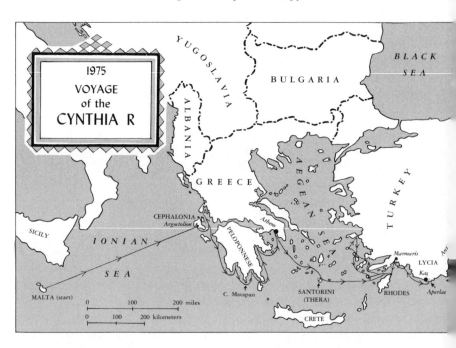

1976		HARBORS VISITED	MILES LOGGED
5/5–6/8	South coast of Turkey	25	450
6/9–8/19	West coast of Turkey	45	1000
8/20–10/12	South coast of Turkey	31	700
			2150

PASSAGES: None

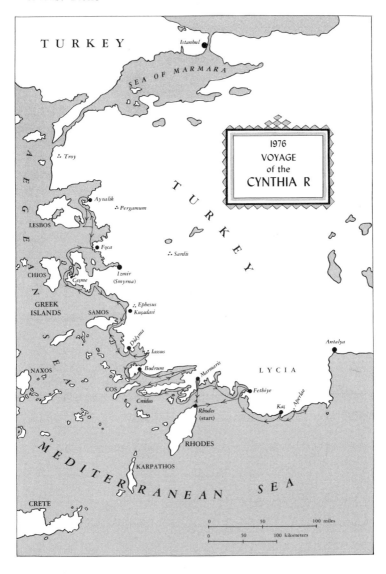

1977		HARBORS VISITED	MILES LOGGED
5/11–6/3	Aegean Islands	19	450
6/4–9/23	South coast of Turkey	56	1600
9/24–10/12	Aegean Islands	19	400
			2450

PASSAGES: None

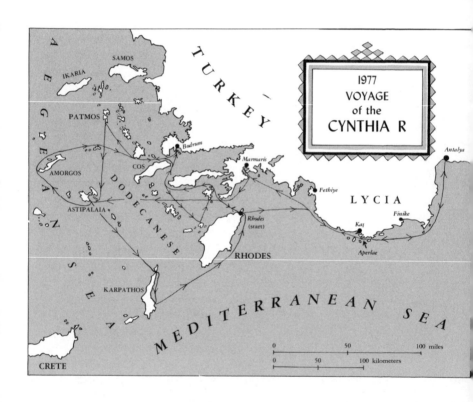

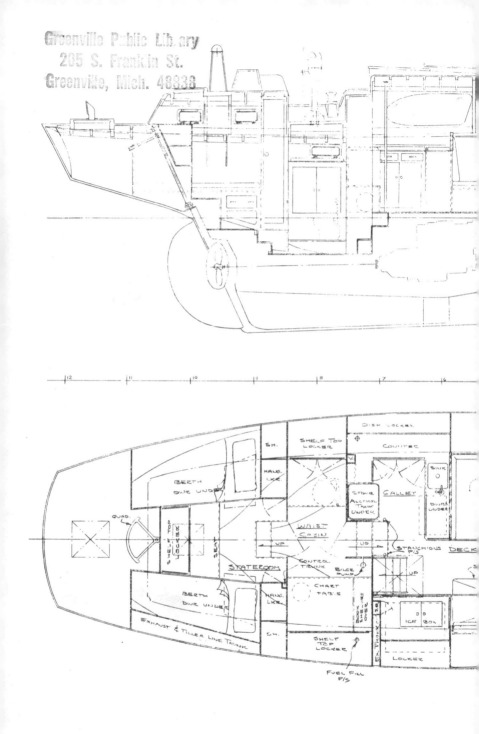